2014

Dad,

♡ Dominique

2014

Dad,

THE Big LEBOWSKI

An Illustrated, Annotated History of the Greatest Cult Film of All Time

by

Jenny M. Jones

Voyageur Press

First published in 2012 by Voyageur Press, an imprint of MBI Publishing Company, 400 First Avenue North, Suite 300, Minneapolis, MN 55401 USA

Voyageur Press titles are also available at discounts in bulk quantity for industrial or sales-promotional use. For details write to Special Sales Manager at MBI Publishing Company, 400 First Avenue North, Suite 300, Minneapolis, MN 55401 USA.

To find out more about our books, visit us online at www.voyageurpress.com.

ISBN-13: 978-0-7603-4279-4

Library of Congress Cataloging-in-Publication Data

Jones, Jenny M.
 The big Lebowski : an illustrated, annotated history of the greatest cult film of all time / Jenny M. Jones.
      p. cm.
  Includes bibliographical references and index.
 ISBN 978-0-7603-4279-4
 1. Big Lebowski (Motion picture) I. Title.
 PN1997.B444J66 2012
 791.43'72—dc23
                            2012008079

Frontis: *It's Just a Game, Man*, by Max Dalton. *Courtesy of the artist, www.maximdalton.com*
Title page: *Oath of the Horatii (After David)*, 2010, by Joe Forkan. *© Joe Forkan*
Opposite: *The Dude 1*, by Greg Gossel. Acrylic, silkscreen, collage, graphite, and spray paint on canvas. *Courtesy of the artist, greggossel.com*

Editor: Grace Labatt
Design Manager: Cindy Samargia Laun
Designer: Brad Norr Design

Printed in China

10 9 8 7 6 5 4 3 2

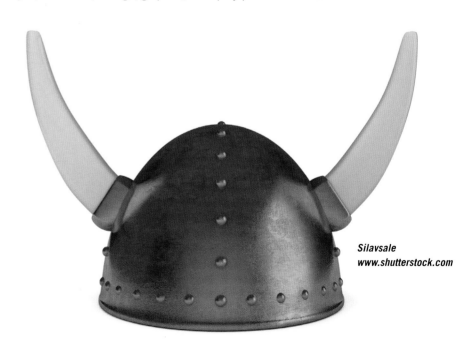

Silavsale
www.shutterstock.com

"This is not 'Nam. This is bowling.
There are rules."

Contents

*© AF Archive / Alamy.
Courtesy of Universal
Studios Licensing LLC*

Ve Cut Off Your Chonson,
by Visual Etiquette.
Courtesy of Visual Etiquette

This Here Story I'm about to Unfold

I first saw *The Big Lebowski* upon its 1998 release in a moderately full movie theater in a Portland, Oregon, mall. I left the theater both confused and exhilarated, as well as a little wobbly—upon initial viewing, *Lebowski*'s sensibility can leave you feeling off-kilter.

It's a movie that I have now seen countless times in a variety of settings: at White Russian parties and packed movie houses and alone in front of my TV (originally on VHS). Like the best literature and films—for me Faulkner's *The Sound and the Fury* and Coppola's *The Godfather*—*The Big Lebowski* changes, expands, and deepens with time. I initially found Walter's constant yelling abrasive; now I consider his dialogue and Goodman's delivery of it to be the funniest and most interesting in the film.

Each showing reveals a little something new—a reference, a joke previously missed (because laughing drowns it out), a parody, a philosophy. I'll watch it and decide it's about masculinity . . . no, friendship . . . no, language . . . no, just plain silliness . . . no, it's a genre film that turns the genre on its head. Well, it's all these things, and more.

This film, created by those sly, witty instigators who come from my home state of Minnesota, had a muted opening that has become a groundswell. Timed for the fifteenth anniversary of the movie, *The Big Lebowski: An Illustrated, Annotated History of the Greatest Cult Film of All Time* is a celebration of all things *Lebowski*: the high and the low of a film that is now among the elite in the pop-culture canon.

Jenny M. Jones, St. Paul, 2012

PROLOGUE
What Makes a Man?
Achieving vs. Abiding

An army of Dudes, by Dax Norman.
Courtesy of the artist, www.daxnorman.com

"Lord save little children! The wind blows and the rains are cold. Yet, they abide. . . . They abide and they endure."

—Rachel, in *The Night of the Hunter* (1955), a favorite of Joel and Ethan Coen

At the conclusion of *The Big Lebowski*, the film's narrator, the Stranger, says he takes comfort in the fact that the Dude "abides"—that is, he endures without yielding. That the Dude abides, which is the nature of his character, spirit, makeup—or to quote the Coen brothers' *Raising Arizona*, his "goddamn *raison d'etre*"—is at the crux of the film. It's a loving characterization, that of the Coens' Dude, and this consummate ability to simply abide may be why this disheveled, foul-mouthed, paunchy layabout has become an inspiration to legions of people worldwide.

Despite operating through a fog of creamy alcohol and reefer smoke, the Dude is no dummy. Off the cuff, he makes hilarious observational quips: to Bunny Lebowski's offer of a blowjob for a cool grand, he deadpans, "I'm just gonna go find a cash machine"; he answers the Big Lebowski's question about what makes a man with "a pair of testicles"; and he jokes that he still "jerks off manually" to pornographer Jackie Treehorn. Even when under threat, he manages to tell the thugs holding his head in the toilet that the money they're looking for must be "down there somewhere. Let me take another look." He also has a fearless streak— when the Big Lebowski refuses to compensate him for his rug, he goes right ahead and takes one for himself.

Even beyond his smarts and innate sense of humor, the Dude is eminently likeable, certainly to generations of young people living in post-1950s conservative America. The Dude values friendship and peace. He takes time to see his landlord Marty's inept modern dance cycle in a near-empty theater, and shows as much patience as can be mustered with the blowhard Walter Sobchak, despite his friend's very unpeaceful, militaristic view on life. Even when exasperated, he tells Walter he loves him. The Dude sympathizes with those he perceives to be weak or under threat. The rival bowler Smokey is fragile, with emotional problems; Bunny's life was in the Dude's hands, and he feels responsible that the kidnappers are going to "kill that poor woman."

Not a workaholic by any stretch of the imagination, the Dude maintains a consistent Zen-like attitude; *New Yorker* critic David Denby characterized the film as "a slacker hymn of praise." He is comfortable with who he is, and he takes life as it comes. While in many ways he is a figure from the past—he defines himself by his 1960s and early 1970s political activism, antiestablishment leanings, and drug use—he isn't actually living in the past, as he berates the mercurial law-and-order nut Walter for doing. The Dude lives in the moment. He does not feel pressure to achieve. As Joel and Ethan Coen wrote when first describing the character in their script, "His rumpled look and relaxed manner suggest a man in whom casualness runs deep." And at a

time when young people with higher education cannot get more than entry-level jobs—despite which money, status, and achievement are still prized by American society— this astute and generally content character, who shrugs off such trappings, is refreshing, even restorative. As an article in *Sidevue* says, *The Big Lebowski* is "casually radical in its joyful explosion of the myth of the American movie hero," a concept the Stranger seems to confirm when he opens the film with the drawled lines, "I won't say a hee-ro, 'cause what's a hee-ro?"

"There's a freedom to *The Big Lebowski*," said Philip Seymour Hoffman (who plays the sycophantic character Brandt) in *Rolling Stone* magazine. "The Dude abides, and I think that's something people really yearn for, to be able to live their life like that. You can see why young people would enjoy that." In the wake of the film, this unique view on life has become a movement—one that chooses abiding over achieving.

But, as the Stranger says, "Aw hell, I done innerduced him enough." To fully embrace *The Big Lebowski*, one must go back to the beginning, to two precocious kids growing up in a Midwestern suburb, and how they began by entertaining themselves and ended up entertaining the rest of us—to beat the band.

© Moviestore Collection / Alamy.
Courtesy of Universal Studios Licensing LLC

Joel and
Ethan Coen.
© AF Archive / Alamy

PART I
B.L.: The Coens before *Lebowski*

 ## The Coen Brothers: The Early Years

Natives of St. Louis Park, at the time an undeveloped Jewish suburb of Minneapolis, Joel and Ethan Coen (born 1954 and 1957, respectively) grew up with a traditional, self-proclaimed "mundane" existence. Their grandparents observed the Jewish Sabbath (like Walter Sobchak, they wouldn't "drive on Shabbos"), and their parents were both professors, Edward Coen of economics and Rena Coen of art history. Early on in their childhood, the boys became aficionados of the locally produced *Mel Jass Matinee Movie* television show, which broadcast wildly disparate films, from a Fellini movie one day to a Hercules flick the next. Such contrasting viewing fare cultivated their taste for both the high- and lowbrow, serious art-house and simple entertainment and informed the filmmaking efforts of their youth.

The boys mowed lawns to cobble together enough money for a Vivitar Super-8mm camera, and the stars were born. Joel and Ethan first experimented with their calling by literally filming the television screen (while a Raymond Burr jungle movie, *Tarzan and the She-Devil*, played). From there they branched out into other areas, sometimes filming their antics—going down slides, jumping out of trees—while playing with neighborhood kids. Joel has since characterized their earliest films as surreal: "In winter, Minnesota, where we were born, resembles a frozen wasteland. There were fields covered with snow and the scenery was very abstract" (*Positif* magazine, from an interview reprinted in *The Coen Brothers Interviews*). Using whatever props and locations they had around them, they

---

"I don't know where the boys come up with these ideas."

—Mrs. Coen, after seeing *The Big Lebowski*, to John Turturro

---

produced such early classics as *Lumberjacks of the North* (making the most of their wardrobe of plaid shirts) and *Zeimers in Zambezi*, a remake of Cornel Wilde's 1966 adventure film *The Naked Prey* that starred their pal Mark "Zeimers" Zimmering. Also included in their early filmography was a five-minute, silent adaptation of the 1959 Allen Drury novel *Advise and Consent* (they had neither read it nor seen the 1962 Otto Preminger film adaptation, but had heard the story from a friend); a lark about shuttle diplomacy called *Henry Kissinger, Man on the Go* (set at the Minneapolis-St. Paul International Airport and starring Ethan in the titular role); and a remake of *Lassie Comes Home* called *Ed . . . A Dog* (named for their father). There were many movies with chase scenes, and much attention was paid to honing vomit special effects. For all of these early works, the brothers hadn't yet grasped the concept of postproduction editing, and thus they edited the works in camera—that is, rather than cutting the footage together, they would film it, then stop and run over to a new position and shoot from another perspective.

The Coen brothers' upbringing in the wintry wasteland/wonderland of Minnesota gave them ample time for moviewatching, and their tastes were far-flung. Brought up on a steady television diet of Walt Disney features, Joel and Ethan adored Dean Jones and Kurt Russell, as well as Doris Day, Bob Hope, and Jerry Lewis. They spent hours with Tony Curtis, Steve Reeves, and the various actors who played Tarzan and appreciated the madcap stylings of directors Preston Sturges, Billy Wilder, and Frank Capra. Ethan has cited *All Hands on Deck*, a 1961 farce with Pat Boone and Buddy Hackett, as his earliest favorite film, while Joel has listed the more erudite Akira Kurosawa classic *The Seven Samurai* as his childhood

As teenagers, the Coens remade the 1966 adventure film *The Naked Prey* in Super-8. © *AF Archive / Alamy*

All Hands on Deck, a childhood favorite of Ethan Coen.
© *AF Archive / Alamy*

years, then moved to New York to study film at the famed Tisch School of the Arts at New York University (which he chose because he missed the application deadline for other schools, so he says). His thirty-minute thesis film, *Soundings*, centered on a woman verbally fantasizing about a roommate while having sex with her deaf boyfriend.

Ethan was the more soft-spoken, introspective one, who carried around a notebook in high school to jot down observations. (As his college friend William Preston Robertson says about the brothers, when they hear something they find amusing or interesting, they enter it into their "personal database" and it eventually reappears in a film.) Ethan also went to Simon's Rock, followed by Princeton University, from which he received a

favorite—although depending on the day, such pronouncements can vary.

But it was really literature, and not movies, that had the greatest effect on the aspiring filmmakers (perhaps a result of their growing up in an academic household). The Southern Gothic writings of William Faulkner and Flannery O'Connor, with their twisted elements of irony and the macabre, heavily influenced the Coens in their writing and filmmaking styles. As admirers of pulp fiction, their other main literary inspiration was the hardboiled writing of the triumvirate of great noir novelists: James M. Cain, Dashiell Hammett, and Raymond Chandler. Their films reference literature, and in some ways—for instance, in the incredible density of details and the intricacies of language—Coen brother films may resemble literature even more than other movies.

After high school, Joel, the more outgoing of the two, departed for Bard College at Simon's Rock, a private school in Great Barrington, Massachusetts. He attended for two

The Seven Samurai, Joel Coen's favorite film growing up. © *AF Archive / Alamy*

Minnesota Roots, and Will the Real Lebowski Please Stand Up?

The Coens frequently insert names from their childhood into their films, in references that only they and a handful of other St. Louis Park, Minnesota, residents might get. Their production company, Mike Zoss Productions, is named after a local amiable pharmacist from their childhood. In *Fargo*, the character Mike Yanagita, with an ex-wife named Linda Cooksey, meets Marge at a Radisson restaurant. At St. Louis Park High School, in the era of the Coens, there were students named Gary Yanagita and Sue Cooksey. In *A Serious Man*, the Gopniks' neighbor is the sexy Mrs. Samski, the same name (if not the same physical appearance) as the Coen family's own neighbor, Vivian Samski. And, in the Coens' childhood neighborhood, there was a big, tall, somewhat goofy boy nicknamed "Guy" (with the French pronunciation *Ghee*) Lebowski—with a brother named Jeffrey Lebowski. According to William Preston Robertson, a friend of Ethan's from college and a writer who has participated in several of their films, "There are certain names, things that they would glom onto. . . . I can actually remember several ideas, where they kept kicking around opportunities to use the name Lebowski. So the name stuck with them and was looking for just the right home."

Although a distinctly Californian story, *The Big Lebowski* also includes several nods to the Coens' home state of Minnesota, a locale of intemperate climates and a high number of residents of Scandinavian descent, mostly Norwegian. Lingonberries, ordered as a pancake accompaniment by most of the nihilists in the diner, are a staple of Scandinavian cuisine. Joel Coen once referred to Minnesota as "Siberia with family restaurants."

The name Rolvaag, as in "Duty Officer Rolvaag," who telephones the Dude to tell him his car has been recovered, has a Norwegian etymology, and there's a Rolvaag River in Norway. (The Coens didn't want to hire an actor for this voice work. Their frequent crew member Bruce Pross, the foley mixer—a specialist in sound effects—on *Lebowski*, had a recording studio, so he "volunteered" to fill in. His faxed instructions from Ethan included only one crucial direction: that "Rolvaag" should rhyme with "log.")

Finally, fellow "Shamus" Da Fino—played by Jon Polito, a Coen-film regular—tells the Dude of Bunny Lebowski's origin: she grew up on a farm in Moorhead, Minnesota, with her family the Knutsons (also a Scandinavian name). Polito recalls what he brought to the story: "I mispronounced Knutsons and called them 'Kuh-nutsons.' I love that I pronounced the *k* in Knutsons. The Coens thought that was hysterical, when I was of course thinking, 'Hey, *this* guy would pronounce the *k*.' " Da Fino displays a photo from the Moorhead farm—a city, incidentally, located less than two miles away from Fargo; also incidentally, it is the hometown of Jeff Bridges' wife—that exudes such bleakness, one has to question the Coens' home-state pride. As the Dude says, "How ya gonna keep 'em down on the farm once they've seen Karl Hungus?"

BA in philosophy. In his thesis on the German philosopher Ludwig Wittgenstein (the "philosopher of poets and composers, playwrights and novelists," according to literary critic Terry Eagleton), Ethan wrote, with characteristic wit and frankness, "I understand what it means to say that there is an omnipotent, benevolent creator, and that claim strikes me as the height of stupidity."

Postgraduation, the brothers reunited in New York City. Joel entered into the world of film production, while Ethan toiled away as a typist for Macy's, not unlike the Herman Melville hero Bartleby, the Scrivener. Joel worked as an (apparently ineffectual) production assistant on a few industrial films and music videos, then broke into editing on the Frank LaLoggia low-budget horror movie *Fear No Evil* (1981). In the meantime, in their Upper West Side apartment on Riverside Drive, the brothers began to write scripts (while pacing back and forth, a practice that continues to this day).

In 1980, after completing his work on *Fear No Evil*, Joel fortuitously got a job as an assistant editor on Sam Raimi's first feature film,

the now–cult classic *The Evil Dead*, and a very fruitful friendship was born. Raimi taught the Coens a lot, including how best to utilize the "shaky-cam," a technique in which a camera is hand-held, producing footage that creates a sense of unease and apprehension. Most significant, by witnessing Raimi's experience as he made his first film, the Coens learned about a particular kind of financing for an independent movie: forming a limited partnership with many small investors.

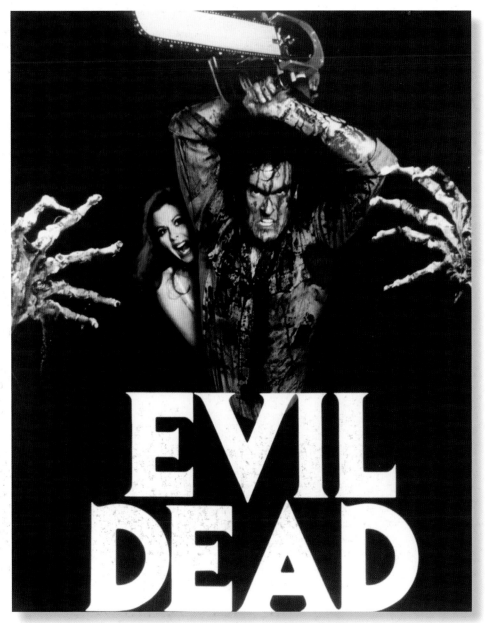

The Evil Dead, on which Joel Coen worked as an assistant editor.
© Pictorial Press Ltd / Alamy

Blood Not So Simple

Joel and Ethan Coen's first jointly made, full-length feature film, *Blood Simple*, had its roots in the noir pulp fiction they grew up on. The title is taken from Dashiell Hammett's 1929 novel *Red Harvest*, which expounds that when you murder someone, it makes you go "blood-simple," or addled in the head. When devising the film's plot, the brothers endeavored to make a modern version of a James Cain (*Double Indemnity, The Postman Always Rings Twice*) story. In 1981, armed with a short clip featuring a character being buried alive, Joel and Ethan headed back to Minnesota to find investors. They contacted members of the Jewish charitable organization Hadassah, took meeting after meeting with businessmen in coffee shops, and garnered a mass of small pledges from private

> "The innocent must suffer, the guilty must be punished, you must drink blood to be a man."
> —Ethan Coen, quoting Sam Raimi to describe the style of *Blood Simple*, at the 1984 New York Film Festival press conference

investors, raising $750,000 over the course of nine months. With that they began production.

It was a trial by fire. Virtually no one in the cast or crew, including the writer-director-editor-producers Ethan and Joel, had spent much time on a film set before. Barry Sonnenfeld, the cinematographer whom Joel had met at NYU and who went on to photograph their next two films, reportedly threw up every day of the eight-week shoot. The threesome spent many sessions at the local Denny's during filming in Texas, methodically plotting out the next day's schedule of what would be shot and how it would be lit. Starring unknowns Dan Hedaya, Jon Getz, and Frances McDormand (later Joel's wife) and featuring veteran M. Emmett Walsh in a role created especially for him, the film is a darkly comic, intricately plotted noir about infidelity and murder. *Blood Simple* has been described by Joel as Hitchcockian with a touch of Chuck Jones, creator of *Looney Toons*.

Although initially rejected by every major studio, the film attracted critical notice at

M. Emmet Walsh in *Blood Simple*. © AF Archive / Alamy

festivals, namely the 1984 New York Film Festival, and finally found distribution, launching the careers of the two known in the film business as "the Coen brothers."

"Two heads are better than none."

—Ethan Coen

The Coens' movies are a cooperative—some might say conspiratorial—enterprise, with Joel and Ethan writing, directing, and editing together (using the crusty pseudonym Roderick Jaynes for the latter role). As a Directors Guild formality, until *The Ladykillers* release in 2004, Joel was credited as director, Ethan as producer, but this belied their truly collaborative process. The brothers have been described by colleagues as a "Two-Man Ecosystem" (Barry Sonnenfeld) and the "Yeah-yeahs" (John Turturro), who operate as one unit, or, as John Goodman has said, "They share a uni-mind." Jack Kehler, who played Marty the Landlord in *The Big Lebowski*, said, "[It's] the old cliché, they finish each other's... not even sentences; they finish each other's thoughts." While Ethan is more dialogue/script-oriented, and Joel's focus tends toward visual matters, they work in close tandem with few, if any, disagreements. When asked by a reporter if they ever fight, Joel replied, "That's not an interesting question." Something else they clearly agree on is not feeling obligated to kowtow to the press.

One way in which the Coens' process is exceptional and unique is in their extensive use of storyboards. They conceive of and envision the entire movie in advance, then storyboard it. Starting with their second film, *Raising Arizona*, they have worked closely with Ohio-based storyboard artist J. Todd Anderson, meticulously planning out each scene and even specific shots in advance. What started out as a necessity—during production of an independent film there is not enough money or time to create the movie as you go—has evolved into their distinctive process. The Coens, Anderson, and cinematographer Roger Deakins met over six weeks to storyboard *The Big Lebowski*. Joel created a shot list, Ethan did thumbnail sketches, and then the group plotted out the movie.

Chris Spellman, the set decorator for *Lebowski* (as well as *Miller's Crossing, Barton Fink*, and *The Man Who Wasn't There*), differentiates the Coens from other directors

"The funny thing about the Coens is, when you read a script from them, you're immediately brought into their world.... But for an actor, it's a sort of a real wonderful playground to jump into. You just find yourself being the character just because you're saying their words. Their words are the magic; their script is the magic."

—Jon Polito, actor and veteran of five Coen films

Storyboarding

"Storyboard. A series of sketches or sometimes photographs that represents the individual shots to be taken for a film production. The individual shots are arranged in the normal sequence of action and represent a visual blueprint of the entire film (or sometimes only parts of the film). Dialogue, sound effects, music, and camera movement are also frequently noted. The sketches might be hung in order on a wall or assembled together in script form. Essential in planning animation works, they are also frequently used in the making of feature films to allow the director and the director of photography to prepare for and carry out various setups and camera movements. With its series of illustrations and captions, the storyboard resembles a cartoon strip." —*The Complete Film Dictionary*, Ira Konigsberg

THE LEAGUE

Storyboard Artist J. Todd Anderson's Rules for a Perfect Movie

1. A Perfect Movie creates the world it exists in.

2. It wholly sustains that world.

3. Regardless of changes in society, it retains its meaning and entertainment value.

4. A Perfect Movie is never placed in any preferential or numerical order. Each film is perfect by its own scale.

© 2008 (with Geo. Willeman)

because they have a "clear vision of what they want before any film rolls." This vision, which is in essence transcribed directly onto the storyboards, enables the Coens to clearly communicate their point of view to the movie crew, transferring crucial knowledge with less than the usual amount of chatter (historically not Joel or Ethan's strong suit). The storyboards for the week are posted for the crew so everyone involved in the production has the opportunity for a very visual peek inside the Coens' brains. From there, movie magic.

The Coens' elaborate works are a mix of pastiche and homage, referencing everything from musicals and old movies to Faulkner to pulp novels and comic books, accentuated by dazzling cinematography and intricate design. One cannot extract the films from their landscapes: the stifling hot Texas of *Blood Simple*; the stultifying, gleaming New York cityscape of *The Hudsucker Proxy*; the dusty Mississippi Delta of *O Brother, Where Art Thou?*; the frozen tundra of *Fargo*; the seedy underbelly that so sharply contrasts the wealthy opulence

> ## "It's like a Beatles song. [Each Coen film] has its own character."
>
> —J. Todd Anderson, storyboard artist, in *The Big Lebowski: The Making of a Coen Brothers Film*

of Los Angeles in *The Big Lebowski*; and so on. Their unique sense of place is flawlessly conceived, right down to the distinctive jargon of their characters, reflecting a stylized form of American vernacular that fits the time and place and genre. As *The New York Times* described it, the Coens create "a postmodern cinematic world...where everything seems vaguely unhinged."

Joel Coen has said, "One of the pleasures of making movies is creating a world." Within

"What I find unique and extremely interesting is that [Joel] has most of the shot setups in his head. Unlike so many other directors I've worked for who feel the need to shoot a scene a hundred times and from every conceivable angle, they shoot it a handful of times and only from a specific angle."

—Peter "Goose" Siragusa, actor who portrayed bartenders in *The Big Lebowski* and *The Man Who Wasn't There*

these worlds the brothers create open-ended stories, often using first-person narration and a cavalry of gifted and oftentimes "wacky" (to use a typical Coen term) actors who sign on for the ride again and again. Frequent fellow travelers—all members of the cast of *The Big Lebowski*—include the intense John Turturro; the consummate everyman Steve Buscemi; and John Goodman, a boisterous and fearless kindred spirit.

Although they have mined many genres throughout their career, film noir seems to be the Coens' touchstone. From the hard-boiled thriller *Blood Simple* to the luminous and moody *The Man Who Wasn't There* to *The Big Lebowski*, with its Philip Marlowe–esque "Dude," they have done noir every which way, filtering its absurdness and sense of disorientation, alienation, and cynicism through their uniquely skewed sensibility. As Ronald Bergan wrote in his book, *The Coen Brothers*, "All their movies are comedies, and all of them, excepting *The Hudsucker Proxy*, are fundamentally *films noirs*, disguised as horror movie (*Blood Simple*), farce (*Raising Arizona*), gangster movie (*Miller's Crossing*), psychological drama (*Barton Fink*), police thriller (*Fargo*), comedy (*The Big Lebowski*), and social drama (*O Brother, Where Art Thou?*)."

An exuberant funny bone also runs through their movies, and they employ brazen slapstick, deliciously clever banter, gallows humor, and even sight gags with relish.

"The Coens are like a mom-and-pop operation. They write it, they edit it, they do the whole thing. They're involved in everything. It's very low stress, working with them. There's almost no stress. If I could make a movie with them every couple of years I would, just because of the pleasure of it."

—John Turturro, in *The Onion*

Nobody Fucks with Da Jesus print, by Visual Etiquette. *Courtesy of Visual Etiquette*

In *The Big Lebowski* this ranges from Walter smashing up the wrong car and provoking the car's owner to seek retribution on the Dude's poor beat-up Gran Torino; to the over-the-top purple-jumpsuited, hairnetted character of Jesus Quintana; to the Dude rubbing a pencil over paper to reveal a dirty picture. (At a 2009 retrospective discussion of their filmography at the Walker Art Center in Minneapolis, viewing this scene prompted a long, infectious bout of laughter from Ethan.) The films seem to embody the pure joy of their creators.

Once dubbed "the Hardy Boys from hell," the Coen brothers have confounded and at times divided critics and audiences alike. While these genre-bending, period-twisting shape-shifters can be difficult to pin down, it's abundantly clear that these are filmmakers whose love for the movies is matched by the vastness of their imagination.

"If somebody goes out to make a movie that isn't designed primarily to entertain people, then I don't know what the fuck they're doing. What's the Raymond Chandler line? 'All good art is entertainment and anyone who says differently is a stuffed shirt and juvenile at the art of living.'"

—Joel Coen, in *Film Comment*

Jeff Bridges and Joel Coen.
© AF Archive / Alamy

The Six Coen Motifs

"Most of the characters in our movies are pretty unpleasant—losers or lunkheads, or both. But we're also very fond of those characters, because you don't usually see movies based around those kinds of people. We're not interested in burly superhero types."—Joel Coen, in *Total Film*

While the Coens' body of work is extremely diverse—Westerns, thrillers, comedies, period pieces from all different times and locales, farces, black-and-white noirs, saturated color odysseys—there are common threads running throughout. William Preston Robertson, who has done voice work in their films and wrote the book *The Big Lebowski: The Making of a Coen Brothers Film*, listed these "recurring motifs" as: "1. howling fat men; 2. blustery titans; 3. vomiting; 4. violence; 5. dreams; and 6. peculiar haircuts." Of these, only vomiting (at least, on screen) and peculiar haircuts (unless the Jesus' hairnet counts) do not fit *The Big Lebowski*.

John Goodman is certainly their favored "howling fat man." As Walter Sobchak, he howls about rules and Shabbos and at Donny. Goodman began as a howling escaped convict in *Raising Arizona* (rising up from the mud in a rainstorm), then howled as Madman Mundt in *Barton Fink* and portrayed a howling Cyclops in *O Brother, Where Art Thou?* As *The New York Times* described, "In all the Coen brothers' movies, [Goodman] plays someone who is either menacing or about to erupt. He's like a tank of volatile, pressurized hydrogen."

Goodman has said, "Let me do a Coen brothers film every other year, and I'll be happy."

Said blustery titans (some of whom howl and some of whom are fat) are mostly rich, white men in positions of power, often issuing commands from behind a desk; this all fits the Big Lebowski. (However, the Coens also employ small, elderly men of power behind outsized wooden desks; see *Intolerable Cruelty* and *A Serious Man*.)

All Coen movies have their own element of violence, like the nihilist losing his ear to Walter's teeth in the parking lot scene in *Lebowski*. *The Big Lebowski* and *The Hudsucker Proxy* are the only Coen brothers films in which nobody is shot. (The Dude's poor car, however, is less fortunate.) Kidnappings appear in most, one at the hands of a siren (*O Brother, Where Art Thou?*), one by alien (*The Man Who Wasn't There*), one by crooks lacking in competence (*Fargo*), and one a faux kidnapping (*The Big Lebowski*). Many, many Coen characters get punched in the face. In fact, the Dude not only gets face-punched but smacked in the forehead with a coffee mug.

Dreams—in the Dude's case drug- and punch-induced fantasies—are indeed a common theme in most Coen works, too. H.I.'s dream in *Raising Arizona* conjures up the Lone Biker of the Apocalypse, and the film ends on a dream of the future. The Coens also use dreams in confounding and disturbing ways. The bait-and-switch dream in *Blood Simple* provokes audible audience screams. In *Barton Fink*, the murder that stuns the main character could be either dream or reality.

The Early Filmmaking Career of the Two-Headed Director

Blood Simple (1984)

With echoes of Hitchcock, *The Postman Always Rings Twice*, and *Double Indemnity*, the Coens' first feature film stunned audiences at the 1984 New York Film Festival. *The New York Times* raved about its "black humor, abundant originality and a brilliant visual style." The atmospherically gothic tale of a double-cross set in a dusty Texas town features Frances McDormand (who got this, her first acting job, when her roommate Holly Hunter bowed out) as an unfaithful wife and M. Emmet Walsh as the amoral private detective Loren Visser. The Coens still enjoy touting *Village Voice* reviewer J. Hoberman's stinging quip—Hoberman said the film had "the heart of a Bloomingdale's window and the soul of a résumé."

"It's probable that most filmmakers love making movies, but few of them express this love with such voracious, crazy ardor. The brothers are a pair of brilliant oxymorons: shaggy-dog formalists, at once obsessed with every detail and apt to let their stories run wild."

—A. O. Scott, in *The New York Times*

Ethan and Joel Coen at the release of *Miller's Crossing,* 1990.
Time Life Pictures / Getty Images

Raising Arizona (1987)

In a tonal about-face from their debut, the Coens next took on the screwball comedy/kidnap caper genre. In *Raising Arizona*, H.I. McDunnough (Nicolas Cage) and his wife, Ed (Holly Hunter), make a desperate grab for the American dream in 1980s suburban Tempe. Made in ten weeks for four times what *Blood Simple* cost to produce, the film incorporated an ingenious vernacular that Joel called, "a mixture of local dialect and a vocabulary we imagined from the likely reading materials of the characters: the Bible, magazines" (*Positif*). Marked by a vivacious soundtrack that combined Beethoven and yodeling and featuring one of the funniest chase scenes ever, *Raising Arizona*'s humor is nonetheless tempered by an apocalyptic undercurrent and grim political climate. After the film was released to some success, the Coens turned down Warner Bros.' offer of millions to direct the next *Batman*.

"It's interesting seeing the same actors in the same films and playing with them over and over. Like having shot John Goodman before in the face with blue paint in *Raising Arizona,* and then he's back again to blow dust all over the Dude in *The Big Lebowski.*"

—Peter Chesney, mechanical effects designer on eight Coen films and counting

Raising Arizona is another Coen film with a sizeable cult following.
© Pictorial Press Ltd / Alamy

The future Jesus Quintana in *Miller's Crossing*, in which the phrase "Jesus, Tom" is something of a catchphrase.
© AF Archive / Alamy

Miller's Crossing (1990)

Originally referred to by the Coens as *The Bighead* (named for the lead character played by Gabriel Byrne), their adaptation of Dashiell Hammett's *Red Harvest* and *The Glass Key* is a classic Prohibition-era gangster noir, with Irish and Italian mobs going to war over internecine double-dealing. Gorgeously shot, this fable of friendship and loyalty is awash in period atmosphere. It is highlighted by a tour-de-force performance by last-minute fill-in Albert Finney, who came on board when Trey Wilson (Nathan Arizona in *Raising Arizona*) unexpectedly died just before filming commenced.

Miller's Crossing has the most complicated of all the Coens' plots. It marked the end of their short streak of modest hits and the beginning of a string of box-office flops.

The Haunting Hat Image in *Miller's Crossing*

William Preston Robertson also suggests "lost hats" as another motif in the Coens' films. It may be that there are more lost heads in their films, but at any rate the most famous hat in all their work is the elusive black fedora that's windswept along a leafy forest glade in *Miller's Crossing*—a truly breathtaking visual. Longtime Coen mechanical effects man (mechanical effects are created in front of the camera rather than optically added later) Peter Chesney demystifies the magic behind the image, proving that some of the seemingly smallest filmic gestures can be the most arduous to produce.

"Like a lot of things on their shows, there are subtle effects that [the Coens] are very specifically interested in. On *Miller's Crossing*, one of the opening sequences is the hat in the woods. Remember, back then, you couldn't go for the easy CGI, and this was a very specific image that they really wanted to have. It was actually done by string—a rather large set-up for a small gag! We had a fishing rod loop put about fifty feet up a tree in the background in the center, and the line went to the hat and then came back to a speed control motor and a machined spool that gave me the right diameter for the right speed. . . . We had to get a series of winches and winch the trees out of the way so they wouldn't get in the way of the string. There were like six trees, and we weren't allowed to hurt the trees, so we put big lines up and lock and tackle and cable winches and winched the top of about a half a dozen trees over so that the overhead string wasn't getting snagged by these overhead branches, one of the key components to making the string work. And then the hat needed to tumble to get going because you're trying to make this look like a puff of wind blew it but you didn't want to use wind because then you would disturb the leaves, and then you would have sourced it. So if you look closely, you'll see there are three tiny twigs sticking out of the ground. We stuck them in just tall enough to catch the brim of the hat, so that it would catch those little tiny twigs and then start to tumble. And as it tumbled you would ramp up the speed several times during the course of the travel so you got that sense of it being blown through the woods by a breeze that wasn't there. And we actually spent probably three or four hours doing it, until the Coens got the one that they wanted—many takes, and actually the one that's in the film is one that's probably six takes before we thought we had enough. But it's that kind of subtlety that they sometimes would go for on images that the audience doesn't really know are difficult."

Barton Fink (1991)

Joel and Ethan wrote *Barton Fink* in a mere three weeks when they experienced writer's block while crafting the script of *Miller's Crossing*. The film portrays the socially conscious New York writer Barton Fink (John Turturro), who, on the cusp of World War II, reluctantly comes to Hollywood to pen a wrestling picture for studio exec Jack Lipnick (Michael Lerner, Oscar-nominated for this character based on Jack Warner, Louis B. Mayer, and Harry Cohn). Fink's writer's-block frustration builds into madness, embodied by the glue-oozing wallpaper in his room at the Hotel Earle, his torture by California's only mosquito, and his interactions with the increasingly volatile insurance salesman Charlie Meadows (John Goodman). A true original that plumbs the depths of the creative process, *Barton Fink* was the first film in the forty-four-year history of the Cannes Film Festival to win all three major awards. (Roman Polanski presided over the Cannes jury; *Fink*'s chilling mood evokes Polanski's 1976 thriller *The Tenant*.)

Another *Lebowski* principal featured in the film was Steve Buscemi, in the small but memorable role of Chet! (The character never

John Turturro as Barton Fink.
© Moviestore Collection Ltd / Alamy

Michael Lerner as *Barton Fink* movie-biz honcho Jack Lipnick, a blustery titan in the vein of the Big Lebowski.
© AF Archive / Alamy

misses the opportunity to append an exclamation point to his name.) Buscemi later said in an interview in *Bomb*, "[The Coens] get such a kick out of actors. In *Barton Fink*, I was doing this scene where I was picking up the shoes to put on the cart, you know, and then like I hear a noise and kind of stop, and then continue. They had me do that six or seven times because they enjoyed that scene."

Both Turturro and Goodman's parts were written with them in mind, and according to the Coens, the interplay between these disparate characters in part inspired the unlikely pair of the Dude and Walter Sobchak in *The Big Lebowski*. Another foreshadowing between the two productions: the wrap party for *Barton Fink* was held at a bowling alley.

The Hudsucker Proxy (1994)

Set in 1958 but evoking Frank Capra films of the 1930s and 1940s, *The Hudsucker Proxy* was a stylishly written and conceived picture about naïve Norville Barnes (Tim Robbins), who comes to the big city with big dreams. As feisty newspaper reporter Amy Archer, Jennifer Jason Leigh channeled Rosalind Russell from *His Girl Friday*, and the incomparable Paul Newman rounded out the cast as calculating executive Sidney J. Mussburger. Roger Ebert hailed it as "a feast for the eyes and the imagination," but the film was criticized as having all style and no substance. Cowritten with the Coens' friend Sam Raimi, the feature had their biggest budget by far at $25 million, but took in a mere $3 million.

Fargo (1996)

After the tepid response to their previous several films, the Coens seemingly laughed in the face of reason by taking on a project that on its surface was their most inaccessible and darkest yet. The reaction: worldwide acclaim, a breakthrough hit, and perhaps utter mystification on the part of the Coens. Roger Ebert simply declared it "one of the best movies I've ever seen." In general inspired by real events from their home region, but almost completely invented despite its faux documentary–style announcement that "This is a true story" in the opening credits, *Fargo* is a thriller noir stuck in a Minnesota deep freeze (although production on the film commenced during one of the least snowy Minnesota winters ever, necessitating snow machines). This taut tale of a kidnapping gone awry incorporated dark humor and a haunting score by Coen regular Carter Burwell. *Fargo*'s brilliantly penned personalities, including the sap Jerry Lundegaard, played by William H. Macy, and inept kidnapper Carl Showalter (Steve Buscemi), are balanced by perhaps the most humane character in any Coen film: small-town police chief Marge Gunderson, played

Coen Heroes, Talkers, and Weirdos

Among the distinct character types found in multiple Coen films is the apocalyptic, fire-and-brimstone type, incarnated in *Raising Arizona*'s Lone Biker of the Apocalypse, who was "especially hard on the little things"; *Barton Fink*'s Charlie Meadows, who while surrounded by flames in a hotel hallway shouts, "I'll show you the life of the mind!"; and *No Country for Old Men*'s Anton Chigurh, who is ominously apocalyptic in, well, everything he does.

On the flip side are the Coen heroes—typically, antiheroes. These are the lovable (and some not so) losers who go against type, such as the pathetic car salesman Jerry Lundegaard in *Fargo* or the addled, pot-smoking Dude in *The Big Lebowski*.

Rounding out the Coens' stable of characters are the gabbers, the Laurel and Hardy–inspired "dopes." There's the run-off-at-the-mouth Carl Showalter (Steve Buscemi) in *Fargo*, blockhead personal trainer Chad Feldheimer (Brad Pitt) in *Burn After Reading*, and any character George Clooney has ever played in a Coen brothers film. (Reportedly, after *Burn After Reading* wrapped, Clooney announced, "That's it boys, I've played my last idiot!")

The brothers toy with audience expectations with their variations on good guys and bad guys and with inherently comic juxtaposed pairings: big men next to small men; fast talkers conversing with deliberate enunciators; and, of course, the great coupling of a militaristic blowhard Vietnam vet and a longhaired, pot-smoking hippie—friends who inexplicably yet somehow understandably have come together through a shared interest of bowling.

Steve Buscemi and the Coens

Steve Buscemi (which he pronounces "Bu-semmy" as opposed to the correct Sicilian pronunciation of "Bu-shemmy") has been cast in six Coen brothers films—more than any other actor. They are *Miller's Crossing, The Hudsucker Proxy, Barton Fink, Fargo, The Big Lebowski*, and their short within the compilation *Paris Je t'aime (2006)*. Most of these were small parts until *Fargo*, in which his quick-talking, "funny-looking" sociopathic character is killed off in a most memorable and gruesome way—via woodchipper. In fact, his characters are often killed off by the Coens, as in *Miller's* and *Lebowski*.

© AF Archive / Alamy.
Courtesy of Universal Studios Licensing LLC

pitch perfectly by Frances McDormand. Confounding many critics' opinion that the Coens lack respect for their own characters, Marge is a well-rounded, intelligent, and eminently sympathetic woman, with, of course, quirky attributes—her heavy Minnesota accent and prodigious pregnant belly provide ample fodder for laughs.

Fargo garnered Joel the Best Director award at the Cannes Film Festival and went on to win the Best Original Screenplay Oscar (accepted by Joel and Ethan) and the Best Actress Oscar for McDormand, for which she famously thanked "the cowriter, director, and producer of *Fargo*, Mr. Ethan Coen, who helped make an actor of me; his brother,

Mr. Joel Coen, who made a woman of me; and our moon and our son, Mr. Pedro McDormand Coen, who's made a real mother of me."

The wins came in the midst of work on their next film, *The Big Lebowski. Lebowski* had been written at the same time as *Fargo*, but production was delayed in order for the stars' schedules to align. Peter Siragusa, an actor on the *Lebowski* set, recalls, "They are extremely low-keyed guys, and I remember that the morning after they won the Oscar for *Fargo* was no different than any other morning on set. VERY casual."

Fargo has since been selected for preservation by the National Film Registry.

STRIKES & GUTTERS

Following *Fargo*'s success, there were plans for the film to be made into a television series starring Kathy Bates, which never materialized. Needless to say, the Coens weren't involved in this enterprise.

Peter Stormare and Steve Buscemi (future nihilist and Donny, respectively) in *Fargo*.
© *Photos 12 / Alamy*

The Big Lebowski,
print by Jim Horwat,
2009.
Courtesy of the artist,
www.jimhorwat.com

PART II
The Seeds of Production: Origin of *The Big Lebowski*, an L.A. Story

When the Coen brothers imagine a tale, they often have a strong, specific sense of where it's going to take place—and the locale of a film is frequently what generates the plot in the first place. It's hard to know exactly what came first for the Coens in the development of *The Big Lebowski*—the setting or the story—but for many reasons California, and Los Angeles specifically, fits *Lebowski* to a T. The people the movie's characters were inspired by were L.A.-based, as were aspects of the story. Bowling and Googie space age–style architecture (see page 69 for more on Googie architecture) from the 1940s and 1950s were centered in L.A., as was 1960s and 1970s psychedelic drug consumption (the Dude's element). Add to the City of Angels mix the crime fiction of Raymond Chandler noir stories, which formed the foundation of the *Lebowski* plot and in which the city itself is practically a character.

> **"For us it was above and beyond all else a Californian story."**
>
> —Ethan Coen, in *Positif*, reprinted in *The Coen Brothers Interviews*

The Coens are mad for utilizing clashing juxtapositions in their films. The very opening of *The Big Lebowski* features the cowboy-twanged voice-over of Sam Elliott's the Stranger, musing on the Dude and the specific place where he lives. The incongruity between his western talk and the city are immediately apparent in this speech: "Maybe that's

Sunset Bowling Center on the Warner Bros. lot, 1945.
© *Lake County Museum / Corbis*

why I found the place s'durned innarestin'." The Coens have a similar perspective on L.A. They live in New York and have always considered themselves tourists in L.A., which they see as more surreal in situations, settings, and eclectic personages than New York.

The Coens knew an abundance of "characters" in L.A. Whereas *Fargo* only purports to be a "true story," *The Big Lebowski* was in reality inspired by actual L.A. people and their experiences—and some of the strangest plot elements contain nuggets of truth.

Hollywood Boulevard in the 1940s.
Photograph by Philip Gendreau / © Bettmann / Corbis

A Rug That Tied the Plot Together

In the late 1980s, Joel and Ethan Coen were at an L.A. dinner party at the home of Peter Exline, now a script consultant, to whom producer Barry Sonnenfeld had introduced them through an NYU connection during *Blood Simple* fundraising. At the party, "Uncle Pete" waxed poetic ad infinitum about how his beat-up, faux Persian rug "tied the room together," a joke that tickled the Coen brothers. The rug and the associated phrase,

Locations

1 **Exteriors of the Dude's bungalow/limousine sequence/run-in with Da Fino:** Strip of houses, 606-609 Venezia Blvd., Venice Beach (interiors in Hollywood sound stage).

2 **Wooden bridge:** Santa Clara River Valley just off Hwy 126 at Torrey Road, just outside of Fillmore. *In the movie, located in Simi Valley.*

3 **Tumbleweed:** Rolls up a hill in Pear Blossom, California, outside Palmdale. Merges with L.A. cityscape from perspective of Simi Valley, NW of the Burbank Airport. It rolls past a 101 freeway overpass at Santa Monica Blvd., a Benitos taco stand at 3rd Ave. at Edinborough, an empty Sunset Blvd., and finally a deserted beach along Santa Monica Bay at night.

4 **Hollywood Star Lanes:** 5227 Santa Monica Blvd.

5 **Dinah's Family Restaurant:** 6521 South Sepulveda, Culver City. Open during the production.

6 **Donny's eulogy:** Along the shores of Palos Verdes, which separates the south bay of L.A. from Long Beach. *In the movie, located along Malibu coastline.*

7 **Johnie's Coffee Shop:** Closed in 1997. Intersection of Wilshire Blvd. and Fairfax Ave.

8 **In cab after being at the Malibu Police Station:** Culver City, along streets Duquesne and Jefferson. *In the movie, located along Pacific Coast Hwy of Malibu.*

9 **Larry's house:** Stearns Drive between West Pico Blvd and West 18th Street, in the Fairfax District. *In the movie, located in North Hollywood on Radford, near In-N-Out Burger.*

10 **Jesus' Walk:** North Kenmore Ave. between Monroe Street and Lily Crest Ave., Hollywood.

11 **Auto Circus:** Downtown Los Angeles impound lot, West 18th Street at St. Andrew's Place. (First day of shooting.) *In the movie, located in North Hollywood.*

12 **Sobchak Security:** 6757 Santa Monica Blvd. minimall (near North Highland Ave.), near where Hollywood Star Lanes used to be (also a Benitos in this mall).

13 **Dude's car crash, while Creedence plays:** Up Cahuenga Blvd. in Hollywood, left onto La Mirada Ave., heading toward Vine Street.

14 **Maude's Loft / Landlord Modern Dance Quintet:** Downtown L.A., Palace Theater, corner of 6th and South Broadway.

15 **Jackie Treehorn residence:** Sheats Goldstein Residence, 10104 Angelo View Drive in Benedict Canyon.

16 **The Big Lebowski's mansion:** Interiors are in the Greystone Mansion, 905 Loma Vista Drive.

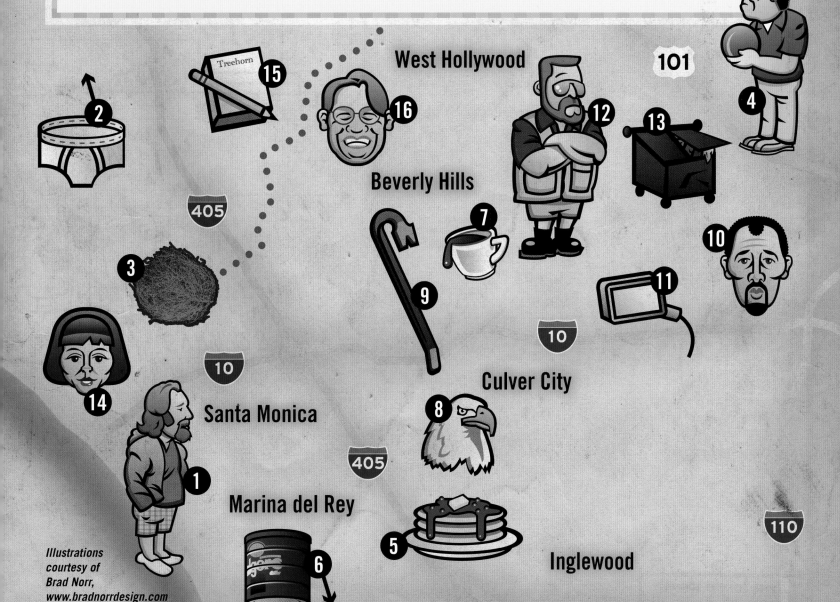

Illustrations courtesy of Brad Norr, www.bradnorrdesign.com

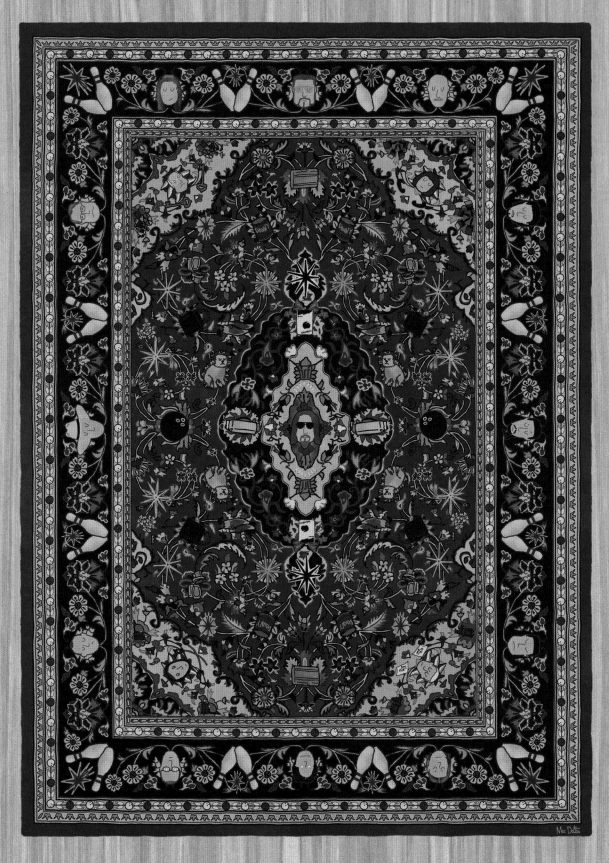

The Rug, by Max Dalton.
Courtesy of the artist, www.maximdalton.com

which underscores the incongruity of such a ratty rug making an aesthetic difference in a room, became the activator for the *Lebowski* plot—the Dude's response to heavies soiling his rug propels the story.

A story that Exline told the Coens at that pivotal dinner party provided another key plot turn. In about 1986, Exline's Mazda was stolen. It was later recovered and when he picked it up in a police impound lot, he discovered a damning piece of evidence. Left behind amidst hamburger wrappers was the graded homework of one fourteen-year-old Jaik Freeman— with address included.

While a studio exec at Universal, Exline had met "Big" Lew Abernathy, who had some connections to the movie biz (and who paid for film school by moonlighting as a private investigator). They tracked the adolescent down and arrived unannounced at his house. (In a scene reminiscent of the movie, Freeman's father was in a hospital bed at the time.) Abernathy made a big show of it, arriving in a suit and dramatically pulling Freeman's homework, which was sealed in an evidence bag, from his briefcase. Freeman never admitted to any wrongdoing. In an interview with *Rolling Stone*, Joel recalls hearing the story: "I remember when Pete told us that [homework] story and thinking there was something quintessentially L.A. about it, but L.A. in a very Chandler-ian way."

> ## "All the characters are pretty much emblematic of Los Angeles—they're all types who seem like people you would meet there."
>
> —Ethan Coen, in *Total Film*

The Real Little Larry
In their book, *I'm a Lebowski, You're a Lebowski*, the originators of the Lebowski Fest tell of tracking down the real "Little Larry" for an interview. Although Jaik Freeman had seen *The Big Lebowski*, until their phone call he had never connected the story in the film to his real-life adolescent encounter with the men who showed up at his house to "brace" him about a stolen car. (And, in case you're wondering, no, he wasn't "about to crack.")

© AF Archive / Alamy. Courtesy of Universal Studios Licensing LLC

"A couple of the characters in *The Big Lebowski* are, very loosely, inspired by real people. We know a guy who's a middle-aged hippie pothead, and another who's a Vietnam vet who's totally defined by, and obsessed with, the time he spent in Vietnam."

—Ethan Coen, in 1998 (reprinted in *Rolling Stone*)

Welcome to the Hotel California: The *Lebowski* Characters as Elements of L.A.

His Dudeness. Duder. El Duderino.

The Dude was loosely based on the loud, boisterous, jovial, and eccentric Jeff Dowd, a film producer. First nicknamed the "Dude" as a kid playing baseball in California, Dowd has called himself "the Pope of Dope," went through a period of heavy White Russian–drinking and bowling-alley hanging out, and was a member of the Seattle Seven during the Vietnam War (as in the film, it was him and "six other guys"). His political activism led to him being indicted and tried for conspiracy to destroy federal property, but he was exonerated due to a mistrial. Dowd met Joel and Ethan on their

Pencils by One Up Designs.
Photo courtesy of One Up Designs, www.one-updesigns.com

first trip to L.A. to fundraise for *Blood Simple*, and his first impression of them, as he said in *The Boston Globe*, was that they were "a couple of grungy guys, walking back and forth and smoking cigarettes." The brothers loved to riff on Dowd's nickname. Often they would call him up and banter about his nickname in an analogous way to *The Big Lebowski*: "His Dudeness, Duder, or El Duderino, if you're not into the whole brevity thing."

The Coens were entranced by the idea of the Dude—the person least apt to comprehend how to untangle a complicated situation ("lotta ins, lotta outs, lotta what-have-yous") and who absorbs what's going on around him through the prism of dope—as a protagonist who is unwittingly thrust into a complex web of mistaken identity, rife with intrigue.

"They took that period of the Dude, froze him in time and moved him up to 1991. On a fundamental level, Jeff Bridges got my body language down entirely . . . the semimumbling talking, going off on tangents and stuff like that. I'm an easy mimic."

—Jeff Dowd, in *Rolling Stone*

"I took stuff from him [Dowd] for the Dude . . . but, to be honest, it's mostly just me. . . . I drew on myself a lot from back in the Sixties and Seventies. I lived in a little place like that and did drugs, although I think I was a little more creative than the Dude."

—Jeff Bridges, in Ronald Bergan's *The Coen Brothers*

The original Dude, Jeff Dowd, was jailed for six months in the early 1970s as a result of his participation in the Seattle Seven. Not because he was found guilty of the charges—conspiracy to riot—but because the judge, clearly no fan of dude-like behavior, found him in contempt of court.
Photograph by Noel Vasquez / Getty Images

The Three Faces of Walter Sobchak

The character of Walter Sobchak is a composite, in part, of Abernathy and Exline; the latter is a Vietnam vet who would frequently mention the conflict, making such blustery pronouncements as, "Well, we were winning when *I* left." Other character traits can be traced to John Milius, the bombastic, gun-enthusiast, camouflage-wearing director of such jingoistic pics as *Red Dawn* and *Conan the Barbarian*, and a cowriter of *Apocalypse Now* (and the quotable, evocative line, "I love the smell of napalm in the morning"). Joel and Ethan had met Milius in L.A. and invited him to play the part of Jack Lipnick in *Barton Fink* (which ended up being played by Michael Lerner). Milius is Jewish (Walter's adopted faith), as well as a self-proclaimed "Zen anarchist." His larger-than-life personality—and his hugely entertaining stories—fleshed out the vivid contours of Walter Sobchak.

Writer-director John Milius, a "Zen anarchist" gun collector.
Photograph by Alberto E. Rodriguez / Getty Images

"Maude (Julianne Moore) has for her blueprints the sixties New York Fluxus artists like Yoko Ono before she met John Lennon, or Carol[lee] Schneemann, who literally threw herself into her projects for physical support. Maude owes her a lot!"

—Joel Coen, in *Positif*, reprinted in *The Coen Brothers Interviews*

A 1960s New York Fluxus happening, led by avant-garde composer Karlheinz Stockhausen. *SSPL via Getty Images*

Maude's art has been commended.
© A.F. Archive / Alamy. Courtesy of Universal Studios Licensing LLC

Maude Lebowski and the Fluxus Movement

California, with its patchwork of alternative populations, is home to a tremendous abundance of artists. In fact, it leads the nation in total number of artists. And of course, Los Angeles is a hub of artistic activity for the state. It only makes sense that the Coens would include in their mélange of L.A. characters an off-kilter Fluxus performance artist: Maude Lebowski. Like other *Lebowski* characters,

Maude is a throwback to the 1960s, when performance art was in its heyday.

Fluxus, meaning "flowing" or "to flow," was an avant-garde art movement of the 1960s heavily influenced by Dadaism. Lithuanian-American artist George Maciunas, who authored the 1963 *Fluxus Manifesto*, said that Fluxus was created to "promote a revolutionary flood and tide in art, promote living art, anti-art." Pioneer feminist performance artist and radical underground filmmaker Carolee Schneemann, a clear influence on the character

1973 installation by German Fluxus pioneer Wolf Vostell, whose art incorporated symbols of the modern era (such as a car). © *Hans Georg Roth / Corbis*

Carolee Schneemann.
© *Christopher Felber / Corbis*

Graziella Martinez emerges from a "fossil egg" by Argentinian sculptor—and Fluxus artist—Rodolfo Krasno, 1972.
Photograph by Spartaco Bodini / Associated Press

of Maude, was associated with the Fluxus Art Movement and the Happenings (events considered art) that occurred at the beginning of the decade. Her work explored the interplay between eroticism and politics, and she created assemblage-style paintings that morphed into Dionysian performance. Her famous piece *Meat Joy* (1964) involved seminude performers rolling around amid various cow organs, sausages, and fish, among other materials.

Up to and Including Her Limits (1973–1976) was a performance in which Schneemann was suspended from a tree surgeon's harness. In a projector's thrown light, she drew with colorful crayons on the walls and floor surrounding her, reaching as far as her outstretched arms would

Up to and Including Her Limits. **Photograph by Shelly Farkas Davis**

allow as she swung through the space, creating a "web" of marks. The piece was a response to Jackson Pollack's technique, and Schneemann's process has since in turn been mimicked by artists such as Matthew Barney. Quite obviously, Maude Lebowski was a shameless borrower of Schneemann's method in her own work.

Interior Scroll (1975) was pivotal in the development of 1970s feminist art. In the work, the nude Schneemann, with paint on face and body, stands on a table, unwraps herself from a sheet, then pulls from her vagina a long, thin scroll. She unrolls it to read a poetic text about gender roles. In a parlance reminiscent of Maude's repeated use of the word "vagina" in reference to her work, Schneemann wrote in her book *More Than Meat Joy: Performance Works and Selected Writings,* "I thought of the vagina in many ways—physically, conceptually: as a sculptural form, an architectural referent, the source of sacred knowledge, ecstasy, birth passage, transformation."

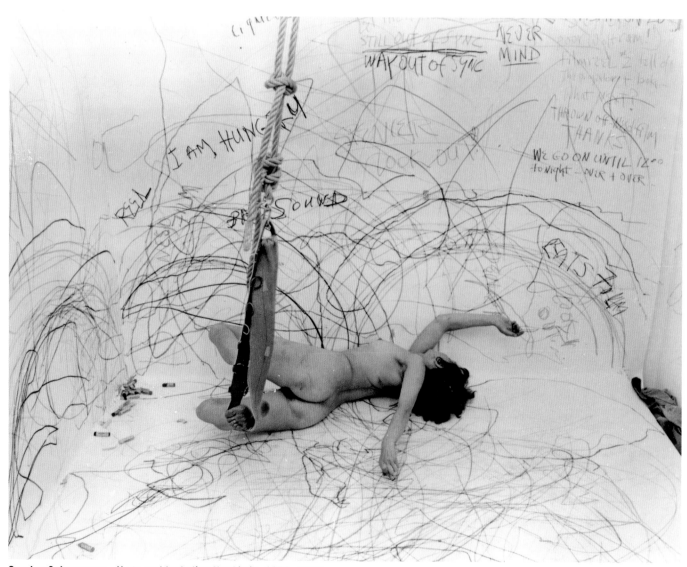

Carolee Schneemann, *Up to and Including Her Limits*, 1973–1976.
Performance, with crayon on paper, rope, and harness suspended from ceiling.
Photograph by Henrik Gard

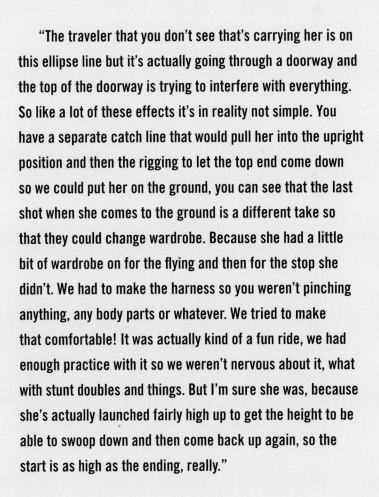

Maude's Flying Harness

"I assumed I was going to be upright. I didn't know I was going to be like Superman. That was terrifying. And I was pregnant, and it was three in the morning, and I was thirty feet in the air, and they had to bring me up really fast. It was really strange, but it was worth it in the end."
—Julianne Moore, *The Boston Phoenix*

From the mechanical effects designer, Peter Chesney: "When Maude paints the canvas, that scene was shot in the middle of the night because the schedule required it. We made a custom harness for her, to carry her in four points on the harness so she would stay horizontal. I had to figure out where the rope should go because it was a very tight location for that because she had to go under a doorway. That was our flying travel rig to fly her over Jeff Bridges to hit the canvas and come back up again. It was actually a method we developed with the same sort of geometry we used way back when on *Forever Young*, a Mel Gibson movie for which we swung a B25 one-third-scale bomber miniature into a landing. We did the same thing with Maude, using a loose line ellipse to figure out a trajectory and then pull up the loose traveler line on a two-wheel pulley system and let it go and then the object of trajectory rolls through an ellipse (a circle generated by two lines that carry the same length from foci at opposite ends).

"The traveler that you don't see that's carrying her is on this ellipse line but it's actually going through a doorway and the top of the doorway is trying to interfere with everything. So like a lot of these effects it's in reality not simple. You have a separate catch line that would pull her into the upright position and then the rigging to let the top end come down so we could put her on the ground, you can see that the last shot when she comes to the ground is a different take so that they could change wardrobe. Because she had a little bit of wardrobe on for the flying and then for the stop she didn't. We had to make the harness so you weren't pinching anything, any body parts or whatever. We tried to make that comfortable! It was actually kind of a fun ride, we had enough practice with it so we weren't nervous about it, what with stunt doubles and things. But I'm sure she was, because she's actually launched fairly high up to get the height to be able to swoop down and then come back up again, so the start is as high as the ending, really."

The Lebowski Cycle

By Joe Forkan

The Lebowski Cycle is a series of paintings and drawings exploring the idea of layered narrative, using masterpieces of European art and *The Big Lebowski* as a starting point.

The series came out of a longstanding interest in narrative painting, particularly paintings from the Baroque and Neoclassical eras. I've always been drawn to complex figurative paintings that depict dramatic story arcs and compress many thoughts, ideas, and emotions into a single image. I was also interested in the human interactions and conflicts, modes of depiction, and formal structures that are operating in those paintings, not just the specific stories.

I wanted to explore a large, unified series, but I was looking for a way to mitigate the grand seriousness that historical and religious paintings often contain.

In wondering how the Old Masters might have handled less lofty subject matter, I started thinking about *The Big Lebowski* (a favorite film, obviously). It seemed that the characters, humor, and preposterous story arc of the film might be enlisted to explore multiple points of view, moods, and intentions, if combined with themes and titles from well-known narrative paintings.

The Supper at Emmaus (1601), by Michelangelo da Caravaggio. © The Art Collection / Alamy

Supper at Emmaus (After Caravaggio), 2010. Paintings in *The Lebowski Cycle* are oil on linen and were created between 2006 and 2011.
© Joe Forkan

The Death of Marat (After David), 2008.
© Joe Forkan

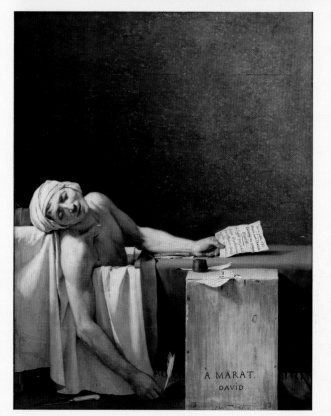

The Death of Marat (1793),
by Jacques Louis David.
© The Art Collection / Alamy

"Uli doesn't believe in anything.
He's a nihilist."
—Bunny Lebowski

"Ah, that must be exhausting."
—The Dude

The Coen brothers were already working with layered genres and archetypes in the film. They constructed a labyrinthine narrative worthy of a Raymond Chandler novel and replaced the hard-boiled detective with an aging pothead. This gave them great storytelling possibilities, playing off of and to the conventions of different genres. If you get all the references, it's great; if not, it's still rich storytelling. The fact that the characters in the film are dead serious about what they are doing—that it's their *actions* that are funny, rather than overt comic acting—was another reason I wanted to use *The Big Lebowski* as

The Raft of the Medusa (1818–1819), by Théodore Géricault. © Exotica.im 16 / Alamy

a source. I liked the collision of humor and drama and the odd ways film and painting language could come together.

None of these large-scale paintings are based on straight screenshots. Characters were combined from different frames, elements were added and subtracted, and compositions changed and expanded, then adapted further in the process of painting.

Trying to find the right balance between the disparate sources and conventions to make hybrid images that reference the film, art history, and contemporary art was the struggle and the fun, hopefully creating a lot of different ways to enter the work.

T Bone Burnett, writing about working on the Coen brothers' *O Brother, Where Art Thou?*, said the tone of that movie was "epic and dead serious on the one hand and comic and affable on the other." I think I respond to that sensibility in the Coen brothers' work, and achieving that sensibility was really one of my goals for the series.

The original fourteen paintings were completed over a five-year period, from 2006 to 2011.

Joe Forkan is an associate professor of art at California State University, Fullerton.

Photographs by Susan Einstein. Courtesy of Joe Forkan

Fife Player (1866), by Edouard
Manet. © *Peter Barritt / Alamy*

Jester, 2011. © *Joe Forkan*

Overleaf:
*The Raft of the Medusa
(After Géricault)*, 2011.
© *Joe Forkan*

The Anti-Hollywood: The Old Pornographers

Los Angeles is known for its movie-star culture, but the flip side of the glamorous Hollywood biz is the considerably less-so multibillion-dollar porn industry. Both commercial enterprises are actually based in the San Fernando Valley (sometimes called "San Pornando Valley," or simply "Porn Valley"). *The Big Lebowski*'s pornographer character Jackie Treehorn (played by a dapper Ben Gazzara) has similarities to cultural icon and *Playboy* mogul Hugh Hefner circa the 1960s–1970s, when he was the host of television shows *Playboy's Penthouse* (1959–1960) and *Playboy After Dark* (1969–1970). What Treehorn says about the effect of the digital revolution on the adult entertainment industry—"New technology permits us to do very exciting things in interactive erotic software. Wave of the future, Dude. One hundred percent electronic"—is true; digitally manipulated and computer-generated pornography is now widespread, and the industry is even moving into the 3-D realm.

Other elements of the porn plotline are also based in reality. The Coens employed actual porn star Asia Carrera, veteran of over 250 hardcore flicks with such titles as *Interview with a Vamp* and *Taxi Dancer*, for the character of Sherry, Bunny's roommate in *Logjammin'*. Reportedly, they added lines for her so she could get her Screen Actors Guild card. Carrera rates *The Big Lebowski* a top score of "5" on her website, but points out that *Logjammin'* "is NOT a real movie!"

Hugh Hefner (in 1966)—the original Jackie Treehorn? *Getty Images*

Logjammin', print by Agnes Barton-Sabo.
© 2010 Agnes Barton-Sabo, www.bettyturbo.etsy.com

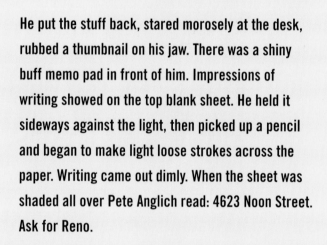

Dirty Pictures

Not in the original script: the hilarious episode in which Jackie writes on a pad of paper and rips off the page before leaving the room. The Dude, thinking he might glean a clue from it, rubs a pencil point over the subsequent sheet to capture the impression—only to discover that Treehorn had merely drawn a dirty picture. The page for this scene was added by the Coens after the script was written and is a riff on a common mystery-movie conceit in which a detective performs the same action as the Dude, but usually with more conclusive results. Similar episodes occur in Hitchcock's *North by Northwest* (1959), Fritz Lang's silent film *Spies* (1928), and Sam Fuller's *Pickup on South Street* (1953), all falling somewhere along the noir continuum. It's a conceit that appears in literature as well, such as the short story "Whistle and I'll Come to You" by M. S. James, the Nancy Drew mystery *Running Scared*, and, of course, in Raymond Chandler's writing. From Chandler's "Pickup on Noon Street:"

He put the stuff back, stared morosely at the desk, rubbed a thumbnail on his jaw. There was a shiny buff memo pad in front of him. Impressions of writing showed on the top blank sheet. He held it sideways against the light, then picked up a pencil and began to make light loose strokes across the paper. Writing came out dimly. When the sheet was shaded all over Pete Anglich read: 4623 Noon Street. Ask for Reno.

During production of the *Lebowski* scene, Ben Gazzara, who really drew the picture that's shown in the film, had to stop and ask the Coens to refresh his memory: "Boys, *why* am I drawing the dick?"

The Nihilists: Believing in "Nossing"

As Walter Sobchak suggests, nihilism isn't so much a philosophical practice as it is the absence of one. From the Latin word *nihil* meaning "nothing," nihilists practice an extreme form of skepticism, leading to the rejection of all laws and institutions—or, as is often repeated in the film, the belief in nothing. Although nihilism's roots are Russian (see the writings of nineteenth-century philosophers Nikolai Chernychevsky and Mikhal Bakunin), the philosopher most closely associated with the nihilist school of thought was German: Friedrich Nietzsche. Thus, the Coens' conceiving of the three nihilist characters as Germans only seems fitting.

Nietzsche wasn't strictly a nihilist, as he actually put forth values and lamented what he called the "death of God." But at the heart of his writings was a sentiment against belief systems, which he claimed deny individual perspectives. Specifically, he considered all religions to denigrate strength by connoting it as "bad" and "evil," thereby celebrating weakness and self-denial. In other words,

> "Nihilists! Fuck me. I mean say what you want about the tenets of National Socialism, Dude, at least it's an ethos."
>
> —Walter Sobchak, *The Big Lebowski*

ROLL SCENE

The Cinematic Reverse Engineering of Falling Flat

The shot of the Dude passing out on Treehorn's glass coffee table had to be done in reverse. It's a complex sequence, because the table needed to be rigged so there was enough room for the camera under it. Also, the crew had to remove Bridges' makeup; otherwise in the film it would have been on the glass before he actually gets there. The scene required the actor to act in reverse—starting with his face on the table (blacked out), and pulling up to a conscious state. As Peter Chesney says, "When you get into the subtleties of actually creating the images there's a little more cinematic engineering involved."

Chesney also tackled this on *The Hudsucker Proxy*, when an employee of Hudsucker Industries tries to jump out the window, unaware that Sidney J. Mussburger (Paul Newman) has installed Plexiglas. The man hits the glass and slides down. This shot was also done as a "reverse." Another reverse occurs when Norville Barnes (Tim Robbins) comes to a screeching halt after falling off the building, just before hitting the ground. In reality, the crew jerked him approximately twenty feet in the air. He also had to act in a reverse chronology, responding to the plummet and unexpected stop first with incredulity, then terror.

Believing in Music and Wardrobe Malfunctions

The title of the techno-pop music Carter Burwell created for the nihilists' boombox in the parking lot scene is a play on their ideology: "Wie Glauben" translates to "We Believe" in German. Also in this scene: in the shot of the nihilist played by Flea crawling away from the burned car, his butt crack inadvertently shows. The crew was planning to fix it, but Joel and Ethan loved the image, and the accident stayed in.

Nietzsche was pro-individual (similar to, but not fully, a "nihilistic" viewpoint).

The diverse population of California is particularly accepting of alternative lifestyles, has antiestablishment leanings, and celebrates an individualist culture—from its direct-participation voting system, to the cult of celebrity that is Hollywood, to the laid-back "sex, drugs, and rock 'n' roll" spirit that pervades many regions—and therefore seems a ripe breeding ground for the small subsection of the population that identifies as nihilists. The California populace also ranks below the national average on several gauges of one belief system tackled by Nietzsche: religion. According to the Pew Forum on Religion and Public Life, fewer Californians consider religion to be important in their lives, attend religious services, or believe in God than members of the populations of other states. As with the rest of the array of colorful characters in *The Big Lebowski*, nihilists fit right into the eccentric soup of the film's Los Angeles setting.

Friedrich Nietzsche, around 1870.
© Pictorial Press Ltd / Alamy

ROLL SCENE

The Nihilists' Studied German Accent

From Torsten Voges, the only actor playing a nihilist in the film who was actually German:

"I have a heavy German accent, and the other guys who portrayed nihilists don't. John Goodman once said, 'They sound like Elmer Fudd when they do the German accent.' But we actually got together and rehearsed the accent a little bit, because Aimee Mann [the nihilist woman] was really into learning the correct accent even though she only had like two or three lines.

"The funny thing was that a couple of years later I was at an audition for a film in which they were looking for German nihilist-types, and the casting director heard me read and said, 'Well, your accent is okay, but it doesn't sound like the German accent of the nihilists in *The Big Lebowski*—can't you sound like Flea, or the other guy, Stormare?' So the accent in the film became its own little specialty."

Pot Culture and the Dude

The Dude as a prototypical stoner aptly fits the Coens' scheme for *Lebowski* for many reasons. In its very essence, this recreational activity goes along with his mellow, abiding attitude. Joel and Ethan Coen delighted in the idea of making the familiar character of Philip Marlowe—often played by the indomitable Humphrey Bogart—a pothead. Although Marlowe was hard-drinking and wise-cracking in the same vein as the Dude, pot-smoking seems incongruent with the classic characterization of the detective as a tough yet highbrow man's man. Contrast the Dude's attire when he visits the Big Lebowski

"AS FOR MAN, HIS DAYS ARE AS GRASS. AS A FLOWER OF THE FIELD, SO HE FLOURISHETH. FOR THE WIND PASSETH OVER IT, AND IT IS GONE."

—Ps. 103:15, posted in gold letters on a wall in the mortuary from which the Dude and Walter take Donny's ashes

to Chandler's description of Marlowe in the opening lines of *The Big Sleep*: "I was wearing my powder-blue suit, with dark blue shirt, tie and display handkerchief, black brogues, black wool socks with dark blue clocks on them. I was neat, clean, shaved, and sober, and I didn't care who knew it. I was everything the well-dressed private detective ought to be. I was calling on four million dollars." Not exactly equivalent to a stoner's appearance.

Pot-smoking had its heyday in the 1960s, the quintessential Dude period. Marijuana use corresponds with other 1960s countercultural activities, including some that the Dude himself dabbled in, such as protest movements, being a conscientious objector, and having antiestablishment views in general (calling the Malibu Chief of Police a "fascist," for instance). The Dude's look and language also match both the stoner culture and the culture of the 1960s—sometimes an indistinguishable distinction. The longhaired Dude is nonviolent;

STRIKES & GUTTERS

The Special Effect of the Big Red Scissors
In the dream sequence when the nihilists are chasing the Dude with giant red scissors, the prop was a genuinely large pair of scissors. The scissors had to be supported on fine wires and surgical tubing in order for them to appear to "float" out in front of the actors. To create the illusion that they were simultaneously running and chopping the scissors, the actors ran on blacked-out treadmills.

Sign near the Dude's home in Venice Beach, California.
TFoxFoto / www.shutterstock.com

although he makes acerbic retorts to both the Treehorn thugs and the Chief of Police, he doesn't fight back against their physical abuses. And in answer to the threat of another villain of the film, Jesus Quintana, the Dude replies in very hippie-like parlance, "Yeah well, you know, that's just, like, your opinion, man." Throughout the film, his speech is peppered with such terms as "man" and "like."

Finally, the Dude's frequent marijuana use and laid-back demeanor (chicken or the egg?) are fitting for this California story. The history of cannabis use has been traced back as far as the third millennium BCE, and the drug has been relatively widely used in various cultures throughout larger history. The plant is native to Central and South Asia and has been documented throughout Asia and the Middle East. Ancient Hindus in India and Nepal called it *ganjika*, which later became "ganja." A plant known by various names, the Hebrew *qannabbos*, meaning "aromatic cane," became "cannabis." The moniker "marijuana" was developed from Mexican Spanish. Although illegal in most of the United States (and the world) the United Nations has estimated that 4 percent of the world's population partakes of pot annually.

It is the West Coast that is known for illicit and psychotropic drugs in this country. In 1997 marijuana ranked fourth out of all U.S. cash crops, and in a handful of states, including California, marijuana stands as the largest revenue-producing crop. It is allowed in some form in sixteen different states and in Washington, D.C., but it was California that first legalized marijuana for medical purposes, in 1996.

The Dude listens to whale songs while partaking.
Melissaf84 / www.shutterstock.com

Uli, print by Mikey Hester.
Courtesy of the artist, www.mikeyhester.com

The Dude Rolls

The Dude smokes marijuana four times in the film—that we can observe. In the Great Room scene, he asks the Big Lebowski, "Mind if I do a jay?" He puts a joint in his mouth and takes it out to seal the joint paper together. As he smokes, he reads the ransom note, his interior narration slowing down as the Big Lebowski's words fade out—capturing the experience of his altered mind. When he tells the Big Lebowski, "This is a bummer man, that's a bummer," his voice chokes slightly as he tries to hold the smoke in.

Backdropped by a bottle of Mr. Bubbles, the Dude also smokes a marijuana cigarette in his pink bathtub, again coughing a little, while surrounded by candles and listening to the soothing sounds of "Song of the Whale" on cassette. He is interrupted by the marauding nihilists.

In a hilarious transition from the doctor telling the Dude to slide his shorts down to the Dude pounding on his car roof in time

---

"This is a very complicated case, Maude. Lotta ins, lotta outs. You know, fortunately I'm adhering to a pretty strict, uh, drug regimen to keep my mind, you know, limber."

—the Dude

"No lava lamps or that kind of shit. No Day-Glo posters on the wall of his house. No Grateful Dead music on the soundtrack. And though I personally am a Cheech and Chong enthusiast, and would often attempt to pull Jeff Bridges's chain by telling him we were basically just making a Cheech and Chong movie . . . we didn't want it to look like a Cheech and Chong movie."

—Ethan Coen, about not beating the pothead jokes to death, *The Big Lebowski: The Making of a Coen Brothers Film*

---

to Creedence Clearwater Revival's "Lookin' Out My Back Door," the Dude again tokes the end of a joint. Spotting a tail following him, he tries to flick the joint out of the car, only to have it bounce against the closed window and fall into his lap, burning him. He tries to douse it with beer, and ends up crashing into a dumpster.

Lastly, the Dude ignites a match on the bedpost and lights a marijuana cigarette held with a roach clip while in bed with Maude. It is a scene that recalls the classic romantic-movie trope of a character smoking sensually in bed after coitus (complete with a light piano music soundtrack). When Maude asks what he does for "recreation," she turns her head to look at the joint. One of his answers is a drug reference: "the occasional acid flashback." When he inhales too deeply, the pot smoke catches in his throat and he hacks it out.

There are more subtle allusions to pot sprinkled throughout the movie. Although there isn't any obviously discernible paraphernalia around the Dude's apartment, when the cops interview him, one picks up a small bowling pin out of the ashtray and examines it closely; it looks to be some kind of pipe. The Dude has two hallucinogenic, almost psychedelic dream sequences. He frequently makes pot references; early in the film he tells Brandt he spent his time in college "smoking a lot of Thai Stick" (a Thai variety of marijuana, usually wrapped around bamboo, sometimes soaked in hashish). He calls the Big Lebowski a "human paraquat," a toxin sprayed on marijuana plants by the U.S. government since the 1970s. Indirect mentions include calling himself the "Bagman," a term for a person who transports money, often used in reference to a drug exchange.

Even other characters, inadvertently or not, use the language of pot culture. "Blow" (as in Bunny's refrain "G'ahead. Blow") can refer to cocaine or smoking marijuana. The oft-repeated phrase of no "funny stuff," usually said by the nihilists, is slang for marijuana. "Johnson," an appendage the Dude is terribly afraid of losing, has also been

defined by various sources as a 1960s term for a joint or getting high. The word "loaded," used for Walter's gun and the Big Lebowski's money, also means being high. A "joyride," as the police deduce to have taken place in the Dude's car, also means "going out and getting high," according to the *Marijuana Dictionary*.

There is an amazing frequency with which bowling and pot terms correspond. "Bowl" itself can be a measurement of marijuana or the part of the pipe where the marijuana sits. "Bowling" is smoking several bowls of pot. "Pot bowling" is bowling with a pot of money at stake. To "roll" means to assemble a joint. "Score" is the act of obtaining drugs. Even "split," which in bowling means leaving nonadjacent groups of one or more pins standing after a roll, is a pot term: according to the *Urban Dictionary*, it's "a state of high that surpasses the norm."

Also surpassing the norm: the frequency with which the film is watched under the influence of marijuana—perhaps in a show of kindred spirit to the Dude. Perhaps this practice contributes to the film's rewatchability, discussed further in Part V.

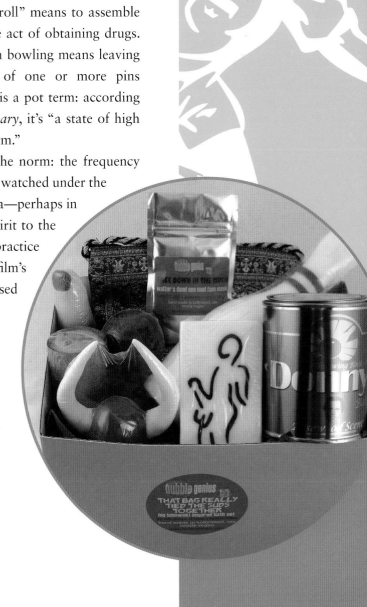

Bath products inspired by *Lebowski*, including a bowling pin soap on a rope, Walter's Face Down in the Muck dead sea mud mask, and Donny's ashes bath salts. Recommended for use while listening to whale songs.
Courtesy Paula Bonhomme, © 2009 Bubble Genius LLC

Polishing the Ball

Mechanical effects designer Peter Chesney explains why the Dude is seen polishing his nails in a *Lebowski* scene: "The image of the Dude with clear fingernail polish, while they're drinking their beer, at the bowling alley: that's something that bowlers do, they try to keep their nails undamaged from the bowling ball. . . . It shows the attention to detail in the film."

Evolution of the Style: The Retro Look of Brunswick Bowling and Googie Architecture

In midcentury Los Angeles, the popularity of bowling and the Brunswick-Balke-Collender Company (which became the Brunswick Corporation in 1960) was on the rise, as was the trend toward Googie architecture. With their parallel futuristic elements, these two movements inspired the aesthetic of *The Big Lebowski*.

The Wide World of Bowling Sports

In the 1980s, pivotal *Lebowski* persona Pete Exline participated in an amateur Hollywood softball league. Games often resulted in spirited arguments; *Who's the Boss?* star Tony Danza reportedly once walked off the field during play. The Coens considered softball for the main activity of *The Big Lebowski*, but eventually deemed it too boring, at least for a movie plot.

They ultimately settled on bowling, for numerous reasons. For one, it's a sport that doesn't require physical fitness; in fact, drinking and smoking are often encouraged. A predominantly male activity, bowling fits the concept of *The Big Lebowski* as a classic buddy movie (with wildly divergent buddies). Bowling is a "retro" and particularly American sport in that it really flourished during the 1950s and 1960s in the western United States, specifically Los Angeles. Visually, the sleek lines yet shabby appearance of bowling alleys evoke a period, vintage style, which suits the main characters, who are throwbacks to the 1960s and 1970s:

"The idea was to shoot those bowling rituals almost in slow motion. The credits sequence was conceived to make you enter that world and understand the importance of bowling to the movie."

—Joel Coen, in *Positif*, reprinted in *The Coen Brothers Interviews*

Bowling in 1894. The vines around the mirror are reminiscent of a certain interpretive dance. *Library of Congress*

Brunswick-style ball returns resemble F-86 Sabre jets.
Associated Press

Walter to the Vietnam War, the Dude to the peace movement, and even Maude Lebowski to the Fluxus art movement.

So the Coens seized on bowling as a central narrative thread, a sport for all ages and sizes and temperaments, a unifier of such incongruent friends as Walter, the Dude, and Donny. The bowling alley became an integral setting, and the crew set to work incorporating bowling into the look of *The Big Lebowski*.

Rick Heinrichs, the movie's production designer, had many conversations with the Coens about the intricacies of the style of bowling. Together they discussed the "kinetic energy" of bowling, with balls and pins flying down multiple alleys at once; the beauty of the long, sleek wood floors; and the retro appearance of the 1940s Brunswick styling, with its space-age-like ball returns that are reminiscent of 1940s jet fighter aircrafts. The color scheme of Brunswick included orange,

Championship Rings

The United States Bowling Congress (USBC) offers rings for bowling certain high-scoring games (300, 299, or 298) or series (800 or 900—the rare instance of three consecutive 300s). If a bowler repeats one of these scores, "chips," or precious stones, are added to the original ring. In *The Big Lebowski*, the character of Jesus Quintana wears several of these rings, proudly displaying his bowling prowess.

Boys working in a bowling alley in Trenton, New Jersey, 1909.
Photograph by Lewis Wickes Hine / Library of Congress

"Brunswick: The No. 1 Name in Bowling"

Brunswick bowling alley in San Francisco, 1941.
© Universal Images Group (Lake County Discovery Museum) / Alamy

Since the mid-nineteenth century, bowling and the Brunswick Corporation have been linked. Founder John Moses Brunswick tried to take the sport out of the realm of the elite to make it more family- and public-friendly. He moved to the United States from Switzerland at the age of fourteen and started the Cincinnati Carriage Making Company in a small workshop. The company expanded to include cabinets, tables, and chairs, and in 1845 produced its first billiards table. After many name changes, the company merged with another to become the largest billiards equipment operation in the world: The Brunswick-Balke-Collender Company. In the 1890s, Moses Bensinger, Brunswick president (and John Moses Brunswick's son-in-law), saw great potential in the then-disorganized sport of bowling. He began making wooden lanes, pins, and bowling balls. He would also play an important role in establishing the American Bowling Congress in 1895.

In 1906, with the revolutionary Mineralite ball, the company began manufacturing bowling balls made of rubber. Brunswick claims to have launched the first mechanical automated pinsetter in 1956, although another such pinsetter was first shown to the public at the ABC National Championships in Buffalo in 1946. By the mid-1960s, the bowling boom went bust, and Brunswick took physical possession of 131 bowling centers as payment for bowling equipment. Today, Brunswick is in the marine, fitness, and bowling and billiards industries. The Brunswick Bowling and Billiards division produces recreation centers in addition to manufacturing goods.

A Brunswick television commercial from the 1950s epitomizes the mid-twentieth-century American fantasy. A housewife, wearing an apron, arranges TV dinners in the freezer, while her husband reads the paper and the children play with rocket ships. This scene transitions into images of the Brunswick equipment: gleaming balls sliding along the silver path of the ball return; shining lanes; and the smooth, hi-tech mechanization of the pin turret. The voiceover is pure 1950s kitsch:

Introducing the American way of life, on the threshold of the golden sixties: color, style and convenience. Recreation, fun—these are the ultimate desires of today, tomorrow, and the years ahead of us. And these are the very same features that Brunswick is building into the new dynamic recreation centers. Six basic colors to provide the proper atmosphere for recreation: The richness of gold, the pleasure-packed attractiveness of tangerine . . . the improved exclusive Brunswick telescore is unmatched in the field. Brilliant, crisp projection, it has that Brunswick stamp of quality from stem to stern, with a hand dryer built in at terminal end. Brunswick's exclusive pin turret ensures immediate spotting of ten new pins following each strike or second ball.

The commercial clearly demonstrates Brunswick's move to turn bowling into a more mainstream, family-oriented activity.

browns, and creams, which the crew used as inspiration to tint the set. (Even the Dude's clothes roughly adhere to this color palette.) To counteract these rich, earthy hues, Heinrichs added metal-flake blue as an accent.

The *Lebowski* bowling scenes were filmed at the legendary Hollywood Star Lanes near Santa Monica. Chris Spellman, set decorator for the film, was tasked with finding all the props, furnishings, and decorations to create the right atmosphere. Spellman reports: "At that time, we weren't really using computers to find items or . . . track things down. It was pure detective work, on our own—trying to track down the proper people at Brunswick to refurbish the bowling alley. I went to a lot of bowling alleys, ones that had shut down recently, or were about to shut down, and made treks all over southern California to go to some of the bowling alleys . . . and negotiate for items. Getting immersed in the whole bowling culture was kind of fun."

To teach the cast how to bowl, bowling great Barry Asher was hired as a consultant. Asher set a Professional Bowlers Association record that stood for ten years when he averaged 247 at the 1971 South Bend Open, using a rubber bowling ball, no less.

If you watch carefully you'll notice that Jeff Bridges never once rolls a ball in the alley (except in his dream)—not a stroker, cranker, nor tweener. Nonetheless, both cast and crew spent a lot of time at the bowling alley during production. Assistant accountant Kristina Soderquist remembers taking a phone call one day: "'Do you think you could bring my per diem down to the bowling alley?' It was Jeff Bridges, and I decided that yes, I needed to take his per diem down to him personally. He couldn't have been nicer, as he always

was when I saw him during production. He and John Goodman were having a great time bowling."

Hollywood Star Lanes, built in 1960, was demolished in 2003. Spellman reports that the starburst light fixtures, which were created for the movie, were saved from the wrecking ball and moved to the Lucky Strike Lanes in downtown Los Angeles. In an homage to *The Big Lebowski*, Lucky Strike also purchased Lane #7 from the fabled Hollywood alley and used the materials to build their "Hollywood's bar." Lucky Strike bowling alleys have since multiplied into twenty locations around the country, while the former bowling playground of the Dude, Walter, Donny, and Jesus Quintana is now the site of an elementary school.

Jeff Bridges at the *Lebowski* premiere party, Chelsea Piers, New York. *NY Daily News via Getty Images*

Jeff Bridges is Not a Bowler, Although He Plays One in the Movies

Jeff Bridges portrayed the president of the United States in *The Contender* (2000). In one scene, he bowls while talking to an advisor (Sam Elliott). Unbeknownst to the director, Rod Lurie, who wrote the scene in order to woo Bridges to the project, the actor isn't a bowler. He did appreciate the connection, though—upon agreeing to play the role, Bridges said to Lurie, "Wow, Dude's gonna be president."

Bowling, the Everyman Sport

The blond man stoops to unzip the satchel. He pulls out a bowling ball and examines it in the manner of a superstitious native confronting an artifact of a more advanced civilization.

BLOND MAN
. . . The fuck is this? . . .

DUDE
Obviously you're not a golfer.

—excerpted from *The Big Lebowski* (published shooting script)

In 1930 the British anthropologist Sir Flinders Petrie and his team of archeologists found the first-known evidence of bowling equipment. In the tomb of an Egyptian boy dating back to 3200 BCE, Petrie and his team discovered a set of balls and pins.

Primitive forms of the game, in which stones were thrown at pebbles or sticks (similar to the sport of bocce ball), have been played in Germany since 300 CE. The sport has also been played in England since 1100, but was outlawed by Edward III in the mid-1300s in order to promote archery. Bowling came back into vogue in England in the sixteenth century, when the gluttonous King Henry VIII favored the activity.

Around this time, the Dutch introduced early forms of nine-pin bowling, or "Dutch Pins," to America. (The area of Bowling Green in Manhattan got its name from nine-pin bowling also known as "Bowl on the Green," because of the frequency with which the game was played there.) Bowling became associated with low forms of entertainment (gambling and taverns), and legend has it that the tenth pin was added to get around the law banning ninepins in Connecticut—giving rise to the modern game. Today the sport of bowling is played by over one hundred million people in more than ninety different countries.

Women compete at a British league charity competition in 1936.
© Hulton-Deutsch Collection / Corbis

The Jetsons Stylings of Googie Architecture

Googie, also known as "Coffee Shop Modern" architecture, was a prominent feature of post–World War II American design, in particular in 1940s and 1950s coffee shops and bowling alleys. Los Angeles was the hub of the movement. The city's workforce included employees of NASA, the air force, Boeing, and the fantastical Disneyland. Its West Coast culture was open to bucking tradition, which fed into the sudden popularity of the Googie style. With its bold and ultramodern diagonal lines, bright signs, boomerangs, and cantilevered extensions, Googie was the look of the future.

"Probably never in the history of the human race has a culture equaled ours in the dreariness and corrupted fantasy of a major part of its building."

—*Architectural Forum*, 1957, critiquing Googie architecture

Bowl Premiere Lanes in Santa Fe Springs, California, preserves the Googie look that was so popular in the region during the 1950s.
© David Zaitz / Alamy

Googie sign at a used car shop in California.
© LHB Photo / Alamy

Several settings in *The Big Lebowski* feature Googie architecture, such as Dinah's Family Restaurant, where the nihilists eat their lingonberry pancakes and pigs in blankets. This location was denoted by the Coens in the script as "Denny's" (a restaurant the brothers have frequented since their *Blood Simple* days). Denny's, which began its long life as a string of coffee shops named Danny's, has its roots in Googie. Prominent architects Louis Armét and Eldon Davis designed several Danny's—and subsequently, Denny's—and their work became touchstones of Googie style.

Jackie Treehorn's house is set in the palatial Sheats Goldstein Residence of Beverly Hills, designed and built between 1961 and 1963 by John Lautner, a famed southern Californian architect. (The term "Googie architecture" was coined in 1952 after a *House and Home* editor drove by Lautner's Googie's Coffee Shop at the corner of Sunset Strip

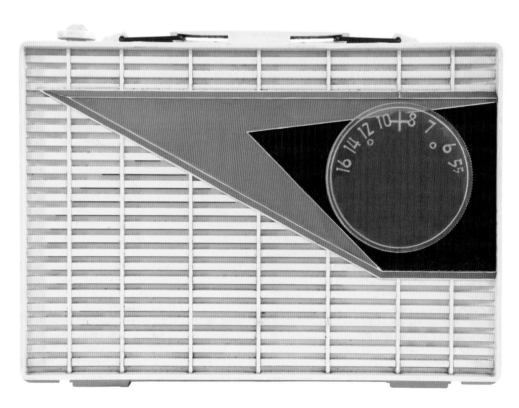

1950s Googie-style radio.
© trekandshoot / Alamy

Exterior of the Sheats Goldstein Residence.
© Arcaid Images / Alamy

and Crescent Heights.) Although the house exemplifies Organic Architecture, it does feature some space-age elements, including 750 skylights in the living room where the Dude passes out.

Although In-N-Out Burger doesn't appear onscreen, it is referenced repeatedly, and Walter and Donny are munching the establishment's tasty burgers after unsuccessfully leaning on Little Larry. This Southern California chain, whose first location opened in 1948 in a Googie-style building, has been touted as the first drive-through (a statement in dispute). Johnie's Coffee Shop, where Walter and the Dude drink coffee (which only Walter stays to finish), is located in an iconic Googie building; the original coffee shop closed in 1997 and is now used solely as a movie location. Perhaps most subtly, the style of Googie was incorporated into the movie's star motif, or as Rick Heinrichs called it, the "radiating icon" of the film.

The Sheats Goldstein Residence is not on the beach, as depicted in *Lebowski*, but on a hill overlooking L.A.
© Arcaid Images / Alamy

The coffee-shop scene with the nihilists is the only scene in the entire movie that doesn't include the Dude.

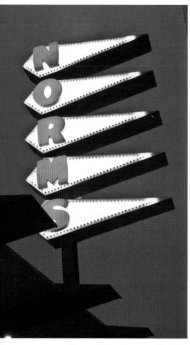

Norms Restaurant in L.A.
© Michael Going / Alamy

As Alan Hess wrote in his book, *Googie: Fifties Coffee Shop Architecture*: "The dingbat, the starburst, the sputnik, the frozen sparkler are all descriptions for a symbol widely used in signs and ornaments in the fifties. It depicted energy caught in the act of explosive release, like a coruscating diamond. The space imagery inherent in the shape reflected the optimism of an age that topped itself by going from amazing feat to unparalleled wonder." Such retro star shapes are seen throughout the film. For instance, neon stars of various shapes form the title sequence. Stars were created by the production team for the interior and exterior walls of the bowling alley (coincidentally shot at Hollywood Star Lanes). The Dude sees stars that form the L.A. nightscape when he is knocked out prior to his first dream, and his second dream sequence (the "musical" number) has a star background.

Pulling the Disparate Pieces Together

For Director of Photography Roger Deakins, a veteran of many Coen movies, it was a challenge to find a balance between these two disparate styles of the real and the unreal. For *Fargo*, the Coens went for a naturalistic, almost documentary-like atmosphere, with flat lighting, whereas films such as *The Hudsucker Proxy* had a more embellished, artificial look. The crew's task for *The Big Lebowski* was to take a wide variety of sets—the Dude's grungy apartment, the Big Lebowski's opulent mansion, the bowling alley in all its retro glory—and create some kind of visual unity that would in turn balance the shaggy-dogness of the plot with the stylization of the dream sequences.

The Los Angeles In-N-Out.
© E. J. Baumeister Jr. / Alamy

The Big Lebowski: The Making of a Coen Brothers Film, written by Coen cohort William Preston Robertson and edited by *Lebowski* editor (and Ethan's then-wife) Tricia Cooke, outlines how Deakins approached the cinematography of the film. He struggled with finding that unity, as the dream sequences had to look crisp and light, but the Dude's house needed to be dark and dingy. Most of the movie was shot on high-speed stock, adding a "grittiness" to the image.

While noir plays heavily into the plot, it doesn't really contribute to the visual mood

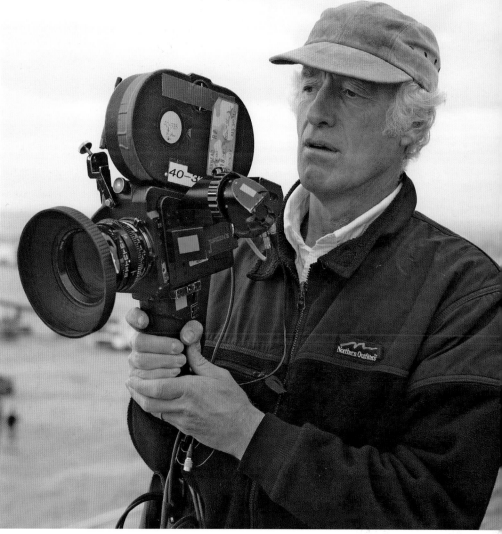

Roger Deakins on the set of 2005's *Jarhead.*
© AF Archive / Alamy

"*The Big Lebowski*'s photography is more naturalistic and raw, and probably a lot more contrasty than *Fargo*. On the other hand, the camera moves are less observational than *Fargo*. The camera moves are more stylized, but the lighting and the look of it are more realistic and gritty."

—Roger Deakins, in *The Big Lebowski: The Making of a Coen Brothers Film*

of the film—*The Big Lebowski*, by its nature, and the nature of its protagonist, is on the whole a mellow, happy movie. For that reason, as Ethan says, they wanted it to be "bright and poppy." Deakins ultimately decided on using the night as a visual bridge between the disparate looks. He used special lighting for the night scenes—orange, rather than the typical blue. The effect is an adept visual cue, whether it's used in the eerie bacchanalian scene at the pornographer's pad or in the bowling-alley parking lot, where the grungy, past-their-prime, heavy-metalesque nihilists threaten the protagonist and his buddies while wielding chainsaws.

PART III
The Making of *The Big Lebowski*

 ## Wordsmithing the Script

 rmed with the idea of a genre twist—molding the tropes of noir with a hero (or rather, antihero) whose thinking and detective work is filtered through a haze of dope—the Coens set about writing. *The Big Lebowski* was penned at the same time as *Fargo* and while they were in production on *Barton Fink*, but because the brothers had to wait for their desired *Lebowski* actors' schedules to align, they filmed *Fargo* first.

At 119 pages, *The Big Lebowski* shooting script was all Coen precision. There's very little deviation from the script in the completed movie, in contrast to many films in which elements of the finished product aren't determined until the actual production. (Francis Ford Coppola's *Apocalypse Now* famously never really had an ending, certainly not one written in advance. An overweight Marlon Brando showed up in the Philippines jungle without having read the conclusion-lacking script and improvised, and Coppola pounded out pages on his typewriter until the wee hours of the morning—for scenes that were to be shot the next very day.)

William Preston Robertson, who had been on the sets of many of the Coens' earlier movies, expounds upon Joel and Ethan's scriptwriting process in relation to *The Big Lebowski*: "There's such an absolute structural integrity to [their movies], and everything is down on paper already, and there's tremendous control of it, and they know exactly what they want at the moment they've written it. And what made *The Big Lebowski* unique among the movies that they've written is that it actually tries (and succeeds quite well) to make a movie that doesn't follow that." Movies from the 1970s—case in point, Robert Altman's *The Long Goodbye*, a direct precursor to *Lebowski* in its neo–Philip Marlowe character and Chandlerian plot—have a much looser, less precise tenor. Robertson continues, "What makes *The Big Lebowski* so ingenious is that the Coens mimic that casual, lax style except for the fact that the film still follows the kind of control

"I remember reading the script. This was the follow-up to *Fargo*, and I'd been a big Coen brothers fan, and I remember reading the script and thinking, 'Hmmm, really? This is the next one after *Fargo*?' And I wasn't all that impressed, I didn't know if it would go anywhere. It was a well-written script, obviously, but the story didn't really resonate too much with me. And then when I saw it in the cast and crew screening, I was utterly and totally blown away. I remember going up to Joel and saying, 'Oh my god, you guys know how to make a movie!' because visually and in every other sense this was something that my imagination never touched on in a million years."

—actor Mark Pellegrino, Blond Jackie Treehorn Thug (and, later, the very different character of Jacob on the TV show *Lost*)

and exactness that all of their projects do. It just happens to also include a lot of 'ums' and 'you knows' and this kind of stuff—but every 'um' and 'you know' in the movie is *also* in the script. Part of its genius is its specific, controlled and successful effort to represent this kind of lax, casual, relaxed, all-over-the-place, meandering kind of film, so you get the best of both worlds, in a sense. And they haven't done anything else like that."

This appearance of a relaxed film (and thereby production) is very much in keeping with the protagonist's laid-back persona. However, there's very little improvisation on a Coen set, which hasn't always sat well with their actors. (Nicolas Cage, in particular, is said to have struggled with the rigidity of sticking to the script during the filming of *Raising Arizona*.) The principal cast of *Lebowski*, however, did their utmost to follow the Coens' vision. Jeff Bridges adhered closely to the script—word by word, ellipsis by ellipsis—because he felt that when he strayed from what they wrote it just didn't sound right. John Goodman remembers the only truly improvised line coming when the Dude calls the Big Lebowski a "human paraquat," a word referring to the pesticide sprayed on Mexican marijuana fields in the late 1970s under U.S. insistence, and a political concept definitely in keeping with the character of the Dude. Julianne Moore described the script's exactness in an interview with *Rolling Stone*: "Everything in the script has intention to the point that it's rhythmic. I remember Ethan just coming up and giving a direction where he asked me to remove [a word]. Those are the kind of directions they would give because they have that much specificity."

You're Entering a World of Pain, by Misha. Acrylic on velvet canvas board.
Courtesy of the artist, www.misha-art.com

The Coens don't always start writing a script with the plot in mind. For example, with *Raising Arizona*, they were first intrigued by the comic implications of the large cacti that exist in Arizona (a place they had never been), came up with the movie title, and only then began to think up the plot. Likewise, they often devise a bizarre image or concept they want to incorporate into a film, and then have to figure out how to fit it into the script. The severed toe in *Lebowski* was one such image. They were captivated by the idea of it, but then had to determine whose appendage it could be.

 ## Casting the Principal Players (The League)

Polygram, the funders of *Fargo*, and Working Title Films, the production company for *The Hudsucker Proxy*, *Fargo*, and four subsequent Coen films, came on board with a $15 million budget. It was a pretty paltry amount in modern moviemaking terms, but the Coens typically settled for small budgets in order to retain creative control and ultimate approval, or "final cut," of the finished film, something only a handful of American directors working within the mid- to large-sized studios have. Having final cut ensures that there are fewer strings attached to the films' financiers. The Coens learned a hard lesson early on with *Crimewave* (1985), which they wrote (Sam Raimi directed) and considered to be ultimately butchered by the studio.

The Coens often write characters with specific players in mind. For *The Big Lebowski*, they expressly wrote the parts of Walter Sobchak for John Goodman (a veteran of three Coen pics at the time), Theodore Donald "Donny" Kerabatsos for Steve Buscemi (Coen player in four features then), and Jesus Quintana for John Turturro (who had appeared in two previous Coen films).

The toe turns out to belong to the female nihilist, played by musician Aimee Mann.
Photograph by Douglas Mason / Getty Images

THE LEGEND

Creating Jesus

"It was an early element in the script and we knew that we wanted John to play him. I had seen him about ten years ago in a play at the Public Theater called *Ma Puta Vita* [sic; correct title is *La Puta Vida*] in which he played a pederast. Well, maybe that's taking it a little too far . . . [but] there was a kind of lewd section with weird overtones. I was very impressed by it. So we thought, let's make Turturro a pederast. It'll be something he can really run with."

—Joel Coen, in Ronald Bergan's *The Coen Brothers*

The Stranger was identified specifically as Sam Elliott in the script (although apparently they originally misspelled his name), possibly because the Coen brothers liked the sound of his voice, which has a classically rough Western cadence to it (an asset in his earlier films *Tombstone* and *Gettysburg*). In the shooting script his second appearance is described thusly: "He is middle-aged and craggily handsome—Sam Elliott, perhaps." Sam Elliott, indeed. Elliott didn't quite understand his role in the film, and would say to the Coens during shooting, "I don't know what I'm doing here, boys."

While writing *The Big Lebowski*, the Coens didn't immediately envision who should inhabit the part of the Dude, and when the script was done they initially approached Hollywood star Mel Gibson. Needless to say, that would have made for a very different movie.

The Coens then contacted character actor Jeff Bridges, who had made a name for himself in such disparate films as the black-and-white

Sam Elliott in *Buffalo Girls* (1995) with Angelica Huston.
© Moviestore Collection Ltd / Alamy

The Jesus screen-print, by Darin Shock.
Courtesy of the artist, State of Shock Studios LLC, www.stateofshockstudios.com

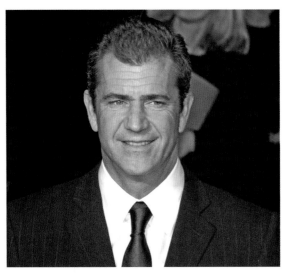

This guy as the Dude? As Walter would say, "Now that is just ridiculous." © Pictorial Press Ltd / Alamy

drama *The Last Picture Show* (1971) and the sci-fi classic *Tron* (1982). Bridges initially resisted taking the role, and it took some convincing from the Coens to get him on board. They went to his house and explained how perfect he'd be for the part, to which he responded in disbelief, "Really?" Although now Bridges acknowledges the many similarities between himself and Jeffrey Lebowski (at least in his youth), he initially could not envision himself as the Dude.

The Coens often reminisce about how Bridges would ask before each scene, "Did the

"He just sort of got it."

—Ethan Coen, on Jeff Bridges' rendition of the Dude

Dude burn one on the way over?" and when they answered affirmatively, he'd rub his eyes to make them red. Bridges has stated firmly that while marijuana was a part of his life in the past, he wasn't a method actor during

 ## STRIKES & GUTTERS

Fun Casting Facts

- Mel Gibson was not the only big-time movie star considered for *Lebowski*. Charlize Theron auditioned for the part of Bunny Lebowski.

- Jesus Quintana's bowling partner, Liam O'Brien, was played by novice James G. Hoosier, who answered a flyer seeking an Irish-looking bowler.

- When first reading the script, Steve Buscemi wasn't particularly interested in playing the part of Donny, but he ended up being the best bowler of the principles.

- *Eternal Sunshine of the Spotless Mind* writer/producer Charlie Kaufman makes a cameo—he's in the audience during Marty's danse moderne.

- Carlos Leon, who plays Maude Lebowski's Thug #1 (who punches the Dude), was a celebrity trainer before becoming an actor. He's also the father of Lourdes Maria Ciccone Leon, whose mother is Madonna. *The Big Lebowski* was one of his first big movies, and he is always surprised when people recognize him on

Jerry Havela as Saddam Hussein.
© Moviestore Collection Ltd / Alamy.
Courtesy of Universal Studios Licensing LLC

the street. "It's funny they do, because I'm on screen for only two to three minutes, but still it's crazy how much I get recognized: 'Hey man, you were in *The Big Lebowski*!' They want me to sign their DVDs. They're fanatics about it!"

- Jerry Haleva, who portrayed Saddam Hussein, has acted in six movies, *all* as Hussein.

Lebowski production—he never actually used the illegal substance while making the film. He did, however, happily put on weight for the part. He also contributed much of his own wardrobe, which helped shape the indelible character of the Dude.

Actual production did not begin until the actors' schedules coincided. John Goodman was working on his successful television show *Roseanne*, while Jeff Bridges was shooting the Western *Wild Bill*. Julianne Moore was in production on *The Lost World: Jurassic Park* when she first read the script for *The Big Lebowski*. She only worked for two weeks on the film, early and late during the production.

STRIKES & GUTTERS

Jellies and Undies

"There's a quality of looseness, a quality of worn-in softness to the fabric and color choices. A washed-out quality. The Dude is somebody who may own a piece of clothing for ten years. And he doesn't separate his darks from his lights."—Mary Zophres, in *The Making of The Big Lebowski*

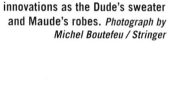

Lebowski costume designer Mary Zophres (shown with her work for *Catch Me If You Can*) helped establish character through such innovations as the Dude's sweater and Maude's robes. *Photograph by Michel Boutefeu / Stringer*

Mary Zophres, costume designer for *The Big Lebowski*, spent a lot of time creating the wardrobe for the Dude. She wanted to accentuate his gut, so she outfitted him in baggie pants that ran below his stomach and tight shirts with seams that dropped. As validation of a theory that he was born to play the part, Bridges also wore bits and pieces from his own wardrobe, such as the baseball shirt he wears in the ransom note scene with Sadaharu Oh, the "Babe Ruth" of Japanese baseball, on it (and which he also wears in a scene in *The Fisher King*, 1991). According to *Rolling Stone*, Bridges still owns the beige and brown zigzag cable-knit sweater so memorably displayed by the Dude.

The Coens had decided that the Dude should wear Munsingwear underwear (they loved the name of the Minneapolis-based underwear and military garment manufacturer from their youth), i.e., "tightie whities," with the name on the waistband often peeking out.

Determining the Dude's footwear was an arduous process. Flip-flops had the right look, but they made a slapping sound on the ground and exacerbated Bridges' back problems. One day he wore jelly shoes—or jellies—to the set. These fit the Dude's personality perfectly. As they were no longer manufactured in the United States, however, the crew had to order his shoes from Trinidad (although they can now be purchased on any number of *Big Lebowski* merchandise websites).

The Dude's sweater looks different on the model. It's inspired by sweaters made by the Cowichan tribes of British Columbia. *Photo courtesy of Pendleton Woolen Mills, www.pendleton-usa.com*

"Obviously you're not a golfer"

The Dude paper doll, by Claudia Varosio.
Courtesy of the artist, www.etsy.com/shop/claudiavarosio

Jeff Bridges: The Elite Everyman

By Gail Levin

What came first, the character or the actor? The casting or the part? The great British director Stephen Frears has said it's all in the casting. "You can't make a fat man thin."

Then there's the word *act*. And the word *character*. *Act* fits into *character*. Tidy.

And then there are the parts—those really *great* parts. The ones that come from who knows where—the brilliance of the writer, the serendipity of the plot, the perfect storm of influences? Some are simply the parts themselves. Hamlet, Lear, Scarlett O'Hara, Charles Foster Kane, Stanley Kowalski—all are great, really apropos of nothing but their own inherent traits, depicting archetypes, if you will. And of course there are the defining actors who played those parts: Richard Burton as Hamlet, Vivien Leigh, Orson Welles, Brando! This cloaks the part with its own veneer. The actor who played the character thus immortalizes it and makes the two indistinguishable.

Then there are the really great parts that are of their time with such uncanny precision as if to toll the hour. Duddy Kravitz, Willy Loman, Terry Malloy, Mr. Tibbs, the young lovers in *Breathless*, Annie Hall. Those are the parts that seem to pluck something out of the atmosphere and create the original, the prototype. They earn a place in the pantheon because they are perfect little archeological excavations, consummate specimens. What makes them art is that they endure.

What makes all of these parts so particularly exquisite is that they join character, actor, and role in a more exalted way than we usually see. Actor and character become indistinguishable. Actualization is so consummate as to brand itself. These are encapsulations of an ethos, a whole cultural arrival; they are not simply a person or a plot device.

And then there's the Dude.

In the summer of 2010 I had the great rush to be asked to direct a film for the prestigious PBS series *American Masters* on Jeff Bridges. One of the Hollywood scions. Famous father, famous legacy, famous famous. And honestly, I knew the canon and the revered place *The Big Lebowski* holds among Jeff Bridges fans, and I had long loved him, as I think many women have, as that sort of very good-looking, surly, but still-so-seductive guy in films like *The Last Picture Show, Against All Odds*, and *The Fabulous Baker Boys*. Kind of dreamy and out of reach and sigh-making. Though that may sound a bit overromanticized, it's pretty true for many of his female fans.

It is worth mentioning that Jeff Bridges holds a singular spot as an actor. He's an extraordinarily natural cocktail of the guy the girls want, the guy the guys want to be, a god to slackers of all stripe, and even a reluctant sci-fi hero. He was in *Tron* early, when all that digital, virtual movie stuff was new; add prescient to the list of his traits.

But it is the innate, effortless space that Jeff inhabits that makes his character unique.

So, what condition was his condition in?

In his filmography *Lebowski* falls sort of right in the middle in terms of big acts. He had a smashing out-of-the-gate start with Peter Bogdanovich's *The Last Picture Show* in 1971, for which he garnered an Oscar nomination. Then he did some very fine films with some very fine directors, including *Fat City* under the eye of the great John Huston and *Bad Company*, directed by

Robert Benton. A couple of gigantic flops—*King Kong* and *Heaven's Gate*—followed, though these were not without their own Hollywood pedigrees. Jeff followed these with the small but mighty *Cutter's Way* in 1981 and *Tron* a year later. *Tron* is distinguished more by its resonance now than by anything it achieved at the time of its release.

A few more middling films, such as *Starman*, *Jagged Edge*, *The Morning After*, and *Tucker*, followed. These were middling in the sense that they were always among someone's favorites, but they were not really noteworthy save for the fact that Jeff worked with several more outstanding directors and picked up a few more Oscar nods. Then came *The Fabulous Baker Boys* and *The Fisher King*,

Jeff Bridges in *The Last Picture Show*, his breakthrough role.
© AF Archive / Alamy

both memorable. In 1989's *Baker Boys*, alongside his very superb brother Beau and Michelle Pfeiffer, he roils and rages about his "condition," and in *The Fisher King*, that condition darkens in a role ridden with grief and guilt. But all the way through we still encountered the spoiled, beautiful Jeff, who is able to get away with all that self-indulgent *sturm und drang*. In truth, it's not an especially compelling type—attractive as a guy perhaps, but attractive as a character? Not terribly.

This is to take nothing from Jeff. He is a consummate performer, consistent and reliable, well-placed, always a draw, with a shiny surface and an electric charm. And all those parts were well-suited to his bad-boyish image and his movie-star stuff.

So what exactly suggested to Joel and Ethan Coen, by the time *Lebowski* started gleaming in their eye, that this guy could be the Dude? I mean, why him?

Jeff Bridges is an everyman, but an elite one. He's not prone to this type of part, a Coen brothers part. He's not one of the sort of twisted crowd of regulars that the Coens are so adept at realizing and utilizing, the John Turturros and Steve Buscemis and John Goodmans, those out-there guys, wild character types who play roles that are more actor-driven somehow than movie-driven. Jeff seems pretty straight in that crowd.

Or maybe that's exactly what attracted them. That this guy, Jeff Bridges, might just be, in his real life, his real character, something else. Something unexpected, something a little messier, the slacker's slacker—lazy and cocooned, "fat" and happy, a stoner for all time. Just maybe, somewhere lurking in that Hollywood frame, was the soul of a true bum!

One thing is for sure, the Dude had to be able to say "fuck" like it was Shakespeare, and Jeff could certainly do that!

But still, nothing leading up to *Lebowski* suggested Jeff Bridges—at least not to the layman's eye. And that is what makes genius, if I may be so bold as to suggest that genius is reached through happy accidents of acute observation. *The Big Lebowski* itself had such happy accidents converge: razor-sharp exposition, incredible isolated moments, perfect pitch, and perfect casting. Any one of those qualities is extraordinary to achieve; to get them all in one place can make a masterpiece—a classic. And *Lebowski* is, in every respect, a classic. A classic script, a classic character.

Jeff Bridges is the Dude. Who'da thunk it?

If this were a film, fade out.

Now fade up.

So, who is Jeff Bridges? I can't pretend to really know. But in making our film, of course, I did talk to him and he did tell me things, so here goes. Here's Jeff in his own words.

I do my damnedest to swerve. I really try hard to swerve....My M.O. is funny as far as picking projects—I really do my best to *not* work, not be engaged....You never know what's going to be right around the corner that was going to be a great opportunity, but you can't do it 'cause this is happening....And I know what hard work making a movie is and I do have a bit of the Dude in me, you know, a little....I consider myself kind of lazy. It's funny, it's a funny thing. I would like to think of myself as a person who is more proactive in creating things but it's the opposite of that. It's this resistance and reticence, you know.

This comment is a bit surprising when one considers the vastness of Jeff's filmography, and yet alas! What's this? Aha! The Dude stirs!

The Coens encountered this ambivalence as well. Again Jeff:

I remember the Coens said, "We're writing something for you." And I said, "You're kidding me, great! I can't wait to read it." They said, "Yeah, you're going to like it." And then I read it and I said, "What's this? Man, this is like nothing I've ever done before. This is like, did you crash one of my high school parties?" I could kind of relate to this younger version of myself. But then I was a little bit concerned because I had daughters, young teens, and if this were a hit movie then they've got that big pothead father. And you know, I'm the son of a famous father myself.

The loneliness of the elite everyman—so much to protect and yet much to evoke; much to preserve, yet much to liberate. Woody Allen has said as much, bringing to mind the famous—and unconfirmed—declaration by Rodin that one sculpts an elephant by chipping away at everything that is not an elephant. So too did Jeff allow himself to chip away at perhaps everything that was movie-star Jeff, and leave room for the Dude to emerge. The character was honed so close to home that its mastery almost feels like a documentary.

Character is destiny!

Jeff has spoken of the exactness of the script. As amazingly improvisational as *Lebowski* feels, it is not. The script was hewn with a scalpel in which every pause is provided, every syllable is significant, every one of those "fucks" is poetry.

And yet, have you ever read a film script? No matter how good they are, the words look

Julianne Moore and Jeff Bridges at the *Lebowski* premiere party in New York, February 1998.
Photograph by Catherine McGann / Getty Images

oddly paltry on a page by themselves, little scratchings in search of an actor.

Which brings us back to that question—what came first, the character or the actor?

Without the words, without the vertebrae, without the creation of character, no one can step into the role. Again one can't help but muse on what made the Coens mark this one for Jeff in the first place. How did they know? Perhaps they didn't; genius is a roll of the dice too.

Jeff, of course, does not disappoint. His is a performance full of candor and generosity. All the slick stuff is gone. Jeff is without vanity or safety, really. He is not trim and shiny and Jeff-like, but rather lumpy and needing a shower and hilarious! He embodies the Dude fully and again with such unerring accuracy and superb glibness that you feel as though you're actually smoking a joint with him. And with that seeming ease, that seeming effortless affect, Jeff has made a character for all time.

The actor *is* the character. The actor *is* the part. There is no distance. And in the annals of great roles, those really great roles that give the audience something fresh but inevitable—something wholly unexpected, and yet the only possible choice—this character, portrayed by this actor, is undeniable. He was the *only* possible choice.

"Sometimes there's a man."

Jeff Bridges *is* the Dude.

One little postscript from John Goodman—Jeff's partner in *Lebowski*, the inimitable Walter Sobchak—another example of that elusive, elite, everyman.

After the picture was wrapped, about nine months later I think, we did a photo shoot for *Esquire* magazine. And Jeff showed up and I didn't know him. He was totally Jeff Bridges, actor—it was a new guy. And it kinda hurt. Where's the Dude, you know? Or where's the guy I knew? He just wasn't there. He was onto something else I guess. He cleaned up real good, but I missed the Dude.

Soon after, Jeff played President Jackson Evans in *The Contender*. He received an Oscar nomination. But the President and the Dude shared one very important trait—they loved bowling.

The Dude abides!

Emmy Award–winning filmmaker Gail Levin directed the PBS American Masters documentary Jeff Bridges: The Dude Abides.

LEBOWSKI

"Family" Tree

(That Was Me... and Six Other Guys: Professional Connections from *The Big Lebowski*)

Jeff Bridges (The Dude)

Coens: *True Grit*
John Turturro: *Fearless*
John Goodman: *Masked and Anonymous*
David Huddleston: *Bad Company*
Leon Russom: *True Grit*
Carter Burwell: *True Grit*
Marko Costanzo: *True Grit, The Mirror Has Two Faces, The Door in the Floor, The Morning After, Nadine, See You in the Morning*
Peter Kurland: *True Grit*
Mary Zophres: *True Grit*

Peter Stormare (Uli the Nihilist)

Coens: *Fargo*
Steve Buscemi: *Armageddon, Fargo, 13 Moons*
Julianne Moore: *The Lost World: Jurassic Park*
Warren Keith: *Fargo*
David Thewlis: *Damage*
Carter Burwell: *Fargo, Mercury Rising*
John Cameron: *Fargo*
Marko Costanzo: *Fargo*
Tricia Cooke: *Fargo*
Peter Kurland: *Fargo*
John S. Lyons: *Fargo*
William Preston Robertson: *Fargo*
Mary Zophres: *Fargo, Playing God*

Steve Buscemi (Donny)

Coens: *Miller's Crossing, Barton Fink, The Hudsucker Proxy, Fargo, Paris je t'aime, Romance and Cigarettes (Turturro-directed, Coen-produced), Sawbones (play)*
John Turturro: *The Search for One-Eyed Jimmy*
Peter Stormare: *Armageddon, Fargo, 13 Moons*
John Goodman: *Monsters, Inc., Barton Fink, The Hudsucker Proxy, The Equalizer (TV)*
Julianne Moore: *Tales from the Darkside*
Warren Keith: *Fargo*
Jean Ann Black: *Big Fish, Barton Fink, The Hudsucker Proxy*
Carter Burwell: *Miller's Crossing, Barton Fink, The Hudsucker Proxy, Fargo, Airheads*
John Cameron: *Fargo, The Hudsucker Proxy*
Marko Costanzo: *Boardwalk Empire, Fargo, Barton Fink, The Hudsucker Proxy, New York Stories, Big Night, Mystery Train, Blind Date, Handsome Harry, The Imposters, Bloodhounds of Broadway, Call Me*
Tricia Cooke: *Fargo, Miller's Crossing, Barton Fink, The Hudsucker Proxy, The Grey Zone*
Peter Kurland: *Miller's Crossing, Barton Fink, The Hudsucker Proxy, Fargo, Bloodhounds of Broadway*
John S. Lyons: *Fargo, Miller's Crossing, Barton Fink, The Hudsucker Proxy*
William Preston Robertson: *Fargo, Miller's Crossing, Barton Fink*
Mary Zophres: *Fargo, Ghost World, The Hudsucker Proxy*

David Thewlis (Knox Harrington)

Peter Stormare: *Damage*
Jean Ann Black: *Seven Years in Tibet*
Marko Costanzo: *The New World*
John S. Lyons: *The Trial*

John Goodman (Walter Sobchak)

Coens: *Raising Arizona, Barton Fink, The Hudsucker Proxy, O Brother, Where Art Thou?, Sawbones*

Steve Buscemi: *Monsters, Inc., Barton Fink, The Hudsucker Proxy, The Equalizer (TV)*

John Turturro: *O Brother, Where Art Thou?, Barton Fink*

Jeff Bridges: *Masked and Anonymous*

Jon Polito: *Barton Fink, Roseanne (TV), The Hudsucker Proxy, The Adventures of Rocky and Bullwinkle, C.H.U.D.*

Warren Keith: *Raising Arizona*

Jean Ann Black: *O Brother, Where Art Thou?, Barton Fink, The Hudsucker Proxy*

Carter Burwell: *Raising Arizona, Barton Fink, The Hudsucker Proxy, O Brother, Where Art Thou?, What Planet Are You From?*

John Cameron: *O Brother, Where Art Thou?, The Hudsucker Proxy*

Marko Costanzo: *O Brother, Where Art Thou?, Raising Arizona, Barton Fink, Bringing Out the Dead, The Hudsucker Proxy, C.H.U.D., What Planet Are You From?*

Tricia Cooke: *O Brother, Where Art Thou?, Barton Fink, The Hudsucker Proxy*

Peter Kurland: *Raising Arizona, Barton Fink, The Hudsucker Proxy, O Brother, Where Art Thou?*

John S. Lyons: *Raising Arizona, Barton Fink, The Hudsucker Proxy*

William Preston Robertson: *Raising Arizona, Barton Fink*

Mary Zophres: *O Brother, Where Art Thou?, The Hudsucker Proxy*

William Preston Robertson (voice actor)

Coens: *Blood Simple, Raising Arizona, Miller's Crossing, Barton Fink*

Jean Ann Black: *Barton Fink, Blood Simple*

Carter Burwell: *Blood Simple, Raising Arizona, Miller's Crossing, Barton Fink*

John Cameron: *Fargo*

Marko Costanzo: *Fargo, Raising Arizona, Barton Fink*

Tricia Cooke: *Fargo, Miller's Crossing, Barton Fink, Weeping Shriner*

Peter Kurland: *Blood Simple, Raising Arizona, Miller's Crossing, Barton Fink*

John S. Lyons: *Fargo, Miller's Crossing, Raising Arizona, Barton Fink*

Mary Zophres: *Fargo*

John Turturro: *Miller's Crossing, Barton Fink*

Jon Polito: *Miller's Crossing, Barton Fink*

Steve Buscemi: *Fargo, Miller's Crossing, Barton Fink*

John Goodman: *Raising Arizona, Barton Fink*

Warren Keith: *Fargo, Raising Arizona*

Peter Stormare: *Fargo*

Julianne Moore (Maude Lebowski)

Steve Buscemi: *Tales from the Darkside*

Peter Stormare: *The Lost World: Jurassic Park*

Philip Seymour Hoffman: *Magnolia, Boogie Nights*

Carter Burwell: *The Kids Are All Right*

Marko Costanzo: *Short Cuts, Surviving Picasso, A Map of the World*

John S. Lyons: *Boogie Nights*

John Turturro (Jesus Quintana)

Coens: *Miller's Crossing, Barton Fink, O Brother, Where Art Thou?, Romance and Cigarettes (Turturro-directed, Coen-produced)*

Jeff Bridges: *Fearless*

Steve Buscemi: *Mr. Deeds, Miller's Crossing, Barton Fink, Romance and Cigarettes, The Search for One-Eyed Jimmy*

Jon Polito: *Miller's Crossing, Barton Fink*

John Goodman: *O Brother, Where Art Thou?, Barton Fink*

Jean Ann Black: *Oh Brother, Where Art Thou?, Barton Fink*

Carter Burwell: *Miller's Crossing, Barton Fink, O Brother, Where Art Thou?*

John Cameron: *O Brother, Where Art Thou?*

Marko Costanzo: *O Brother, Where Art Thou?, The Good Shepherd, What Just Happened, Do the Right Thing, Barton Fink, The Color of Money, Hannah and Her Sisters, Miracle at St. Anna, He Got Game, Jungle Fever, Summer of Sam, Margot at the Wedding, Clockers, Desperately Seeking Susan, Cradle Will Rock, Gung Ho, Mo Better Blues, Girl 6, Grace of My Heart*

Tricia Cooke: *O Brother, Where Art Thou?, Miller's Crossing, Barton Fink*

Peter Kurland: *O Brother, Where Art Thou?, Miller's Crossing, Barton Fink*

John S. Lyons: *Miller's Crossing, Barton Fink*

William Preston Robertson: *Miller's Crossing, Barton Fink*

Mary Zophres: *O Brother, Where Art Thou?*

David Huddleston (The Big Lebowski)

Jon Polito: *Death of a Salesman on Broadway*

Carter Burwell: *Joe's Apartment*

Marko Costanzo: *Life with Mikey, Finnegan Begin Again*

Peter Kurland: *Something to Talk About*

John S. Lyons: *Life with Mikey*

Jon Polito (Da Fino)

Coens: *Miller's Crossing, Barton Fink, The Hudsucker Proxy, The Man Who Wasn't There*

David Huddleston: *Death of a Salesman on Broadway*

Jon Turturro: *Miller's Crossing, Barton Fink*

John Goodman: *Barton Fink, Roseanne (TV), The Hudsucker Proxy, The Adventures of Rocky and Bullwinkle, C.H.U.D.*

Steve Buscemi: *Miller's Crossing, Barton Fink, The Hudsucker Proxy*

Leon Russom: *L.A. Dragnet (TV)*

Jean Ann Black: *The Man Who Wasn't There, Barton Fink, The Hudsucker Proxy*

Carter Burwell: *Miller's Crossing, Barton Fink, The Hudsucker Proxy, The Man Who Wasn't There*

John Cameron: *The Man Who Wasn't There, The Hudsucker Proxy*

Marko Costanzo: *The Man Who Wasn't There, Barton Fink, The Hudsucker Proxy, Death of a Salesman, C.H.U.D., Compromising Positions, Dream Lover*

Tricia Cooke: *Miller's Crossing, Barton Fink, The Hudsucker Proxy, The Man Who Wasn't There*

Peter Kurland: *Miller's Crossing, Barton Fink, The Hudsucker Proxy, The Man Who Wasn't There*

John S. Lyons: *Miller's Crossing, Barton Fink, The Hudsucker Proxy*

William Preston Robertson: *Miller's Crossing, Barton Fink*

Mary Zophres: *The Man Who Wasn't There, The Hudsucker Proxy, View from the Top, Bushwhacked*

Philip Seymour Hoffman (Brandt)

Coens: *Sawbones*
Julianne Moore: *Magnolia, Boogie Nights*
Carter Burwell: *Before the Devil Knows You're Dead*
Marko Costanzo: *The 25th Hour, Charlie Wilson's War, Doubt, Synecdoche New York, Capote, The Savages, Jack Goes Boating*
Peter Kurland: *Punch-Drunk Love*
John S. Lyons: *Boogie Nights, Hard Eight*

Leon Russom (Malibu Chief of Police)

Coens: *True Grit*
Jeff Bridges: *True Grit*
Jon Polito: *L.A. Dragnet (TV)*
Carter Burwell: *True Grit*
Marko Costanzo: *True Grit, Silver Bullet*
Peter Kurland: *True Grit*
Mary Zophres: *True Gri*

Peter Kurland (sound)

Coens: *ALL*

Jean Ann Black: *Blood Simple, Barton Fink, The Hudsucker Proxy, O Brother, Where Art Thou?, The Man Who Wasn't There, Intolerable Cruelty, No Country for Old Men, Burn After Reading, A Serious Man*

Carter Burwell: *ALL Coen movies*

John Cameron: *Fargo, O Brother, Where Art Thou?, Miller's Crossing, The Man Who Wasn't There, Barton Fink, The Hudsucker Proxy*

Marko Costanzo: *Barton Fink, Fargo, O Brother, Where Art Thou?, The Man Who Wasn't There, Intolerable Cruelty, The Ladykillers, A Serious Man, True Grit, Men In Black, Men In Black II, Wild Wild West, Big Trouble, For Love or Money, Bloodhounds of Broadway, Full Moon in Blue Water*

Tricia Cooke: *Miller's Crossing, Barton Fink, The Hudsucker Proxy, Fargo, O Brother, Where Art Thou?, The Man Who Wasn't There*

John S. Lyons: *Raising Arizona, Miller's Crossing, Barton Fink, The Hudsucker Proxy, Fargo, For Love or Money*

William Preston Robertson: *Blood Simple, Raising Arizona, Miller's Crossing, Barton Fink*

Mary Zophres: *Fargo, O Brother, Where Art Thou?, The Man Who Wasn't There, Intolerable Cruelty, The Ladykillers, Burn After Reading, A Serious Man, True Grit*

Jeff Bridges: *True Grit*

John Turturro: *O Brother, Where Art Thou?, Miller's Crossing, Barton Fink*

Jon Polito: *Miller's Crossing, Barton Fink, The Hudsucker Proxy, The Man Who Wasn't There*

David Huddleston: *Something to Talk About*

Steve Buscemi: *Miller's Crossing, Barton Fink, The Hudsucker Proxy, Fargo, Bloodhounds of Broadway*

John Goodman: *Raising Arizona, Barton Fink, The Hudsucker Proxy, O Brother, Where Art Thou?*

Philip Seymour Hoffman: *Punch-Drunk Love*

Warren Keith: *Fargo, A Serious Man, Raising Arizona*

Leon Russom: *True Grit*

Peter Stormare: *Fargo*

Warren Keith
(Francis Donnelly, Funeral Director)

Coens: *Raising Arizona, Fargo, A Serious Man*

Peter Stormare: *Fargo*

Steve Buscemi: *Fargo*

John Goodman: *Raising Arizona*

Jean Ann Black: *A Serious Man*

Carter Burwell: *Raising Arizona, Fargo, A Serious Man*

John Cameron: *Fargo*

Marko Costanzo: *Fargo, A Serious Man, Raising Arizona*

Tricia Cooke: *Fargo*

Peter Kurland: *Fargo, A Serious Man, Raising Arizona*

John S. Lyons: *Fargo, Raising Arizona*

William Preston Robertson: *Fargo, Raising Arizona*

Mary Zophres: *Fargo, A Serious Man*

John S. Lyons (casting director)

Coens: *Raising Arizona, Miller's Crossing, Barton Fink, The Hudsucker Proxy, Fargo*

Jean Ann Black: *Barton Fink, The Hudsucker Proxy, Amos & Andrew*

Carter Burwell: *Raising Arizona, Miller's Crossing, Barton Fink, The Hudsucker Proxy, Fargo, It Could Happen To You, Framed*

John Cameron: *Fargo, The Hudsucker Proxy*

Marko Costanzo: *Raising Arizona, Miller's Crossing, Barton Fink, The Hudsucker Proxy, Fargo, It Could Happen to You, For Love or Money, Life with Mikey, Hello Again, Household Saints*

Tricia Cooke: *Fargo, Miller's Crossing, Barton Fink, The Hudsucker Proxy*

Peter Kurland: *Raising Arizona, Miller's Crossing, Barton Fink, The Hudsucker Proxy, Fargo, For Love or Money*

William Preston Robertson: *Fargo, Miller's Crossing, Raising Arizona, Barton Fink*

Mary Zophres: *Fargo, The Hudsucker Proxy*

John Turturro: *Miller's Crossing, Barton Fink*

Jon Polito: *Miller's Crossing, Barton Fink, The Hudsucker Proxy*

David Huddleston: *Life with Mikey*

Steve Buscemi: *Fargo, Miller's Crossing, Barton Fink, The Hudsucker Proxy*

John S. Lyons: *Raising Arizona, Barton Fink, The Hudsucker Proxy*

Philip Seymour Hoffman: *Boogie Nights, Hard Eight*

Warren Keith: *Fargo, Raising Arizona*

Peter Stormare: *Fargo*

Julianne Moore: *Boogie Nights*

David Thewlis: *The Trial*

Mary Zophres (costume designer)

Coens: *Fargo, O Brother, Where Art Thou?, The Man Who Wasn't There, Intolerable Cruelty, The Ladykillers, Burn After Reading, A Serious Man, True Grit*

Jean Ann Black: *No Country for Old Men, Burn After Reading, O Brother, Where Art Thou?, A Serious Man, Intolerable Cruelty, The Man Who Wasn't There, Born on the Fourth of July, The Hudsucker Proxy*

Carter Burwell: *Fargo, O Brother, Where Art Thou?, The Man Who Wasn't There, Intolerable Cruelty, The Ladykillers, Burn After Reading, A Serious Man, True Grit, This Boy's Life*

John Cameron: *Fargo, O Brother, Where Art Thou?, Intolerable Cruelty, The Man Who Wasn't There, The Ladykillers, The Hudsucker Proxy*

Marko Costanzo: *True Grit, Fargo, O Brother, Where Art Thou?, A Serious Man, Intolerable Cruelty, The Man Who Wasn't There, The Ladykillers, The Hudsucker Proxy*

Tricia Cooke: *Fargo, O Brother, Where Art Thou?, The Man Who Wasn't There, The Hudsucker Proxy*

Peter Kurland: *Fargo, O Brother, Where Art Thou?, The Man Who Wasn't There, Intolerable Cruelty, The Ladykillers, Burn After Reading, A Serious Man, True Grit*

John S. Lyons: *Fargo, The Hudsucker Proxy*

William Preston Robertson: *Fargo*

Jeff Bridges: *True Grit*

John Turturro: *O Brother, Where Art Thou?*

Jon Polito: *The Man Who Wasn't There, The Hudsucker Proxy, View from the Top, Bushwhacked*

Steve Buscemi: *Fargo, Ghost World, The Hudsucker Proxy*

John Goodman: *O Brother, Where Art Thou?, The Hudsucker Proxy*

Warren Keith: *Fargo, A Serious Man*

Leon Russom: *True Grit*

Peter Stormare: *Fargo, Playing God*

Jean Ann Black (makeup)

Coens: *Blood Simple, Barton Fink, The Hudsucker Proxy, O Brother, Where Art Thou?, The Man Who Wasn't There, Intolerable Cruelty, No Country for Old Men, Burn After Reading, A Serious Man*

Carter Burwell: *Twilight Breaking Dawn (pt. 1 & pt. 2), Blood Simple, Barton Fink, The Hudsucker Proxy, O Brother, Where Art Thou?, The Man Who Wasn't There, Intolerable Cruelty, No Country for Old Men, Burn After Reading, A Serious Man*

John Cameron: *Dazed and Confused, O Brother, Where Art Thou?, Intolerable Cruelty, The Man Who Wasn't There, The Hudsucker Proxy, The Tie That Binds*

Marko Costanzo: *O Brother, Where Art Thou?, A Serious Man, Greenberg, Intolerable Cruelty, The Man Who Wasn't There, Barton Fink, The Devil's Own, The Hudsucker Proxy, Before and After, Love Hurts*

Tricia Cooke: *O Brother, Where Art Thou?, The Man Who Wasn't There, Barton Fink, The Hudsucker Proxy*

Peter Kurland: *Blood Simple, Barton Fink, The Hudsucker Proxy, O Brother, Where Art Thou?, The Man Who Wasn't There, Intolerable Cruelty, No Country for Old Men, Burn After Reading, A Serious Man*

John S. Lyons: *Barton Fink, The Hudsucker Proxy, Amos & Andrew*

William Preston Robertson: *Barton Fink, Blood Simple*

Mary Zophres: *No Country for Old Men, Burn After Reading, O Brother, Where Art Thou?, A Serious Man, Intolerable Cruelty, The Man Who Wasn't There, Born on the Fourth of July, The Hudsucker Proxy*

John Turturro: *Oh Brother, Where Art Thou?, Barton Fink*

Jon Polito: *The Man Who Wasn't There, Barton Fink, The Hudsucker Proxy*

Steve Buscemi: *Big Fish, Barton Fink, The Hudsucker Proxy*

John Goodman: *O Brother, Where Art Thou?, Barton Fink, The Hudsucker Proxy*

Warren Keith: *A Serious Man*

David Thewlis: *Seven Years in Tibet*

John Cameron (producer)

Coens: *The Hudsucker Proxy, Fargo, The Man Who Wasn't There, Intolerable Cruelty, The Ladykillers*

Jean Ann Black: *Dazed and Confused, O Brother, Where Art Thou?, Intolerable Cruelty, The Man Who Wasn't There, The Hudsucker Proxy, The Tie That Binds*

Carter Burwell: *The Hudsucker Proxy, Fargo, The Man Who Wasn't There, Intolerable Cruelty, The Ladykillers*

Marko Costanzo: *Fargo, Men in Black, O Brother, Where Art Thou?, Intolerable Cruelty, The Man Who Wasn't There, The Ladykillers, The Hudsucker Proxy, Get Shorty*

Tricia Cooke: *Fargo, O Brother, Where Art Thou?, The Man Who Wasn't There, The Hudsucker Proxy*

Peter Kurland: *Fargo, O Brother, Where Art Thou?, Miller's Crossing, The Man Who Wasn't There, Barton Fink, The Hudsucker Proxy*

John S. Lyons: *Fargo, The Hudsucker Proxy*

William Preston Robertson: *Fargo*

Mary Zophres: *Fargo, O Brother, Where Art Thou?, Intolerable Cruelty, The Man Who Wasn't There, The Ladykillers, The Hudsucker Proxy*

John Turturro: *O Brother, Where Art Thou?*

Jon Polito: *The Man Who Wasn't There, The Hudsucker Proxy*

Steve Buscemi: *Fargo, The Hudsucker Proxy*

John Goodman: *O Brother, Where Art Thou?, The Hudsucker Proxy*

Warren Keith: *Fargo*

Peter Stormare: *Fargo*

Tricia Cooke (assistant/co-editor)

Coens: *Miller's Crossing, Barton Fink, The Hudsucker Proxy, Fargo, O Brother, Where Art Thou?, The Man Who Wasn't There*

Jean Ann Black: *O Brother, Where Art Thou?, The Man Who Wasn't There, Barton Fink, The Hudsucker Proxy*

Carter Burwell: *Miller's Crossing, Barton Fink, The Hudsucker Proxy, Fargo, O Brother, Where Art Thou?, The Man Who Wasn't There*

John Cameron: *Fargo, O Brother, Where Art Thou?, The Man Who Wasn't There, The Hudsucker Proxy*

Marko Costanzo: *Fargo, O Brother, Where Art Thou?, The Man Who Wasn't There, Barton Fink, The Hudsucker Proxy, The Notorious Bettie Page*

Peter Kurland: *Miller's Crossing, Barton Fink, The Hudsucker Proxy, Fargo, O Brother, Where Art Thou?, The Man Who Wasn't There*

John S. Lyons: *Fargo, Miller's Crossing, Barton Fink, The Hudsucker Proxy*

William Preston Robertson: *Fargo, Miller's Crossing, Barton Fink, Weeping Shriner*

Mary Zophres: *Fargo, O Brother, Where Art Thou?, The Man Who Wasn't There, The Hudsucker Proxy*

John Turturro: *O Brother, Where Art Thou?, Miller's Crossing, Barton Fink*

Jon Polito: *Miller's Crossing, Barton Fink, The Hudsucker Proxy, The Man Who Wasn't There*

Steve Buscemi: *Fargo, Miller's Crossing, Barton Fink, The Hudsucker Proxy, The Grey Zone*

John Goodman: *O Brother, Where Art Thou?, Barton Fink, The Hudsucker Proxy*

Warren Keith: *Fargo*

Peter Stormare: *Fargo*

Carter Burwell (music)

Coens: *ALL*

Jean Ann Black: *Twilight Breaking Dawn (pt. 1 & pt. 2), Blood Simple, Barton Fink, The Hudsucker Proxy, O Brother, Where Art Thou?, The Man Who Wasn't There, Intolerable Cruelty, No Country for Old Men, Burn After Reading, A Serious Man*

John Cameron: *The Hudsucker Proxy, Fargo, The Man Who Wasn't There, Intolerable Cruelty, The Ladykillers*

Marko Costanzo: *Barton Fink, Fargo, O Brother, Where Art Thou?, The Man Who Wasn't There, Intolerable Cruelty, The Ladykillers, A Serious Man, True Grit, Before Night Falls, Fur: An Imaginary Portrait of Diane Arbus, It Could Happen To You, What Planet Are You From?, The Beat*

Tricia Cooke: *Miller's Crossing, Barton Fink, The Hudsucker Proxy, Fargo, O Brother, Where Art Thou?, The Man Who Wasn't There*

Peter Kurland: *ALL Coen movies*

John S. Lyons: *Raising Arizona, Miller's Crossing, Barton Fink, The Hudsucker Proxy, Fargo, It Could Happen To You, Framed*

William Preston Robertson: *Blood Simple, Raising Arizona, Miller's Crossing, Barton Fink*

Mary Zophres: *Fargo, O Brother, Where Art Thou?, The Man Who Wasn't There, Intolerable Cruelty, The Ladykillers, Burn After Reading, A Serious Man, True Grit, This Boy's Life*

Jeff Bridges: *True Grit*

John Turturro: *Miller's Crossing, Barton Fink, O Brother, Where Art Thou?*

Jon Polito: *Miller's Crossing, Barton Fink, The Hudsucker Proxy, The Man Who Wasn't There*

David Huddleston: *Joe's Apartment*

Steve Buscemi: *Miller's Crossing, Barton Fink, The Hudsucker Proxy, Fargo, Airheads*

John Goodman: *Raising Arizona, Barton Fink, The Hudsucker Proxy, O Brother, Where Art Thou?, What Planet Are You From?*

Philip Seymour Hoffman: *Before the Devil Knows You're Dead*

Warren Keith: *Raising Arizona, Fargo, A Serious Man*

Leon Russom: *True Grit*

Peter Stormare: *Fargo, Mercury Rising*

Julianne Moore: *The Kids Are All Right*

Marko Costanzo (foley artist)

Coens: *Barton Fink, Fargo, O Brother, Where Art Thou?, The Man Who Wasn't There, Intolerable Cruelty, The Ladykillers, A Serious Man, True Grit*

Jean Ann Black: *O Brother, Where Art Thou?, A Serious Man, Greenberg, Intolerable Cruelty, The Man Who Wasn't There, Barton Fink, The Devil's Own, The Hudsucker Proxy, Before and After, Love Hurts*

Carter Burwell: *Barton Fink, Fargo, O Brother, Where Art Thou?, The Man Who Wasn't There, Intolerable Cruelty, The Ladykillers, A Serious Man, True Grit, Before Night Falls, Fur: An Imaginary Portrait of Diane Arbus, It Could Happen To You, What Planet Are You From?, The Beat*

John Cameron: *Fargo, Men in Black, O Brother, Where Art Thou?, Intolerable Cruelty, The Man Who Wasn't There, The Ladykillers, The Hudsucker Proxy, Get Shorty*

Tricia Cooke: *Fargo, O Brother, Where Art Thou?, The Man Who Wasn't There, Barton Fink, The Hudsucker Proxy, The Notorious Bettie Page*

Peter Kurland: *Barton Fink, Fargo, O Brother, Where Art Thou?, The Man Who Wasn't There, Intolerable Cruelty, The Ladykillers, A Serious Man, True Grit, Men In Black, Men In Black II, Wild Wild West, Big Trouble, For Love or Money, Bloodhounds of Broadway, Full Moon in Blue Water*

John S. Lyons: *Raising Arizona, Miller's Crossing, Barton Fink, The Hudsucker Proxy, Fargo, It Could Happen to You, For Love or Money, Life with Mikey, Hello Again, Household Saints*

William Preston Robertson: *Fargo, Raising Arizona, Barton Fink*

Mary Zophres: *True Grit, Fargo, O Brother, Where Art Thou?, A Serious Man, Intolerable Cruelty, The Man Who Wasn't There, The Ladykillers, The Hudsucker Proxy*

Jeff Bridges: *True Grit, The Mirror Has Two Faces, The Door in the Floor, The Morning After, Nadine, See You in the Morning*

John Turturro: *O Brother, Where Art Thou?, The Good Shepherd, What Just Happened, Do the Right Thing, Barton Fink, The Color of Money, Hannah and Her Sisters, Miracle at St. Anna, He Got Game, Jungle Fever, Summer of Sam, Margot at the Wedding, Clockers, Desperately Seeking Susan, Cradle Will Rock, Gung Ho, Mo Better Blues, Girl 6, Grace of My Heart*

Jon Polito: *The Man Who Wasn't There, Barton Fink, The Hudsucker Proxy, Death of a Salesman, C.H.U.D., Compromising Positions, Dream Lover*

David Huddleston: *Life with Mikey, Finnegan Begin Again*

Steve Buscemi: *Boardwalk Empire, Fargo, Barton Fink, The Hudsucker Proxy, New York Stories, Big Night, Mystery Train, Blind Date, Handsome Harry, The Imposters, Bloodhounds of Broadway, Call Me*

John Goodman: *O Brother, Where Art Thou?, Raising Arizona, Barton Fink, Bringing Out the Dead, The Hudsucker Proxy, C.H.U.D., What Planet Are You From?*

Philip Seymour Hoffman: *The 25th Hour, Charlie Wilson's War, Doubt, Synecdoche New York, Capote, The Savages, Jack Goes Boating*

Warren Keith: *Fargo, A Serious Man, Raising Arizona*

Leon Russom: *True Grit, Silver Bullet*

Peter Stormare: *Fargo*

Julianne Moore: *Short Cuts, Surviving Picasso, A Map of the World*

David Thewlis: *The New World*

The Big Lebowski Production and Postproduction

Before *Lebowski* went into production, the actors spent several weeks rehearsing with one another. The Coens hoped to film a good portion of the movie in a single three-shot of the principals (three people in frame, often at medium range) without editing, and they wanted all the dialogue cues to be picked up so the banter between the Dude, Walter, and Donny would seem improvised—which made it necessary for the actors to memorize the script like a play.

The eleven-week shoot began on January 27, 1997, and included a lot of location shooting in and around Los Angeles. Although Joel got directing credit and Ethan was credited for producing, the brothers actually split the duties down the middle. Filming finished one day ahead of schedule, which, according to the assistant accountant Kristina Soderquist, is "almost unheard of in this business."

"It's the most fun I ever had working on a film. I went to the set on my days off."

—John Goodman, at the 2011 *Big Lebowski* cast reunion

Marko Costanzo, the foley artist (specialist in sound effects), described the unique experience of working in the editing room with the Coens, who come in with a very specific vision for each film. "Everything I do is in postproduction," said Costanzo, "so once we get the film we look at it in the studio and then we start making the sounds. With *The Big Lebowski* we got a rough cut of the film, and a rough cut with the Coens is not like a rough cut with a Martin Scorsese movie. A Scorsese movie is three hours to cut down to two. With the Coens, a rough cut is an hour and thirty-five minutes and cut down to an hour and thirty-four minutes. Because they are also the editors, they know how much they need; they don't get excess footage. They are always precise."

Members of the sound crew speak of the Coens' generosity with the postproduction staff. Typically on a Coen film, the first day of the mix (combining the individual sound tracks for dialogue, music, and sound effects into a composite master) would include a "porridge breakfast," with a more lavish "meat dinner" coming at the end of the mix. According to Costanzo, "if you expected to get invited to the meat dinner you had to eat a bowl of porridge. Silly stuff, but everyone downed their porridge and we were able to go to the meat dinner." Al Zaleski, who got his start as an apprentice sound editor for *The Big Lebowski* and has gone on to become a supervising sound editor on many films, discusses the importance of such acknowledgment of the crew's work by the filmmakers: "It's an amazing opportunity for us sound people who sit in dark closets and listen to things on headphones to actually get to sit next to some of the actors in the films. I ate dinner with Frances McDormand . . . and just to have access to these people as well as the directors was fun."

The Stranger, The Jesus & Walter,
2011, by Joshua Budich.
Courtesy Joshua Budich,
www.joshuabudich.com

The Art of Color Timing

"As a color timer, I am asked to explain 'what is timing?' But when I do, the eyes of the person asking the question invariably glaze over and they lose consciousness. So without delving into the usual ninety minutes of technical jargon, here is an extremely abbreviated explanation:

Color timing establishes the overall look of a film, but has to begin with the Director of Photography's correct exposure of the film. The color balance is achieved by blending the scene-to-scene colors in seamless continuity….

The intention of color correction is to alter the overall color of light. Some lighting may appear undesirable, and appear more natural by rendering the scene with a different color, thus creating a more pleasing artistic effect. Color timing therefore can completely change the mood, create a style, or simply enhance the look of the motion picture.

After completing the timing of *Kundun* for Roger Deakins in 1997, he asked me to do this 'little bowling picture.' I knew this picture wasn't going to be anything small, any more than when Roger had asked me in 1994 to color time a picture "about a little jailbreak" that turned out to be *The Shawshank Redemption*.

In any case, I never imagined bowling to be so universally popular.

From a technical standpoint, Roger's camera angles, composition, and lens work were always impeccable on all his titles. He created a flawless, perfectly exposed film negative enabling all requested possibilities of color changes.

As a result, the visual transitions were smooth, indistinguishable, and seamless; the color timing was done completely photo chemically and therefore complemented Roger's work, just as it should."

—David Orr, color timer for *The Big Lebowski* and over two hundred other films

Scene Scrutiny: Micturating Thugs, Flying Carpets, and Dancing Landlords

Each section of *The Big Lebowski* has its own idiosyncratic behind-the-scenes anecdotes. What follows is a more in-depth breakdown of three in particular: the Dude's bungalow scenes, his first dream sequence, and the captivating modern dance performed by Marty the Landlord.

Roll Scene 1:
The Dude's Bungalow

Along with the bowling alley, the Dude's domicile is the most-used location in the film, with seven scenes taking place there:

> First appearance of the Treehorn thugs: "Ever thus to deadbeats, Lebowski!"
> Various phone messages and Marty the Landlord
> The Dude gets punched in the face while listening to the 1987 Venice Beach League Playoffs
> The police stop by for a visit and close the file on one of two cases

The Dude's Abode.
Courtesy Damn Good Doormats, Spoon Popkin and Lee Sinoski, www.damngooddoormats.com

© Moviestore Collection Ltd / Alamy.
Courtesy of Universal Studios Licensing LLC

> Bathtub soak, interrupted by "marmot"
> Second appearance of the Treehorn thugs (who, oddly enough, have swapped clothing): "You're not dealing with morons, here!"
> The Dude "loves" Maude, mixes a drink, then has an epiphany

Other than the set for the dream sequence, the bungalow interior was the only actual set (artificially constructed setting) that was created for the film. Cinematographer Roger Deakins lit it in such a way to make it look grittier, seedier. In outfitting the Dude's drab abode, the film's set

Lebowski's Sports Bar and Grill in Cicero, New York, the kind of bar the Dude might hang out in.
Photo by Doug Mayer

decorator, Chris Spellman, discusses the crew's thought process: "We knew what part of town the Dude lived in, which was Venice; we knew what kind of places he hung out in, bowling alleys; we knew the kind of bars he hung out in; and we talked about how much money this guy actually had and made and where he got his things from. We wanted to make it realistic, and wanted to make it look like some of the items in his house he found in a back alley—like he saw some table or chair as he was driving home from the bar or bowling alley—so that's how [the design and props for the interior] came about." (As a footnote, at the time of *Lebowski*, the Coens weren't attached to a major studio, so when production ended many of the artifacts were sold off to the cast and crew. Spellman bought both Lebowskis' rugs, which reside in his home to this day.)

Built on a stage, the set of the inside of the Dude's bungalow was laid out in a manner

The Dude mistakes a ferret . . .
VitCOM Photo / www.shutterstock.com

that would facilitate access to certain shots. For example, when the Dude is receiving a swirly in the toilet courtesy of Jackie Treehorn's thugs, the camera could shoot all the way through the hallway and into the other room, so the rug could be seen concurrently. (The special effects crew constructed said toilet's seat out of rubber so that Jeff Bridges wouldn't chip a tooth or otherwise injure himself in the process of getting dunked.) The shot of the blond thug dropping the Dude's bowling ball on the bathroom floor necessitated the creation of a whole false floor with a cushion underneath. The tile itself was real, although it had to be breakaway (made to break easily without injury), and rubber was inserted underneath. As special effects man Peter Chesney says about such seemingly simple scenarios in the movies: "Nothing is as you think it is."

. . . for a marmot.
Irinak / www.shutterstock.com

Another of the bungalow bathroom scenes involves the nihilists siccing a so-called (by the Dude) "marmot" on him in the tub. The Dude is mistaken; the creature is actually a ferret (a marmot is a bushy-tailed, stocky rodent like a woodchuck or squirrel). For the scene in which the creature is underwater, the crew drilled into the wall of the tub through the ceramic and iron, then inserted a rubber gasket and bearing

STRIKES & GUTTERS

The Thug's Latin Leanings

Just before micturating on the Dude's rug, Woo proclaims: "Ever thus to deadbeats, Lebowski!" This is a play on the Latin phrase uttered by the murderers of both Julius Caesar and Abraham Lincoln during their assassinations, "*Sic semper tyrannis!*" which translates to "Thus always to tyrants!" That a thug who has so egregiously mistaken the Dude for a millionaire would be attempting Latin wordplay is just one reason this line is particularly clever. Delving further into the etymology, *sic semper tyrannis* is very lofty Latin-speak, but Woo has replaced "tyrants" with the crude "deadbeats." The intermingling of the high and low here lends fuel to the comic fire.

with a rod that maneuvered the stuffed "marmot" on a stick. Chesney lay on the floor in a raincoat holding a Milwaukee drill, revving it up to spin the fake marmot between Bridges' knees as he thrashed about. Because this action splashed water all over the place, the crew only used the stuffed critter for the drop-in and pull-out—Bridges was merely acting the in-between portion of the attack. More than one live ferret had to be used in the filming of the scene, according to Peter Stormare (Uli the Nihilist), as it is against animal-protection laws to submerge the animal repeatedly. (As the film credits state, "Scenes which appear to place an animal in jeopardy were simulated.") As for what happened to the stuffed ferret: the Coens lent it to the third annual Lebowski Fest in Louisville, Kentucky, in 2003.

The bungalow on Venezia Boulevard (significantly renovated since the days of the Dude).
Courtesy Bulldog Realtors / Winston Cenac and Golden Savage

The exterior of the Dude's abode was part of a six-unit compound located in Venice Beach. The ten-thousand-square-foot property, with its landscaped courtyard, was renovated after production wrapped on *The Big Lebowski*. The sprucing up must have been extensive, as the property was put up for sale in 2011 with a list price of $2.3 million. The actual address, 606-608 Venezia Boulevard, appears on the Dude's sixty-nine-cent check to Ralphs for half-and-half.

Cast Stories from the Bungalow Scenes

➤*From the first appearance of the Treehorn thugs*

Apparently, the Coens took to heart their own scripted moniker of "strapping blond man" for the Treehorn heavy. Actor Mark Pellegrino remembers going to the callback with Ethan and Joel seated on a couch and Joel joking, "You're one of the best blond men that we've seen!"

➤ *From getting punched in the face while listening to the League Championships*

Carlos Leon, who portrayed the face-puncher from the second set of thugs (Maude's hired hands), discusses his audition and what it was like to work with the Coens: "[It was] one of my first big movies even though it was a small role, and it was just an honor to work with the guys who created *Fargo*. In the casting process, I told the Coens that I loved their work, we started talking about New York, they both gave me a hug and I left, and eventually got the job. Specifically on set, they had lunch with me—mind you, I was a beginner actor and they actually sat at the lunch table with me, and we talked about New York City rats. That was our topic, that was our intimacy together: how big they were, and [how much] smarter than any other rats."

Courtesy Bulldog Realtors / Winston Cenac and Golden Savage

**Flea performing his day job, as bassist
for the Red Hot Chili Peppers.**
Photograph by Steve Eichner / WireImage

➤ *From the bathtub-soak-interrupted-by
"marmot" scene*

The Coens revel in juxtapositions, like pairing skinny Barton Fink with robust Charlie Meadows in *Barton Fink*, or run-off-at-the-mouth Carl Showalter with silent brooder Gaear Grimsrud in *Fargo*. Although they teased actor Torsten Voges (Franz the Nihilist) on set about his height, one can only assume that the three radically different heights of the nihilists, from Flea's 5 feet 6 inches to Voges' 6 feet 9 inches, was part of Joel and Ethan's conception of the film's visual aesthetic (and their fun)—particularly as the script expressly called for one of the nihilists to be tall. As Voges recounts, "The Coens were always getting at me for being so tall. It started in the audition. When I went in, it was a tiny room, and they said, 'Oh, you're taller than Tim Robbins [from *The Hudsucker Proxy*], you're way too tall, this is not going to work.' Which made me feel really kind of terrible. And there was another situation in the marmot scene, when they had a really hard time getting us all into frame because it was in the tiny bathroom and again I was a bit too tall. And they were making fun of my height occasionally, to tease me."

It seems unlikely that the Dude would agree with Nixon's politics, but he respects the former president's pastime enough to have a poster of Nixon (bowling in the alley in the White House's basement) hanging in his bungalow. *University of Maryland Institute for Advanced Computer Studies, National Archives and Records Administration*

Shutting Up Donny, or Carl?
Legend has it that Walter's oft-quoted *Lebowski* line to his mild-mannered teammate, "Shut the fuck up, Donny," is a direct response to Steve Buscemi's earlier role in *Fargo*, Carl Showalter—a motormouth who couldn't stop himself from talking.

Roll Scene 2: The Thief of L.A.

The first dream sequence begins in the Dude's house (bungalow scene #3) with him serenely listening to the sounds of the 1987 Venice Beach League Playoffs on headphones. Opening his eyes, he views three strangers, one of whom proceeds to punch him in the face. The crack on the jaw transitions him from the "real" of his living space to the "unreal" of a dream, sparking fireworks (that recurring star motif rearing its head again) that coalesce into the city lights of Los Angeles. The Dude soars over the city to the tune of Bob Dylan's "The Man in Me" (presumably the "Bob" referenced as the "B" side of his cassette). Ahead is Maude Lebowski, a person unknown to the Dude at this point in the film, seated on a flying carpet. The scene is reminiscent of the 1940 film *The Thief of Baghdad* (in fact the script specifies

"It all seems like some kind of weird dream I'm having."
—Jeff Bridges, at the L.A. Lebowski Fest

"If you will it, Dude, it is no dream."
—Walter Sobchak, paraphrasing Theodor Herzl, writer/playwright/journalist and the father of modern political Zionism

Donny shuts up (and runs away) when Walter threatens Smokey.
© Moviestore Collection / Alamy. Courtesy of Universal Studios Licensing LLC

Artist Beck Tench scrutinized *The Big Lebowski* in order to draw ninety-five meticulously detailed scenes from the film on a bowling pin. (During Tench's research, she discovered that the Dude drinks nine White Russians in all.)
Courtesy of Beck Tench

the visual to be "like a sheik on a magic carpet"), in which the main character steals the king's magic flying carpet and becomes free to go off on his own adventures.

To achieve the effect of Julianne Moore riding the carpet, the crew used a real rug with steel rods running through it, which was then puppeteered with an overhead string. "One of those things that [the Coens] kind of enjoy is the clunkiness of some visuals, because it has character rather than a perfect CGI kind of look," says mechanical effects engineer Peter Chesney. "So this was a green-screen shot with the rug. If you look at that image for a minute you'll see it's a little bit spastic, and that's very specific to not wanting it to look perfect. It was all sort of fun; there's a lot of wind on it so the little edges ruffle (which probably made the green screen more difficult)."

To portray the Dude's bowling ball giving in to gravity, a "rotisserie" device that had been built for the subsequent bowling alley dream was reconfigured to allow Bridges to pivot rapidly downward. (Interestingly, the dream scenes are the only ones in which Bridges is holding a bowling bowl.) In the next shot, which critic Roger Ebert proclaimed "the first point-of-view shot in history from inside a bowling ball," the camera was mounted on a device akin to a barbecue spit, on which it rolled down the lane.

Chesney also explains how the crew created the visual of the pins flying away from the Dude's head: "In the bowling sequences there were several things that look like they were optical effects [added after filming, altering the original image] but weren't. For instance, the bowling pins actually had a scotchlight

The Tao of the Dude, by Jeremy Couturier.
© Jeremy Couturier, 2009. www.couturierillustration.com

material that reflects light back to the source so they're lit up from the front. They were all lightweight plastic, and they all had a series of fine strings going to a series of rubber bands . . . . At one point when the camera gets to a certain mark the pins are all pulled away up into the air, so it looks like a strike in zero gravity. There was this whole little rig of every single bowling pin that has a wire on it, attached to a rubber band, which when released, is flown off the table, and the pins tumble out of the light so they would appear to go out into black space."

As to the question of why incorporate a dream sequence at all, Ethan Coen said, it's a "cheap, gimmicky, obvious way to depict the character's inner life." Of course, it also corresponds to the hallucinations depicted in the noir stories of Raymond Chandler, illustrates visually the effects of a brain undergoing a strict drug regimen, and ties together elements of the plot—namely, the rug.

© lolloj / Shutterstock.com

Roll Scene 3: The Danse Moderne / Marty the Landlord's "Cycle"

Actor Jack Kehler, who has appeared in such films as *Lost Highway*, *Waterworld*, and *Point Break*, did not have any professional dance experience before being cast in *The Big Lebowski*. Early in his career, for a class at Carnegie Hall (that had just one other male student), he sported brown tights and learned ballet for five weeks, at which point he came to the realization that he could still be an actor without knowing how to dance. Thus ended Kehler's dancing career, until *Lebowski*.

Once cast, Kehler selected Modest Mussorgsky's "Pictures at an Exhibition" out

Modest Petrovich Mussorgsky, the nineteenth-century Russian composer of Marty's dance-piece music.
Hulton Archive / Stringer / Getty Images

"The audition was just the scene at the doorway. And it was really simple, and I remember reading the line, 'I'm performing my dance quintet—you know, my cycle . . .' After I finished saying it, I realized, 'Oh, I guess I'm going to have to do a dance . . .' Just thinking of the actuality of it. And it did turn out to be as physical as I thought it would be."

—Jack Kehler (Marty the Landlord)

of several chosen pieces of music for what the script tongue-in-cheekily described as a "Danse Moderne." Bill and Jacqui Landrum were the choreographer team for the scene. Bill recalls Kehler's inexperience being an asset, because there was no expectation that he would do anything but memorize a certain series of movements. They put him through the paces, then stepped back to allow the movements to come organically from Kehler.

The dance was clearly inspired by groundbreaking choreographer Martha Graham, who is often the stereotypical go-to for any modern dance references. Named "Dancer of the Century" by *Time* magazine, Graham's very dramatic brand of dance (and of discussing it) is legendary. Whenever Marty the Landlord

"It is here in the studio that the dancer learns his craft, the mastery of his instrument, which is the human body. The dancer cultivates an awareness of the head and throat . . . . A dancer's world is the heart of man, with its joys and its hopes and its fears and its love. And a dancer's world is arrived at by days and days of work, weeks of work and years of work."

—Martha Graham, all seriousness, in the short film, *A Dancer's World*

Martha Graham in *Errand into the Maze*, which depicts the Greek myth of Ariadne and the Minotaur, 1947.
Michael Ochs Archives / Getty Images

A-List Choreographers Bill and Jacqui Landrum

The husband and wife team of Jacqui and Bill Landrum worked together for forty years as movie choreographers. Jacqui got her first professional choreography job on the short-lived but influential 1965 music show *Hollywood a Go-Go*, which both "Mickey" singer Toni Basil and Jacqui were brought in to choreograph. *Big Lebowski* dancer Kiva Dawson recalls that Landrum and Basil "ruled" Hollywood and the Sunset Strip, as most jobs at that time for young dancers went through them. In 1977 Jacqui and Bill Landrum, who had met at a dance class eight years earlier (and wed after three months; the marriage lasted thirty-nine years until Jacqui's passing in 2008), created the Landrum Dance Theatre. For seventeen years, they taught stage movement and drama at the University of Southern California. They choreographed such films as *The Doors* and *Great Balls of Fire*. In addition to *The Big Lebowski*, the Landrums collaborated with the Coens on all of their films that required a choreographer (except *The Hudsucker Proxy*): *Barton Fink*, *The Man Who Wasn't There*, and *O Brother, Where Art Thou?* On the latter, for which they were nominated for an American Choreography Award, they choreographed the legendary Ku Klux Klan scene. Like the big dream/dance sequence of *Lebowski*, the scene is reminiscent of a twisted Busby Berkeley dance number. (See page 125.)

"On all of the films that we worked on with the Coen brothers, one of the great pleasures was [that] as directors, they gave you full trust. We'd have a meeting and discuss what they wanted out of the piece—visually, the style, the period, whatever was required. And then they would let us go off and we would come back and say, 'Alright, we've got a good sketch going here, come look at it and give your input.' Which was always fun because they would say, 'Oh my god, this is exactly what we were envisioning, thank you very much!' . . . The great thing about them is that they function so much out of their intuition, rather than being trapped in the intellectual concept, that that too becomes this great energy on set . . . . There is room for improvisation, even though it rarely happens because their original vision is clear and it works that there's no reason to go and try something else. . . . They're like two kids to play with, it's like: 'Oh good, we have this toy, let's go, let's see what it can do!'"

—*Bill Landrum*

puts his hand to his head in the dance, he is referencing the Graham technique, intentionally or not.

The Landrums used a method of assigning names or images to every movement of Kehler's, so that he could find a continuity to the dance that would be comfortable to him as an actor. They inquired how parts of the music made him feel, then instructed him to execute those feelings through dance. Together the choreographers and actor went through the dance moment by moment, as if it were a script. (And similar to an actor learning a script section by section, breaking down the dance into smaller segments allowed Kehler to memorize it more easily.)

For the scene, there were three advance rehearsals of two to three hours each, and Kehler worked on it off the set as well. Bill remembers Kehler lamenting one day that

his neighbors had heard him practicing in his backyard. They looked over their balcony to see him performing a "modern dance," and very probably thought he was crazy. All that rehearsing, however, meant that on the day of shooting the process went quickly. Kehler says, "We didn't do a whole lot of takes because whatever roughness was in the dance was what was called for." The memorable scene lives on in other forms—Jeff Bridges selected the silhouette photograph he took of Marty the Landlord's cycle for the cover of his 2010 music album *Be Here Soon*.

> "Even though the dance movements weren't second nature to [Kehler], he worked so hard at it and rehearsed it endlessly, to make it look as bad as it should have been bad, and it was perfect, it was just great!"
>
> —Bill Landrum, choreographer

In a more recent instance of interpretive (and inspired) dance, in 2009 and 2010, Chicago's Vaudezilla performance troupe put on a production of *Rollin' Outta Here Naked: A Big Lebowski Burlesque*. Unsurprisingly the show, led by group cofounder Red Hot Annie, was a smash hit. *Candice Conner, oomphotography.com*

SACHA, JOHANNA & LA CLIQUE PRÉSENTENT

LE LEBOWSKI SHOW

The fourth annual "Le Lebowski Show" took place in Paris during the 2011 César Awards, France's equivalent to the Oscars. The party combined French chic with bowling; Maude would approve. Print by Andy Rementer. *Courtesy of the artist, www.andyrementer.com*

JEUDI 7 AVRIL 2011 DE 23H À L'AUBE

BOWLING FOCH

2, BIS AVENUE FOCH-PARIS XVI

PART IV
Genre-bending

Throughout their careers, the Coen brothers have dabbled in all manners of genre. *The Big Lebowski* incorporates a multitude within one film, from a kidnap caper (albeit a faux kidnapping) to a cult movie and a mystery. The IMDB website Box Office Mojo places *Lebowski* on two separate lists: Stoner/Slacker and Dark/Black Comedy. Certainly it also fits into the classic genres of period piece, musical, Western, and film noir.

"This will not stand.
This will not stand, this
aggression against Kuwait."
—President
George H. W. Bush

 ## *The Big Lebowski* as Period Piece

Setting their films in other time periods affords the Coens a specificity that would be lacking in a strictly "contemporary" film—in other words, it gives them the means to create an alternate yet identifiable world. These constructed worlds are more difficult for an audience to dispute, as the Coens are using the past to remove the story from a context the audience is immediately familiar with. Additionally, setting a film in a specific bygone time period allows the Coens to incorporate the intricate and subtle details they so lovingly shoehorn into their films.

The brothers set *The Big Lebowski* in 1991, a mere seven years prior to the film's 1998 release. Though the film is not a remote period piece along the lines of *Miller's Crossing* (the 1920s), *Barton Fink* (1941), or *The Hudsucker Proxy* (1956), it nonetheless evokes a distinct "period" in its own right. Many aspects of the film can attribute their legacy to much less recent times: the 1930s and 1940s Los Angeles of Raymond Chandler; the 1950s and 1960s stylishness of bowling and Googie architecture; and the late 1960s- and 1970s-inspired characters (Vietnam vet, former political radical/hippie pothead, Fluxus-reminiscent performance artist). All of these more dated characteristics are filtered through the prism of the early nineties and emphasize the archaic aspects of the characters and setting.

A variety of details date *The Big Lebowski* to the early 1990s. One such detail is certainly the Dude's use of a beeper, a device that was much more popular in American society until the mid-1990s, when mobile phones took off.

The Dude does carry what is called in the movie a "portable phone," but it's huge by today's standards.

Also in the realm of the high tech, Jackie Treehorn discusses the pornographic future as being all about "interactive erotic software . . . One hundred percent electronic." He's a little ahead of his time here, but accurately predictive: in the 1990s such computer-enhanced pornography wasn't mass-produced yet because it wasn't cost-effective, but at the turn of the century the market exploded.

Walter smokes in the bowling alley bar. Smoking was permitted throughout California until a 1995 public ban was instituted in work-places (such as restaurants); a ban on smok-

The Dude and Walter with other '90s icons (and a few from the '80s and '00s as well).
Courtesy of Evanimal (Evan Yarbrough). www.evanimal.com

Notable Events of 1991 (Other than our conflict with Saddam and the Iraqis)

» A new post-apartheid constitution for South Africa
» Balkan Wars begin
» The New York Giants top the Buffalo Bills (four-time Super Bowl losers) in Super Bowl XXV
» The beating of Rodney King by Los Angeles police is caught on video
» The first World Wide Web browser is introduced
» Magic Johnson announces he has HIV
» Super Nintendo Entertainment System is introduced in the United States

» The Soviet Union is dissolved by the end of the year
» Both Mike Tyson and Jeffrey Dahmer are arrested
» Led by Series MVP Kirby Puckett, the Minnesota Twins best the Atlanta Braves in arguably the most exciting World Series of all time
» Richard Linklater's film *Slacker* is released, spawning (or at least showcasing) youthful versions of the Dude

---

ing in bars followed three years later. Today, of course, one can actually smoke marijuana, with the proper medical clearance, in many locations in the state. The contemporary Dude might make a visit to a good and thorough doctor.

The early nineties were an interesting time in the American culture wars. What was considered "political correctness," or the insistence on nonracist and nonsexist language and discussion, was lambasted by the right wing as penalizing white men and creating an air of intolerance in the country. The controversy was highlighted by a Richard Bernstein *New York Times* article in late 1990 called "The Rising Hegemony of the Politically Correct."

This brewing battle—with lines drawn on college campuses across America—is illustrated by the *Lebowski* characters' definitional use of language. The Dude calls the Big Lebowski "handicapped" and stumbles over "crippled" while Brandt loudly corrects, "*disabled.*" Likewise, Walter politely admonishes, "Dude, Chinaman is not the preferred nomenclature . . . Asian American. Please." To which the Dude points out, "Walter, this isn't a guy who built the railroads, here . . . . He peed on my rug."

Why else set the film in 1991? The coinciding Gulf War also gave Walter (another) reason to grumble.

The Dude's Seinfeldian Lexical World

By Mark Peters

If scientists ever develop a unit of measure for the quotability of something, they should consider calling it a Lebowskigram, in honor of one of the most quotable movies of all time. Fans repeat lines like "You mean, coitus?" and "Nice marmot" with a glee seldom seen, except maybe in acolytes of *The Godfather* and *Anchorman*.

But as I watched *The Big Lebowski* for somewhere between the forty-third and kabillionth time, I was struck by not just the quotability of the lines, but something about their content: the movie is obsessed with the meaning and use of words, and the characters make distinctions between words in minute, Seinfeldian ways. Just as Jerry Seinfeld and Larry David on *Seinfeld* and *Curb Your Enthusiasm* delight in dividing the world into low talkers, close talkers, high talkers, and schmohawks, the Dude's universe is an overturned lexical applecart everyone is trying to straighten up. A fella is not a dude. A Chinaman is not an Asian American. The Big Lebowski is disabled, not handicapped. A pervert is not necessarily a sex offender. Lennon is not Lenin, and a mortuary is not a rental house. Lebowski characters navigate this mess as clumsily and entertainingly as *Seinfeld* characters discuss bunk:

> Elaine: If anyone needs any medical advice, Elaine met a doctor. And he's unattached.
> Jerry: I thought the whole dream of dating a doctor was debunked.
> Elaine: No, it's not debunked, it's totally bunk.
> Jerry: Isn't bunk bad? Like, that's a lot of bunk.
> George: No, something is bunk and then you debunk it.
> Jerry: What?
> Elaine: Huh?
> George: I think.
> (Pause as they all look down)
> Elaine: Look, I'm dating a doctor and I like it. Let's just move on.

In *TBL*, such bickering about language is well-suited to the struggles of the characters, who are trapped in a world with too many ins and outs and what-have-yous for even Sherlock Holmes to master, much less the Dude. So the befuddled Lebowskites grasp at lexical straws. Clinging to the "correct" word is one way the characters cling to the hope that their universe makes sense, which of course it does not. Unfortunately for the Coens' characters—and us—using language as a tether to reality is like pulling yourself out of quicksand with a bowl of oatmeal.

That poor woman? That poor slut?

Though *TBL* is a male-driven, testosterone-soaked movie, the female characters—Bunny and Maude Lebowski—drive the plot and are the object of much word-focused chatter.

Take the Dude insisting that Maude Lebowski is his "fucking lady friend," not his "special lady," as Da Fino the private snoop (Brother Seamus) assumes. Since commitment isn't really in the Dude's wheelhouse—and his toilet-up lifestyle isn't very woman-friendly—he resists the term "special lady," which implies a girlfriend, steady sweetie, significant other, and potential wife. On the other hand "fucking lady friend" is unintentionally literal (on the Dude's part, at least) and quite casual.

Seinfeld's characters, like *Lebowski*'s, dissect language yet never reach any sort of linguistic conclusion.
Getty Images / Handout

Despite the old-fashioned formality of "lady," a "fucking lady friend" isn't quite as serious as a girlfriend, yet reeks of stoned chivalry.

Maude herself would likely accept either term, as long as the Dude doesn't consider her a partner. But some distinctions mean more than others. I can feel Maude's pain when the Dude refers to porn actress/stepmom Bunny as her mother. We know nothing of Maude's bio-mom, but we can assume she's not the type who offers $1,000 blowjobs to bathrobe-clad hippies.

Speaking of Bunny—or should I say, Fawn Knutson?—who is she, exactly? The Dude may think she kidnapped herself, but he's still willing to call her "that poor woman" when he fears her rescue has been bungled by himself and Walter. Walter is convinced Bunny is "that poor slut" instead, a word choice that raises the question (or answers it, for Walter) of whether Bunny is someone who sees sex as a "natural, zesty enterprise" or if she is a "compulsive fornicator"

consumed by nymphomania. We do know that Bunny's employer Jackie Treehorn prefers to think of himself as making "publishing, entertainment, political advocacy" rather than smut, and who can blame him? Smut sounds so smutty.

The name Bunny itself is mega-apt for a character obsessed with sex, bringing to mind coitus-obsessed bunnies that roam nature's fields and Hefner's grottos. I have to agree with this August 2011 observation by Twitter humorist A. S. Paul: "People aren't named Bunny anymore. I think this is a step forward for humanity."

Achievers, dudes, and fellas

Then there are the Lebowski males. "What is a man?" asks the wheelchair-bound Lebowski, and a great deal of the movie is spent riffing on possible answers.

In the overstuffed, fake-rich Lebowski's eyes, a man is an *achiever*—one of the central words of the movie. The title character believes he's an achiever, with all the real manhood that implies. He won the Los Angeles Chamber of Commerce Business Achiever Award and sponsors (or at least sports a plaque celebrating) the Little Lebowski Urban Achievers. The mirror issue of *Time* that momentarily reflects the Dude's face features the words, "Are you a Lebowski achiever?" Post-kidnapping, Lebowski denounces the kidnappers as "men who are unable to achieve on a level field of play," and when the Dude botches the money handoff, he accuses the Dude of failing "to achieve, even in the modest task that was your charge. . . ."

The opposite of an achiever is a bum, like the Dude, and as Lebowski claims, "The bums will always lose." The *Oxford English Dictionary* traces this term for a "lazy or dissolute person; an habitual loafer or tramp" back to 1864 and this use: "The policemen say that even their old, regular and reliable 'bums' appear to have reformed." Another term that's opposite *achiever* is *jerk-off*, as the abusive Malibu Chief of Police puts it. The *OED*'s first use in 1968 mentions that it's "a rustic; a simpleton." *Green's Dictionary of Slang* defines *jerk-off* as "a useless, despised person, a lazy incompetent." A vivid use from a 1939 novel gives you the general idea: "He was the half-pint jerk-off, he was godson, he was the titty-drinker." Of course, *jerk-off* was initially a reference

to masturbation, and this insult is perhaps particularly hurtful to the Dude. With his johnson in jeopardy, the Dude would love to remain eligible for this slur.

Though *TBL* has been a huge factor in the success of *dude*, the currents of language change were already pushing *dude* in a direction the Dude could comfortably epitomize. However, the *OED*'s first meaning, found in the late 1800s, is a different beast: "A name given in ridicule to a man affecting an exaggerated fastidiousness in dress, speech, and deportment, and very particular about what is aesthetically 'good form'; hence, extended to an exquisite, a dandy, 'a swell.'" Here's an early use from 1883: "The 'Dude' sounds like the name of a bird. It is, on the contrary, American slang for a new kind of American young man. The one object for which the dude exists is to tone down the eccentricities of fashion. The silent, subfusc, subdued 'dude' hands down the traditions of good form."

Simultaneously, the word was being used for "a non-westerner or city-dweller who tours or stays in the west of the U.S., esp. one who spends his holidays on a ranch; a tenderfoot." This is the *dude ranch* sense of dude, and may explain why the fella-favoring Stranger isn't enamored of the word: out West, a dude was a poser/tourist. Another 1883 quote about that type of dude oddly

Lennon.
Photograph by John Rodgers / Redferns

Not Lennon.
© Archive Pics / Alamy

applies to the Dude too: "The dude is one of those creatures which are perfectly harmless and are a necessary evil to civilization." It would probably please the Dude to know that the *OED* also has examples of *dudedom, dudeness, dudery, dudism,* and *dudish,* all found in the late 1800s—plus two terms for a female dude, *dudess* and *dudine*. Those would fit well next to the Dude's own self-applied nicknames such as *Duder* and *El Duderino*.

It wasn't until the 1900s that *dude* started to resemble its current use. In this 1918 *OED* use, a dude is just a guy: "In a gang of snipes there is generally one dude who is known as the 'king snipe.'" Eventually, the word broadened so much that it can now be used for a man or woman, as in this 1981 example: "We're not talking about a lame chick and a gnarly guy. We're talking about a couple of far-out dudes." Building on this history, *TBL* did its part in making *dude* a versatile, omnipresent word: I don't know who's a real man these days, but we're all dudes.

The parlance of our Seinfeldian, Davidian times

Lebowski characters who bicker about language slip further and further into the muck, like someone sinking into real muck who insists, "This is mire!"

They're a little bit like a stereotypical fifth-grade English teacher, appalled at dialects and text speak and slang (and other realities of our ever-evolving language), who repeat outdated superstitions like "Never end a sentence in a preposition!" or "Terms like OMG are new and ruining English!" (*OMG* actually dates from at least 1917, and English somehow manages to press on.)

When hostages are in play, when carpet-pissers strike, when you've lost a million dollars, sometimes the only things you can count on are that you're the Dude and not Mr. Lebowski, and that your enemies are "fucking amateurs!" But these word struggles reflect deeper struggles and resonate with some of the other best comedies of this era.

Though the Dude and Walter may seem a long way from the soup Nazis and social assassins who populated *Seinfeld* and still appear on *Curb Your Enthusiasm*, the Lebowski-verse is Seinfeldian and Davidian in ways that go beyond language. The characters have a little bit of what I call Larry David Syndrome (LDS): a mostly male affliction with the primary symptom of always paying attention to the wrong thing.

For example, in the *Seinfeld* episode "The Bris," the Larry David–inspired George Costanza shows classic evidence of LDS, as he raves about a parking spot while totally ignoring a newborn child. On *Curb Your Enthusiasm,* many other cases of the disease have been presented, such as when, in "Club Soda and Salt," Larry abandons sex mid-hootchie-kootchie just to show off a way of getting stains out of a carpet. In yet another case of stains distracting Larry from sex (and thus preventing other, more romantic, stains) Larry screws up his long-hoped-for reunion with his wife (in the *Curb* episode "Seinfeld") just to crack the case of who left a stain on Julie Louis-Dreyfus' table.

This peculiar attention can be seen all over *TBL,* like when the Dude is faced with a naked Maude and can only stammer "That's my robe," or when she is talking about vaginas and the Dude says, "I was talking about my rug." Likewise, Walter's obsessions with Vietnam, Judaism, and the minutest rules of bowling ("Over the line!") misguide him into constant trouble. Even when trying to sympathize with the castration-fearing Dude, he screws it up with a bizarre comment about the legality of amphibious rodents. A total LDS moment.

The dudes and dudettes of *TBL* are not just paddling behind a linguistic boat they've missed by a mile. Like so many of us, their tiny brains are obsessed with the inappropriate, the inane, and the insane. Am I a bum or a man? Is this a league game? Does this dog have papers? Like David and Seinfeld, *TBL* makes compelling, hilarious hay out of the limitations that make our tragic lives comic, and vice versa.

Mark Peters is a lexicographer and language columnist for GOOD *magazine and other publications. He runs the blog* Wordlustitude.

In the Parlance of *Lebowski*

"D'ya Have to Use S'many Cuss Words?"

∨

Language repetition is utilized several different ways in *The Big Lebowski*. Some characters, particularly Walter, repeat words, phrases, and sayings over and over. Sometimes a character repeats someone else's words—even if they weren't in the same room to hear it in the first place. The Dude will frequently hear a word or phrase and regurgitate it later, usually in a different context and certainly in his own manner, even if under ridiculous circumstances. For example, after the nihilists threaten to "cut his dick off," the Dude parrots the strong-arm tactic to Little Larry Sellers—a promise he in no way would ever make good on. In this way, the Dude functions as a verbal sponge.

As far as excessively repeated words go, sources vary on how many times "fuck" and its variations are used in the film, but the 2011 limited edition Blu-ray stipulates that the F-word is uttered 285 times. Interestingly, the Family Media Guide points out that the word is only used as a character slur on six of those occasions. Dudeism.com and the Internet Movie Database (imdb.com) count the total number of "man"s to be 147 and the number of "Dude"s at 161, distinguishing that "Dude" is spoken 160 times and seen once, in the title sequence of the *Gutterballs* film dream. On YouTube, enthusiasts (whether it be of the movie or the word) have compiled videos that string together all of the word's variations in a gloriously profane montage of "fuck," "fucks," "fucked," "fucking," "fuckin'," and one "camelfucker." However the word is used, whether as noun, verb, or adjective, it is said at a rate of about 2.4 times for every movie minute of *The Big Lebowski*. Fuck, that's a lot.

CHART #1: Repetition

Who says what, how often? A sampling of repetition in *Lebowski*

WORD/PHRASE	WHO SAYS IT	TO WHOM	WHERE
This will not stand. This will not stand, this aggression against Kuwait.	George Bush	The American people	Ralphs (on TV)
We're talking about unchecked aggression here, Dude.	Walter	Dude	Bowling alley
This will not stand, ya know, this aggression will not stand, man.	Dude	Big Lebowski	The Lebowski mansion
Where's the money, Lebowski? We want that money, Lebowski. Bunny says you're good for it. Where's the money, Lebowski? Where's the money, Lebowski? Where's the fucking money, shithead?!	Blond Treehorn thug	Dude	The Dude's house
Vee vant the money, Lebowski.	Uli Kunkel (nihilist)	Dude	The Dude's house
Where's the fucking money, you little brat?	Dude	Little Larry	Little Larry Sellers' house
Where's the fucking money, Lebowski?	Dude	Big Lebowski	The Lebowski mansion
Vee vant ze money, Lebowski! . . . We still want the money, Lebowski. . . .	Uli Kunkel (nihilist)	Dude, Walter, and Donny	Parking lot of the bowling alley
See? See what happens, Lebowski? You see what happens?	Blond Treehorn thug	Dude	The Dude's house
Son, this is what happens when you FUCK A STRANGER IN THE ASS! . . . Here you go, Larry. You see what happens? YOU SEE WHAT HAPPENS, LARRY?! YOU SEE WHAT HAPPENS?! THIS IS WHAT HAPPENS WHEN YOU FUCK A STRANGER IN THE ASS, LARRY! THIS IS WHAT HAPPENS, LARRY! DO YOU SEE WHAT HAPPENS, LARRY? DO YOU SEE WHAT HAPPENS WHEN YOU FUCK A STRANGER IN THE ASS? THIS IS WHAT HAPPENS. YOU SEE WHAT HAPPENS, LARRY? DO YOU SEE WHAT HAPPENS, LARRY? DO YOU SEE WHAT HAPPENS LARRY WHEN YOU FUCK A STRANGER IN THE ASS?! THIS IS WHAT HAPPENS, LARRY. THIS IS WHAT HAPPENS, LARRY. WHAT HAPPENS, LARRY! THIS IS WHAT HAPPENS WHEN YOU FUCK A STRANGER. . . .	Walter	Little Larry	Little Larry Sellers' house

WORD/PHRASE	WHO SAYS IT	TO WHOM	WHERE
So that there's no reason, there's no *fucking* reason, why his wife should go out and owe money all over town and then they come and they pee on *your* fucking rug.	Walter	Dude	Bowling alley
His wife goes out and owes money all over town and they pee on *my* rug?	Dude	Walter	Bowling alley
She owes money all over town, including to known pornographers.	Dude	Big Lebowski / Brandt	The Big Lebowski's limo
She owes money all over town.	Dude	Walter	Bowling alley
Just as every bum's lot in life is his own responsibility regardless of who he chooses to blame.	Big Lebowski	Dude	The Lebowski mansion
Your revolution is over, Mr. Lebowski. Condolences—the bums lost! . . . The bums will always lose—do you hear me, Lebowski? The bums (muffled) will always lose.	Big Lebowski	Dude	The Lebowski mansion
Bums!	Big Lebowski	Dude	The Lebowski mansion
Start talking and talk fast, you lousy bum. . . . Where's my goddamn money, you bum?	Big Lebowski	Dude	The Big Lebowski's limo
I have no choice but to tell these bums to do whatever it takes to recover their money from you, Jeffrey Lebowski.	Big Lebowski	Dude	The Big Lebowski's limo
Out of this house now, you bums!	Big Lebowski	Dude and Walter	The Lebowski mansion
Smokey, my friend, you're entering a world of pain. You mark that frame an eight, you're entering a world of pain. A world of pain.	Walter	Smokey	Bowling alley
You're entering a world of pain, son.	Walter	Little Larry	Little Larry Sellers' house
Her life is in your hands. Mr. Lebowski asked me to repeat that: Her life is in your hands. Her life is in your hands, Dude.	Brandt	Dude	The Lebowski mansion
Her life was in our hands, man!	Dude	Walter	Walter's car
Her life was in your hands!	Big Lebowski	Dude	The Big Lebowski's limo

WORD/PHRASE	WHO SAYS IT	TO WHOM	WHERE
Shut the fuck up, Donny.	Walter	Donny	Bowling alley
Shut the fuck up, Donny!	Walter	Donny	Bowling alley
Shut the fuck up.	Nihilist	Dude	Walter's car, via the telephone
Donny, shut the f— when do we play?	Walter	Donny	Bowling alley
Shut the fuck up, Donny. . . . Shut the fuck up, Donny.	Walter	Donny	Fountain Street Theater (Marty the Landlord's "cycle")
Shut the fuck up, Donny.	Walter	Donny	Bowling alley
They're a buncha fucking amateurs. . . . But they're amateurs.	Walter	Dude	His car
They're a buncha fuckin' amateurs.	Walter	Dude	Bowling alley
Fuckin' amateurs!	Walter	Dude	Coffee shop
Now that we're competing with those amateurs.	Jackie Treehorn	Dude	His beach house
No Funny STuFF.	Nihilists	Big Lebowski	Ransom note
But only if there is no funny stuff. . . . So no funny stuff. Okay?	Nihilists	Dude	Walter's car, via the telephone
You think veer kidding und making mit de funny stuff?	Kieffer (nihilist)	Dude	The Dude's house
No funny stuff, Jackie, the kid's got it.	Dude	Jackie Treehorn	Jackie Treehorn's beach house
No funny stuff…no funny stuff.	Nihilists	Dude, Walter, and Donny	Parking lot of the bowling alley
Ahh fuck it, Dude. Let's go bowling.	Walter	Dude	Road in the Simi Valley
C'mon, Dude. Fuck it, man. Let's go bowling.	Walter	Dude	On a cliff along the Malibu coastline

WORD/PHRASE	WHO SAYS IT	TO WHOM	WHERE
To use the parlance of our times.	Maude Lebowski	Dude	Maude's loft
In the parlance of our times, you know.	Dude	Big Lebowski / Brandt	The Big Lebowski's limo
He's a good man, and thorough. . . . He's a good man, and thorough.	Maude Lebowski	Dude	Maude's loft
By god, sir. I will not abide another toe.	Big Lebowski	Dude	The Big Lebowski's limo
Yeah, well, the Dude abides.	Dude	Dude	Bowling alley bar
The Dude abides. . . .	The Stranger	Audience	Bowling alley bar
Lotta ins. Lotta outs. Lotta what-have-yous. And a lot of strands to keep in my head, man. A lotta strands in old Duder's head.	Dude	Maude	Maude's loft
Lotta ins. Lotta outs.	Dude	Maude	The Dude's house
Is this your homework, Larry? Is this your homework, Larry? Is this your homework, Larry? . . . Is this yours, Larry? Is this your homework, Larry? . . . Is this your homework, Larry?	Walter	Little Larry	Little Larry Sellers' house
Jackie Treehorn wants to see the deadbeat Lebowski.	Woo (Treehorn thug)	Dude	The Dude's house
Stay out of Malibu, deadbeat!	Malibu Police Chief	Dude	Police Chief's office
You figured, oh, here's a loser, you know, a deadbeat. . . .	Dude	Big Lebowski	The Big Lebowski's mansion

Chart #2: Variations on Repetitions

Another method of spoken repetition in *The Big Lebowski* dialogue is when various and sundry terms are used for the same concept. This practice is often employed by Maude Lebowski, whose staccato, verbal acrobatics match her dramatic painting style.

GOING TO THE BATHROOM

Piss	Urinate	Pee/Peed	Micturated	Use the John	Soiled	Used It as a Toilet
Dude	Big Lebowski	Dude	Big Lebowski	Dude	Brandt	Auto Circus cop

MALE GENITALIA

Cock	A Pair of Testicles	Dick	Rod	Johnson	Chonson (Johnson)	Viggly Penis
Bunny	Dude	Maude, Dude, Walter	Maude	Maude, Dude	Uli (nihilist)	Uli

SEX

Suck Your Cock	Sex	The Physical Act of Love	Coitus	Natural, Zesty Enterprise	Banging	Love Me	Helping Her Conceive
Bunny	Maude	Maude*	Maude, Dude	Maude	Maude	Maude	Dude

X-RATED

Pornography	Beaver Picture	Smut Business	Adult Entertainment
Maude	Maude	Dude	Jackie Treehorn

LOOSE WOMAN

Bitch	Strumpet	Whore	Slut	Nymphomaniac/nympho	Compulsive Fornicator
Walter	Walter	Walter	Walter, Maude	Maude, Dude	Maude

FEMALE ROMANTIC PARTNER

Special Lady	Fucking Lady Friend
Da Fino	Dude

*a phrase also verbalized by Base Commander Jack D. Ripper (Sterling Hayden) in *Dr. Strangelove or: How I Learned to Stop Worrying and Love the Bomb*

The Big Lebowski as Musical

With the Broadway stage musical as its precursor, the musical film is an American genre that incorporates song and dance, to varying degrees depending on interpretation. Musicals are historically considered to emphasize full-scale song-and-dance routines in a significant way, either as part of the narrative or as the opposite: an unnatural interruption (like the "Kafka break" described below) in the plot line. With the advent of sound in films, Hollywood endeavored to create a new and revolutionary musical world. The development of the musical parallels that of sound film—a story depicted in such films as *Singin' in the Rain* (1952), which looks back at the rocky transition to the "talkies," and *The Artist* (2011), with John Goodman. These escapes from reality flourished during the Great Depression, and the chief pioneers were Busby Berkeley and song-and-dance man Fred Astaire. The movie musicals tide has mostly ebbed, but every decade it is revived to some degree through both traditional and innovative offerings at the box office.

The Big Lebowski incorporates music throughout the film, but it is in the second dream sequence, *Gutterballs*, that *Lebowski* completely inhabits the musical genre, in a way that can only be described as "Dude-like."

What Happens When Kafka, Busby Berkeley, and Kenny Rogers Meet in a Bowling Alley

The Coens profess to require a surrealist interlude at a certain point in all of their scripts—a so-called "Kafka break." Fitting the bill for *The Big Lebowski* is the Dude's second dream sequence, spurred on by a Mickey courtesy of pornographer Jackie Treehorn. The dream is framed as a porno film-within-the-film, with the title *Gutterballs* made all the more titillating by a Hollywood-style title sequence composed of a suggestively moving bowling apparatus: a phallic pin gliding between two gleaming bowling balls. The titles are accompanied by (or rather, in accordance with typical Coen style, juxtaposed against) the 1968 song "Just Dropped In (To See What Condition My Condition Was

"Trying to imagine what a pothead who was slipped a Mickey Finn would dream about, what form it would take, that gave us freedom to do just about anything we wanted."

—The Coens, in *The Irish Times*

Kenny Rogers.
© Pictorial Press Ltd / Alamy

One issue with the location of the Big Lebowski's mansion (Greystone Mansion in Beverly Hills) was that Joel Coen hated the black-and-white tile floor—he thought it looked like a giant men's restroom.

In)" by The First Edition with Kenny Rogers, a song, incidentally, written to warn against the dangers of LSD.

The surrealism of the dream intersects the "real" of the plot through an elaborate set and costumes that incorporate elements of the locations the Dude has encountered in his wanderings: the black-and-white floor mirrors the tiles in the Big Lebowski's mansion; his workman overalls and tool belt are reminiscent of Karl Hungus' in the genuine "beaver" film *Logjammin'*; Maude's Norse goddess costume (complete with bowling-ball breastplate) is evocative of the ambient opera music at the mansion; Maude's trident recalls a Romanesque, trident-wielding female statue at the mansion, visible in the scene in which Brandt hands off the kidnapping instructions; and the giant scissors brandished by the menacing nihilists are featured in artwork in Maude's loft. The

FRAME OF REFERENCE

Coen Kafkaesque

"Kafkaesque: Of, relating to, or suggestive of Franz Kafka or his writings; *especially:* having a nightmarishly complex, bizarre, or illogical quality."—*Merriam-Webster Dictionary*

The writer Franz Kafka (1883–1924), best known for this German-language novels *The Metamorphosis* (1915) and *The Trial* (1925), was so influential in his intricate stories of isolation and hopelessness that he has an adjective named after him. Likewise, the term "Coenesque" is often bandied about although never officially defined, unless you count Robertson's "Six Coen Motifs" (see page 24). In a piece on *True Grit*, the Minneapolis *Star Tribune* discussed the film's "Coenesque moments of irony, disconcerting violence and grotesquerie."

"[The Coens] had already picked the music for that particular scene—'Just Dropped In'—and as in all of their pictures, the music is selected to tell a part of a story, and the lyrics in that clip that we used in that section tell that story, you know? And that's the way music is supposed to be used in pictures and quite often it isn't."

—Brian McCarty, music playback operator

giant scissors have extra dreamlike implications—for instance, in Alfred Hitchcock's *Spellbound*, the Gregory Peck character has a highly symbolic dream with giant scissors, designed for the film by surrealist artist Salvador Dalí. Further upping the surreal ante in the Dude's dream is an appearance by Saddam Hussein—previously referred to both on the supermarket television and in one of Walter's tirades—as a bowling-shoe purveyor overseeing a towering stack of bowling shoes (recalling the great upward pan of sheets in the classic 1948 film *The Bicycle Thief*, or even the skyscraper shots in the Coens' *The Hudsucker Proxy*).

The Great Show-Stopping Numbers of Busby Berkeley

"I wanted to make people happy, if only for an hour."—Busby Berkeley

Iconic Hollywood director-choreographer Busby Berkeley, who worked for most of the major studios over a career that spanned nearly three decades, from 1930 to 1954, was known for his opulent, meticulously choreographed scenes of indistinguishable chorus girls in spectacular dance numbers. The innovator of the musical comedy, whose precision was inspired by a stint in the army, his signatures were a kaleidoscopic crane (overhead) shot of dancers in a pattern and a through-the-legs tracking shot, the latter always at medium distance.

Berkeley's numbers have been imitated in countless films, perhaps most surreally in Mel Brooks' *The Producers* (1968, remade in 2005), in which dancers in Nazi uniform sing and dance in the showcase *Springtime for Hitler*. The dance number in

The "Lady with the Tutti Frutti Hat" scene in *The Gang's All Here*, starring Carmen Miranda, 1943. © *Pictorial Press Ltd / Alamy*

The Big Lebowski recalls most directly Berkeley's "Young and Healthy" number in *42nd Street* (1933; listed by the American Film Institute as the thirteenth best musical of all time), complete with the same style of dancers' shoes and a comparable tracking shot through the chorines' legs. Berkeley also directed a Carmen Miranda picture, 1943's *The Gang's All Here*. The Coens have mentioned Miranda as an inspiration for the scene, and the *Lebowski* dancers' bowling-pin headdresses appear to directly reference her oversized banana hats.

As in *The Big Lebowski* dream sequence, Berkeley's numbers always happened as a "break" in the narrative flow. Berkeley's were less of a "Kafka break," certainly, and often incorporated a piece of the set for transition, like a prop bench that sinks into the floor and becomes the dance platform, while *Lebowski* uses cinematic effects to move from the Dude's (semi)consciousness to his dream state. And whereas Berkeley's impromptu dance numbers often reference the architecture of a cityscape such as New York, the dance number in *Lebowski* incorporates its own kind of architecture through the set, props, and costumes: the architecture of the bowling alley.

42nd Street movie poster, 1933. © *AF archive / Alamy*

Thrown into this cacophonic mix is the Dude, long hair waving, gyrating in a Busby Berkeley–style dance number with a troupe of chorines in Brunswick-tinted, red-and-brown 1930s-style costumes and bowling-pin headdresses. In other words: a great Coen brothers' spectacle.

The Big Dance Number

When husband-and-wife choreographer team Bill and Jacqui Landrum were approached with the mandate to recruit thirty-six dancers for *Lebowski*'s "Busby Berkeley" number, with the caveat that the budget would only allow for two days of rehearsal, it seemed a

Carmen Miranda, a direct precursor to the *Gutterballs* girl.
© *AF Archive / Alamy*

"For a dancer, especially in a group, you know you're not really going to be recognized, so to speak, especially if you're all going to be wearing the same exact thing. It really speaks to the character of the other actors and the choreographers if, as a dancer, you feel a part of something, as opposed to just being arbitrary 'props.' From the audition all the way through the end, we were treated well—we weren't just props."

—Kiva Dawson, dancer

tall order. Berkeley, the renowned Hollywood director and choreographer, had a whole studio at his disposal and would rehearse his large-scale synchronized dance numbers for months before they were actually filmed. The Landrums were also instructed that the dancers needed to be as tall as possible—ideally, no less than 5'10"—in order for Jeff Bridges to easily glide through their legs. Bill Landrum recalls panicking, "Oh my god . . . thirty-six dancers over 5'10" who are brilliant and pick up moves in a minute?" But they met their goal with a crop of classically trained dancers, several of whom the Landrums had worked with in the past—enabling any rookies to feed off the veterans' energy. The choreographers' audition tactic was to find dancers who could adroitly pick up and memorize moves. As the scene didn't really require extraordinary dance steps, the most important criterion was the ability to learn the choreography *quickly*.

"The harder part," Bill recalls, "was making sure that thirty-six girls were in unison."

Producing the big dance number also required that the choreographers work closely with the wardrobe department in the design of the elaborate Carmen Miranda–style headgear that substituted bowling pins for Miranda's bananas. Wardrobe created samples made out of Styrofoam based on the Coens' vision, and Jacqui Landrum tested them out with dance moves. Several of the initial passes were so heavy that she knew the dancers wouldn't last half an hour with them on set. The design needed to be tweaked to get the pieces lighter and lighter and ensure that no necks would be

Behind the scenes of the dream sequence.
Courtesy Kiva Dawson (in the middle, kneeling), www.kivadawson.com

broken in the making of the scene. Bill estimates at least five or six were tested before a
final version was deemed manageable, and even
that version was a challenge for the dancers.

The shooting days, in the Barker Airport
Hanger in Santa Monica, were long, and the
dancers constantly had to lie down to rest
their necks. Jamie Green, one of the dancers
in the scene, recalls, "I'm guessing that who-
ever designed those bowling pin headdresses
had never worked in Vegas before because
they were outrageously heavy and difficult to
maneuver with. All the dancers had head- and

The Dude's eyes brighten. *Courtesy of Evanimal (Evan Yarbrough).*
www.evanimal.com

neck-aches. The only way that we could find
relief was to lay flat on the floor where the
floor would hold the weight of the headdress,
so there are lots of photos of us splayed out on
the floor in between shooting, looking pretty
much dead." With heads full of pincurls in
order to keep the headdresses on, their skulls
were squeezed and hair pulled all day long.
Another dancer, Kiva Dawson, notes the strat-
egies employed to survive the day: "At a certain point the headdresses were squeezing on
our brains, and the big joke was that we didn't
fit into the bathroom stalls—we would have to
walk sideways into most doorways and then
trying to use the restroom was really interesting." Bill Landrum recalls, though, that the
women were so excited about the project and
working with the Coen brothers that rather
than the usual amount of grumbling and com-
plaints, they all just gritted their teeth, saying,
"Whatever it takes, let's just do it."

Bridges picked up on the dancers' energy
right away, and immediately delved into the
music and the scene. The choreographers
threw a lot of period vocabulary at him so he
could prepare for his dance steps—the journey
coming down the stairs, for instance, had to be
safe but look "alive." They asked him for hip
movements and "fun" arm moves. After trying
a variety of things, Bridges worked indepen-
dently on the selected moves, and Bill Landrum remembers that it only took two takes
to complete his dancing scene to the Coens'
satisfaction. Julianne Moore, on the other
hand, had trouble with the stiffly layered costume, which was compounded by the fact that
she was pregnant at the time. According to
the choreographer, she self-consciously shied
away from any extraneous movement, limit-
ing her presence in the scene.

For the Dude's movement over the bowling lane in the scene, Bridges lay on a "rotisserie" apparatus created by the special effects team. He needed to be cantilevered his full body length forward so they made a full body cast of him, then created a fiberglass clamshell harness that he was strapped into and that had two steel beams coming out of it and going back to a rotary axel. That axel was on top of a pushcart they could push forward on the bowling alley set. As he moved forward, the crew could actually roll him over upside down and then back again, kind of like he was on a barbeque! There was a tricky choreography to the rotisserie, because as the rig rolled down the dancers actually had to step out of the way or they would have gotten clobbered by the wagon.

A perhaps unanticipated issue in the production of the scene was that all the work the Landrums did to recruit tall dancers couldn't solve for the broadness of Jeff Bridges' shoulders—Bridges just didn't fit neatly through the dancers' legs. The side-angle shot of him floating over the bowling lane between the chorines' legs was therefore constructed in two separate takes. First, a shot was filmed that tracked alongside the women's legs; and second, one of Bridges floating over the lane was captured (executed by mounting the camera on a skateboard-style apparatus that was controlled with a joystick). To create the side-angle view of the sequence, the two shots were composited in a computer, with Bridges slightly shrunk to look as if his body could maneuver cleanly through the row of legs. The other part of this sequence—the overhead shot of the Dude going through the dancers' legs (on a dolly, or a set of wheels on a platform)—was filmed with Bridges actually going

"So when you see [Bridges'] eyes really brighten, it was really real!"
—Kiva Dawson, dancer

through their legs for the take. Which brings us to the now-infamous practical joke.

Are We Gonna Split Hairs Here?

Perhaps if *The Big Lebowski* were made today, the overhead shot of the Dude floating through the legs might have been accomplished through computer-generated effects. Instead, the dancers and Jeff Bridges were all physically present. In advance, the women approached the makeup and hair department with the idea to stuff wigs in their leotards, creating the appearance of an unruly mass of pubic hair that would surprise Jeff Bridges when he looked up their skirts—unbeknownst to anyone else, including the Coens and the choreographers. In fact, on that particular day of shooting Bridges had invited his wife and daughters onto the set to watch, which made the dancers a little cautious about pulling the trigger on the idea. But, as dancer Wendy Braun recalls, the joke was intended to "ease the tension" of the long, difficult shoot. Both Kiva Dawson and Bill Landrum credit Jacqui Landrum's spirit on set with persuading the dancers to go ahead with the joke. As Bill says, "My wife . . . herself was fun and daring and courageous and fearless and she had that kind of rapport with all the girls."

Dancer Jamie Green lays out the story of the joke as such: "The dancers were straddling the bowling lane (not an easy task, by the way, in character shoes). Jeff was to lay on a gurney and roll underneath our alley of legs, being filmed from the top with a blissful smile on his face. One or two of the dancers—hilarious,

> "Who knows what [Jeff Bridges] was thinking at that moment, not knowing the rest of us were in on it. I think he was trying to make sense of what he saw, perhaps thinking, 'Maybe she's European?' But then he was sent through my legs and on down the line, and he just laughed uncontrollably the whole way. Now everyone on the set *still* has no idea what he's laughing at, but instead of making them guess, we all did a unison skirt flash, and half the crew was on their knees, laughing hysterically.... It was a great moment, and one I'll never forget."
>
> —Wendy Braun, dancer

mischievous women that they were—got the idea that we should all wear outrageous, over-the-top pubic hair coming out of our panties underneath our skirts, so they approached the hair/wardrobe department who obliged us with black curly wigs, which we tore apart and shoved in our panties, hanging out the sides like a jungle. So, there is Jeff, laying underneath the first girl in the line-up and he starts smiling, thinking to himself, 'Somebody's not taking care of business.' As he rolls past the first few girls and sees that we all weren't 'taking care of business,' he is now laughing out loud, and the ladies are trying to stifle our laughter, which also makes it difficult for us to balance in heels with a wide straddle. One of the Coens cuts the take. No one knows what's going on except the dancers and Jeff. So the dancers flash the choreographers and they fall on the floor laughing. But the crew and the Coens still don't know what's going on. So we all turn to them and flash them. The crew laughed, but Joel and Ethan were *not* amused. One of them said something to the effect of 'million-dollar-a-day set, people, let's get going.' So, our practical joke was a hit with everyone but Joel and Ethan. Later that year at an L.A. Dance Awards ceremony, we won the award for best practical joke on a movie set. It was quite an honor."

The joke, ill-timed to the production schedule though it may have been, apparently didn't create much discord on set. According to Bridges, the one and only bout of dissent between the Coens that he witnessed on the set of *The Big Lebowski* occurred at the end of the chorine sequence. Prior to filming the scene, Joel instructed Bridges to scowl in pain upon headbutting the pins, to which Ethan objected, imagining the Dude should be on the whole happy about the collision. This gentle disagreement was solved by shooting it both ways. Although the Dude does exhibit a look of surprise in the finished film, his head doesn't seem to actually make contact with the pins. And whether or not he's smiling or grimacing is up for interpretation.

Bill Landrum sums up what it's like to have dancers on set: "There was all this friendliness that permeated all over the soundstage between the crew and Joel and Ethan and Jeff, who [like the Coens] was a dream to work with. And everybody was friends, and the dancers were mixing . . . to the point that after we finished shooting, there were no dancers on set and it was like a morgue, and Joel and Jeff came around and said, 'Oh my god, I can't stand the feel of the set today, we miss the dancers.' So Joel and Ethan turned to the casting lady and said 'Call eight dancers in immediately.' 'We don't need them.' 'Yes we do!' They literally brought eight or ten dancers back just to be on set and hang around and it changed the atmosphere immediately. Which we always found to be true on any film that we've done in which there are musical numbers. It's like it just makes a whole other life to a set because a studio can be so myopic in terms of just focusing in on the day's work, but with dancers there's always energy and conversation and life. . . . [The energy is] contagious when you have dancers on the set. It's great."

STRIKES & GUTTERS

Jeff Bridges still keeps several of the chorine bowling-pin hats in commemoration of the shoot.

The dancers on set. The gurney on which Bridges would ride—and make an unexpected discovery—is in front of the first dancer.
Courtesy of Wendy Braun (second from the front)

Lebowski's Music Condition

By Todd Martens

It all starts with a song. When *The Big Lebowski* opens with the Sons of the Pioneers' "Tumbling Tumbleweeds," it immediately throws off any sense of time and place, a genre-distorting move used regularly by the Coen brothers. The casually paced mid-1930s tune, all Western strings and vocal harmonies, is rescued from an era of black-and-white gunslingers, and used here as a camera follows the uprooted plant into Los Angeles of the 1990s.

The drifting-through-life tumbleweed and lazy-day melody of the Sons of the Pioneers song most obviously reflects the tone of the film's country narrator, the Stranger. Yet it wouldn't be unfair also to draw a comparison between the song and the personality of the Dude. The camera follows the tumbleweed as it rolls over highways and down the center of urban streets, seemingly surviving its way to the beach almost by accident. It's arguably the only scene in the film in which song and image combine for such an easy metaphor.

It doesn't last long. The music shuts up and gets out of the way when the Dude ambles home and gets his face shoved in a toilet. The songs that follow continue to hit the audience with like-minded unexpectedness. The Dude loves some classic rock, but keep him away from the Eagles, and it's a late 1960s, Kenny Rogers–sung psychedelic rock song that scores a trippy dream sequence choreographed with ol'-fashioned movie-musical pizzazz.

When it comes to its soundtrack, *Lebowski* is a rock 'n' roll movie, but one in which the songs don't echo or telegraph characters' thoughts. Instead, they slyly and subtly champion its working-class slacker hero. It isn't the expected stoner or jam bands that mark the Dude's soundtrack, but rather the gritty rhythm & blues rock of Creedence Clearwater Revival. (As for those who seek to manipulate or control his life, they get served with far more musical pretension.)

Some have labeled *The Big Lebowski* a modern Western. Others have called attention to its noir tendencies. Don't look to the music for help in crafting a definition, here or in other Coen brothers films. When the Coens finally did make an indisputable Western in 2010's *True Grit,* it was religious hymns rather than grand orchestral arrangements that scored the genre piece. When they made a crime comedy in 1987's *Raising Arizona*, yodeling took center stage.

Carter Burwell, the Coens' longtime composer, has noted that the filmmakers take pleasure in toying with not only audience expectations but his own. Said Burwell, "*Blood Simple* was an electronic-plus-solo-piano, a dark thriller of a score. Then *Raising Arizona* was all banjos and yodeling, and then *Miller's Crossing* was orchestral. They weren't hiring me because I knew anything about these genres. I didn't.

"I can't answer why they hire me," he continued, "but I know they don't want the same thing again and again. They want each film to be unlike the previous one, and I know they're not looking for any of the same music."

Before the city of Los Angeles used its powers of imminent domain to replace the Hollywood Star Lanes with an elementary school, visitors could drop by to bowl, hang out, and listen to the standard jukebox dive-bar selection. Were one to venture too far from the likes of AC/DC, it wasn't

Dude favorites CCR in 1968.
© Pictorial Press Ltd / Alamy

unexpected for the purchased song to be instantly skipped. That line is written not from research but from personal experience, as an attempt once to play the Chipmunks' "All I Want for Christmas (Is My Two Front Teeth)" during a holiday season was thwarted by the end of the first verse.

The Coens could have easily romanticized such a locale. They could have turned up the Aerosmith and captured the denizens of the Hollywood Star Lanes as some sort of a cliché, which is exactly how others in the film see the Dude. As the Dude himself eventually realizes, Jeffrey Lebowski views the Dude as having a meaningless life, as little more than a pawn to be moved around a board game.

Not so the Coens, who seem to consider his hapless meandering more respectable than the arrogance of the art-house phonies and money-obsessed upperclassmen who suddenly find themselves in the Dude's circle. The first shot of the Hollywood Star Lanes, during the film's opening credit sequences, is one of the most lovingly framed set pieces in the film. It's Bob Dylan's deep 1970 cut "The Man in Me" that introduces viewers to the world of bowling, and it's a song that idolizes the blue-collar work ethic. Sings Dylan, "The man in me will do nearly any task, as for compensation, there's a little he will ask."

The next major bowling alley scene is perhaps even more pivotal, coming just after the Dude leaves the mansion of Jeffrey Lebowski. The latter sought only to humiliate and belittle the Dude, but it was the Dude who won that initial battle, leaving the mansion with a stolen rug. Close listeners are rewarded with the choppy, fuzzed-up guitars of the Monks' "I Hate You," the title serving as a middle finger to Jeffrey Lebowski.

There's more, however, to the use of the Monks than just an excuse to showcase a kiss-off riff. The Monks were an act formed by a band of American soldiers who were stationed in Germany during Vietnam, the war Walter Sobchak is haunted by and obsessed with. Just as the band was founded as a consequence of (and perhaps in protest of) decisions made by more powerful men, so is Walter, seemingly a paradigm of uncontrolled rage, made practically docile by certain influencers in his life. It's easy to cringe when he pulls a gun on a fellow bowler, but the threat is immediately negated—moments earlier it was revealed that Walter has been watching his ex-wife's show dog. The Monks lived in obscurity, enjoyed a small but loyal following, and were forever marked by their service in the military. Likewise Walter, whose ineffectual instrument is a bowling ball rather than a guitar.

What of those who aren't on the Dude's side? The music surrounding them spans from the ridiculous to the ostentatious. There's Jesus, the bowling arch nemesis of the Dude and Walter, whose pomp and circumstance is highlighted by a fanciful Latin take on the Eagles' "Hotel California" by the Gipsy Kings, and then there's Maude Lebowski, who's living her life as if she's forever in art school. Her music collection is on vinyl, natch, and exists more as conversation pieces than for listening.

Porn king Jackie Treehorn, who appears at first to be on the Dude's side, is cool, calm, and chats up the Dude while the orchestral romance of Henry Mancini's "Lujon" plays in the background. Yet that, too, is a façade, as his interests in the Dude are purely selfish, and he leaves the Dude drugged and staggering down the Malibu streets. Similarly, the music that backs Jeffrey Lebowski comes with an air of sophistication that the character himself lacks. As the Dude is given important instructions regarding ransom, the sounds in Lebowski's mansion are that of Mozart's "Requiem in D Minor."

The music, however, that surrounds the Dude comes from little-known greats and outsiders. Even when the song used is that of a name act, it's a left-of-center pick. Few today remember Kenny Rogers for his precountry work, but it's his Southern drug anthem "Just Dropped In (To See What Condition My Condition Was In)" that scores a Dude dream sequence.

Even the choice of Creedence represents the more rebellious side of classic rock. Beyond the spooked rock of "Run through the Jungle," the band's leader John Fogerty was locked in a multidecade fight with the Man (not related to the Dude). Fogerty spent more than thirty years in a bitter, public bout with his record label, one that wasn't resolved until the mid-2000s.

Creedence symbolizes the polar opposite of the band the Dude openly hates, the Eagles. In the mid-1990s, the Eagles became the first mainstream rock band to sell tickets for more than $100. If Creedence had a dash of antiwar insurgency, the Eagles were all Baby Boomer contentment, a feeling encapsulated in the song "Peaceful Easy Feeling."

"I had a rough night, and I hate the fucking Eagles, man," the Dude tells the cab driver enjoying the song. The line gets him kicked out of the cab. But Eagles fans should forgive the Dude for reacting so harshly to "Peaceful Easy Feeling." It was, after all, the Dude's perceived lackadaisical hippie way of life that Jeffrey Lebowski attempted to exploit, and the lazy-day vibe of the Eagles' "Peaceful Easy Feeling," with its desert lovemaking and "sparking" earnings, is hippiedom as filtered by Boomer nostalgia. By this time in the film, it's been made clear that there's far more to the Dude than any peace-and-love cliché. So while a "Peaceful Easy Feeling" may come easy to the Eagles, the Coens understand that those words represent a goal the Dude actually has to fight to maintain.

When music isn't used

Thirty songs are listed in the end credits for *The Big Lebowski.* For some perspective, that's not quite the seventy-five songs that occupy a decidedly more pop-leaning film, 2009's roller-derby drama *Whip It,* but it's more than enough to indicate that music here has a starring role.

A more apt comparison would be the Coens' own 2000 offering *O Brother, Where Art Thou?* The rootsy soundtrack for the latter, for which the Coens also worked with composer/archivist T Bone Burnett, was the unexpected champ of the forty-fourth annual Grammy Awards, taking home five trophies, including Album of the Year. *The Big Lebowski* boasts eleven more songs than *O Brother*, and is arguably the Coens' most music-centric offering.

"They write and direct their films with spaces for music," said composer Carter Burwell. "When you see their films, you can clearly tell which scenes are going to be told by music. They think about telling a story visually and musically. As wonderful as their dialogue is, they enjoy going minutes without dialogue."

In the case of *The Big Lebowski*, the Coens also found ways to interject music when no song is being heard. Just as telling are the scenes in which music works its way into conversation or doesn't arrive when the audience most expects it. Three examples:

The sound of pins collapsing: Thirty minutes into the film and just as the Dude is getting dragged into a drama that will soon spin out of control, we spy him lying on the floor with his headphones on and his Walkman out.

Yet it's not his beloved Creedence Clearwater Revival we hear. No, what the Dude is relaxing to are the sounds of a bowling alley. It's confirmed that this is not a cinematic trick when the camera scans to a cassette case that reads, "Venice Beach League Playoffs 1987." It serves to further mystify the Dude and distort audience perceptions of hippiedom, but this is no mere character quirk. When so much that happens in the Dude's life and mind treads toward the surreal, perhaps it makes perfect sense that escapism for him would be into the sounds of the mundane.

Fun with the Autobahn: A momentary glance at the vinyl collection of uppity avant-artist Maude Lebowski offers a revealing look into her character. The Dude is looking at an album by Autobahn, a defunct German electronic act fronted by Uli Kunkel, the broke, nihilistic porn star friend of Bunny Lebowski. "They released

Kraftwerk, from Düsseldorf, Germany, described their sound as "robot pop."
© Pictorial Press Ltd / Alamy

one album in the late seventies," Maude says of the act. She then adds with the utmost derision, "Their music is sort of an—ugh—techno-pop." Yet LPs don't end up in Maude's carefully curated collection by accident, and her snootiness toward the genre reflects Maude's trendsetting superficiality. The LP for Autobahn—a reference to a song from digital-rock pioneers Kraftwerk—is surrounded by a random mix of oddities, some ironic and some tasteful. We see "Blue River" from lesser-known Greenwich Village folkie Eric Andersen, the Yiddish cabaret of the Barry Sisters, and the jazzy pop of *Whipped Cream & Other Delights* from Herb Albert & the Tijuana Brass Band. No critic or college radio station would complain, but it's a mini-collection that puts the emphasis on impressing others rather than personal passion.

From the SLF to being a roadie for Metallica: When Maude and the Dude have a brief get-to-know-you conversation after she arrives at his place for the sole purpose of getting impregnated, her stereotyping of him is almost—*almost*—turned on its head. She excitedly stirs when the Dude reveals that he briefly worked in the music industry. Yet when the Dude says "he was a roadie for Metallica," her detached mien quickly returns. The Dude doesn't notice, and goes on to say that he worked with the band during the Speed of Sound Tour. (Metallica fans will know that no such tour exists, although the year after the film was made metal-lifers Anvil released an album dubbed "Speed of Sound.") The scene illustrates the Dude's lack of concern for materialistic wealth or the need to define himself via a profession. The liberal artist Maude, however, is bored conversing about music. Her attraction lies solely in the cachet that a career in music represents.

Todd Martens is a music journalist for the Los Angeles Times.

The Dude claims to have worked as a roadie for the nonexistent "Speed of Sound" Metallica tour.
© Le Desk / Alamy

Baptism of Christ (After Carracci), by Joe Forkan. *Courtesy of the artist.*

The Big Lebowski as Western

From the very opening sequence of *The Big Lebowski*, the film conjures up a classic Western. The strains of the emblematic cowboy song "Tumbling Tumbleweeds" emanate under the dialect-twanged narration of "the Stranger," whom the Coens describe in the script as having a "Western-accented voice." The camera tracks along a sandy, scrubby, sagebrush-filled terrain, and the Stranger's gravelly voice describes the story as taking place "way out West." Not until a tumbleweed rolls to the top of a hill, where the bright Los Angeles nightscape suddenly comes into view below, does it become clear: this is not your typical Western.

"We wanted to introduce the story with that panoramic view, which goes hand in hand with the cowboy song, reminiscent of the pioneer spirit. The voice of the Stranger becomes a frame for the story."

—Joel Coen, in *Positif,* reprinted in *The Coen Brothers Interviews*

The subsequent sequence of said tumbleweed rolling past Los Angeles sights (a busy highway, a Benitos taco stand, the ocean) displays the Coens' characteristic affinity for incongruities. This tumbleweed, a symbol of Western pictures connoting barrenness and isolation, instead rolls through the populous urbanity that is L.A.

Beyond the film's opening, *The Big Lebowski* features other Western elements. When the Stranger finally does appear onscreen (accompanied by the strains of "Tumbling Tumbleweeds" on the bar jukebox), we see that he not only talks like a cowboy, he *is* a cowboy, complete with ten-gallon hat and other similar attire; a sweet horseshoe 'stache; some measure of honor, taking the Dude to task for the frequency of his cussing; and an inclination to swill sarsaparilla, a drink associated with the pioneer period (although whiskey might seem a more appropriate beverage of choice in the Wild West). When he uses the saying, "Sometimes you eat the bear [he pronounces it 'bar'] . . . and sometimes the bear, well, he eats you," the Dude asks, "That some kind of Eastern thing?" "Far from it," the Stranger replies, in a tongue-in-cheek play on words.

Walter also intersects referentially with Westerns. *Branded,* the television series primarily written by Little Larry's father, and of which Walter is such a fan, was an 1880s-set Western about a man who travels to the Old West to restore his good name after being accused of cowardice during the Civil War. Always packing heat, Walter himself has a rule-bound moral "code" (however skewed) he vociferously defends: one doesn't step over the line—especially during League play; demand a ransom without a kidnapping; infringe upon

The Stranger offers sage advice to the Dude while drinking his beverage of choice, sarsaparilla.
© A.F. Archive / Alamy. Courtesy of Universal Studios Licensing LLC

First Amendment rights; drive or roll on Shabbos; use racial slurs; or not have an ethos. And what's his, is his.

Jesus Quintana—whose slow-motion introduction, complete with background music written by the Dude's musical nemesis the Eagles, visually articulates his villainy (not unlike how Western director Sergio Leone shot his characters for emphasis)—has been described by Ethan as serving the role of "the Jack Palance character—the gunslinger, the slick guy." Palance was nominated for an

Academy Award for his performance as a hired gunfighter in the classic Western *Shane* (1953), although he is perhaps best known by contemporary audiences for his one-armed pushups when winning the award at age seventy-three (for the modern-day Western *City Slickers*).

But, as the Stranger says, this discussion is prematurely going "on down the trail," so back up, and westward the wagons for an "innerduction" of the genre.

Rolling the Weed

Executing the tumbleweed's rambling travels, a set piece that wasn't in the original shooting script, was a challenge for the crew. As mechanical effects designer Peter Chesney reports, to move the tumbleweed along pavement, two crew members used handheld compressed air movers to blow it down the street, with another running alongside. It was harder to roll the heavy, spiny tumbleweed on a surface as rough and uneven as the beach, so they threaded string through the tumbleweed and used tensioning devices on the string so it wouldn't snag in the spiny plant. To achieve the movement along the sand, two guys ran forward from fifty or a hundred feet away on either side of it. The bush acted like a pinwheel—because of the density of the tumbleweed, the string made it spin like a yo-yo.

The second hurdle to actualizing the Coens' vision of the tumbleweed sequence came in postproduction. The foley team consists of specialists in sound effects that are recorded after editing to fit the images and actions in a scene—often very detailed work. If the production crew doesn't have a sound effect that was properly made, that's where the foley work comes in. Marko Costanzo, foley artist for the film, describes this process in regards to the tumbleweed: "From the get-go, the most difficult [element] was the tumbleweed. I remember seeing the [unfinished] movie and Bruce [Pross, the foley mixer, as well as the voice of Duty Officer Rolvaag] looking at me and saying, 'You know, we've got to get a tumbleweed sound.' I remember for weeks trying to come up with an idea for a tumbleweed. So, I finally went to some kind of a metro florist exchange, and they had this 'twig ball' that we brought into the studio. I was able to roll it on different surfaces and make it sound like a tumbleweed. With the music, you barely hear it—but you *do* hear it. Like many of the sounds that we do, it's so subliminal, but it's there."

EuToch / www.shutterstock.com

Once upon a Time in the Western: A Brief History of the Horse Opera, Oater, or Cowboy Picture

A defining and enduring genre, Westerns are traditionally set in the western United States and take place as early as 1836 (the Battle of the Alamo), though a more typical era is between 1865 and the late 1890s—the time of the "Wild West." The category's air of bold exploration and discovery; its investigation of man versus, yet in union with, the land; the dramatic vistas of expansive and undeveloped landscapes; and the codes of justice, courage, and honor that inhabit its heroes and villains alike, distinguish the Western from any other genre. It embodies a mythic spirit of America in a way no other kind of movie does. Between 1910 and 1960, it was *the* dominant cinematic genre in this country.

> "The essential American soul is hard, isolate, stoic, and a killer. It has never yet melted."
> —D. H. Lawrence

The Western has been a fixture since the early days of the cinema—in fact, the film *The Great Train Robbery* (1903), widely considered the first Western (though shot in New Jersey), was also recognized for other firsts—its revolutionary editing featured crosscutting between scenes, creating the first movie ellipses

---

Musical Tumbleweeds

According to the Internet Movie Database, the earliest film to incorporate "tumbleweed" into its title was, fittingly, *Tumbleweeds* (1925), starring, directed, and produced by William S. Hart, the prolific moviemaker involved in one way or another on over seventy-five movies. In this, his last film, the term "tumbleweeds" refers to a kind of roaming or drifting cowboy. Soon after *Tumbleweeds* the concept seemingly took off on its own to becoming a symbol of the Old Wild West.

In 1934 one of the first Western musical groups, the Pioneer Trio, became the Sons of the Pioneers. The band went on to appear in one hundred films, with inaugural member "King of the Cowboys" Roy Rogers in forty-four of them. Their rendition of "Tumbling Tumbleweeds," which serves as the background music for the opening sequence of *The Big Lebowski* (and later on the jukebox at the bowling alley), was included on the soundtrack of no fewer than two dozen Westerns in less than a decade, from *The Old Wyoming Trail* (1937) to *Don't Fence Me In* (1945).

Tumbling Tumblweeds (1935) was the acting debut of the original "Singing Cowboy," Gene Autry. He warbles the song "Tumbling Tumbleweeds" over the opening credits of the film, and the track is reprised at the conclusion, although the song title does not appear in the credits.

Singing group the Sons of the Pioneers (with Roy Rogers, second from bottom) has been around, with various lineups, since 1933.
© Pictorial Press Ltd / Alamy

The Great Train Robbery, directed by Edwin S. Porter, a former cameraman for Edison Studios.
Getty Images

in time. The film both thrilled and frightened audiences in its "breaking of the third wall" when a gunslinger looked directly at the camera, pointed his pistol and, shockingly, fired, as if at the audience. (The opposite of this may well be *The Big Lebowski*'s inside-the-bowling-ball shot in the first dream sequence: the viewer serves as the "bullet," having the perspective of being "fired" at the pins.)

Westerns were hugely popular in the silent era, even when film was not pervasive but a mere curiosity existing solely in carnivalesque venues. Such names as D. W. Griffith, Buster Keaton, and John Ford (who became one of the greatest directors of Westerns) dabbled in the burgeoning movie style. With the advent of sound, however, the genre lost favor and gained a

pulp status. It was around this time that Marion Robert Morrison acted in his first picture, listed as "Duke" Morrison (Duke was the family dog's name). He was credited as John Wayne in his second film, whose failure at the box office meant ten years before another starring role, in the John Ford–helmed *Stagecoach* (1939). Ford had also taken a break from the Western, and *Stagecoach* was his first with sound. An epic set in Monument Valley—the future setting of hundreds of Westerns and neo-Westerns—this complex, intelligent film catapulted the two Johns and the Western to stardom. At one point in our history, John Wayne was the most recognized actor in the world. John Ford went on to make many Westerns, including what some consider to be the best: *The Searchers* (1956).

The Western is marked by strong and recognizable archetypes, and the hero figures of Westerns are typically gunfighters with a code; they are men who act. Running through Westerns is a "versus" vein: cowboys versus Indians; law and order versus brutality and savagery; community versus outlaws; values versus greed. But the Western is a much more fluid and flexible genre than it seems on the surface, and through the years after *The Virginian* (1902), with its classic powerful-yet-gentlemanly hero, these standards are often flipped—the "heroes," increasingly morally ambiguous, were often the brutal characters. The "versus" conceit was often embodied *within* the protagonist in contradictory ways. These men, although still with their own codes, were both insiders and outsiders, admired and feared, helpful yet dangerous, loners who existed outside of society but were needed by it. They had the power to act, but their actions weren't always enough to save the community. Such contradictions gibe with the historical reality that on the American frontier, the lines between lawman and outlaw were not always clearly drawn.

The Searchers.
© Moviestore collection Ltd / Alamy

Consider some key movies that exemplify this complexity:

> In *Stagecoach* (1939), which had the movie poster tagline "Men and Women on the Last Frontier of Wickedness," the John Wayne "hero" character is both an outsider and outlaw. He helps a party of strangers out of his sense of justice and is rewarded by ultimately escaping jail.

> *Shane* (directed by George Stevens, 1953) features a gunman (played by Alan Ladd) who saves a homesteading family from powerful robber barons who, through violent means, would bring corporate interests into the town.

> *The Searchers* (1956) has John Wayne, a hardened Civil War veteran, spend years looking for his abducted niece. Set during the Texas-Indian wars, *The Searchers* is a complex characterization of a protagonist who is a fugitive, racist, and Confederate—but, again, a man in power who acts. Wayne's character tries to shoot his niece (Natalie Wood) rather than see her become a Comanche—exhibiting a twisted moral code, to be sure.

> Director Sam Peckinpah assembled an inspired cast of Western stars past their prime in *The Wild Bunch* (1969), an extremely violent story of a ragtag group

Clint Eastwood in *The Good, the Bad, and the Ugly*. Like *Lebowski*, Sergio Leone's film got mixed reviews upon its release, only to become a classic in later years.
© Moviestore collection Ltd / Alamy

of outlaws trying to get out of the game with one last score, as the time of the gunslinger is coming to a close. Peckinpah confronts the clash between values and ideals through characters who endeavor to have a code of honor, but must compromise to exist in our nihilistic world.

- Sergio Leone's "The Man with No Name" Trilogy—*A Fistful of Dollars* (1964); *For a Few Dollars More* (1965); and *The Good, the Bad, and the Ugly* (1966)—followed on the heels of the greatest era of Westerns (the 1950s). Leone's "Spaghetti Westerns" (usually shot in Spain by an Italian production team) made Clint Eastwood a star. His character, one who is awash in moral ambiguity, administers his own violent brand of justice.

Revisionist Westerns had their heyday in the 1960s and 1970s, often illustrating the country's more sympathetic view toward Native American culture, with some very excellent offerings (Robert Altman's *McCabe & Mrs. Miller*, 1971) and some not so great (Michael Cimino's *Heaven's Gate*, 1980). The 1980s marked the low point in output of the genre. Despite the death knell being tolled on more than one occasion for Westerns, however, filmmakers keep bringing it back and audiences keep going. A current Western resurgence is evidenced by such filmmakers as Kelly Reichardt, who in *Meek's Cutoff* (2010) reimagines a true tale of Western expansion, through the viewpoint of pioneer women; and, of course, Joel and Ethan Coen, with the Best Picture Oscar–winning *No Country for Old Men* (2007) and their gutsy remake of *True Grit* (2010), in which Jeff Bridges plays the Rooster Cogburn role originally and famously inhabited by John Wayne. So the Dude replaces the Duke, and Bridges' work with the Coens traverses from a film with Western undertones to an out-and-out Western in the classic sense.

STRIKES & GUTTERS

El Borrachón-erino
The protagonist in 1959's *Rio Bravo*, a deputy recovering from alcoholism played by Dean Martin, is named Borrachón, which is Spanish for "drunk." "If the name bothers you," the character announces, "they used to call me 'Dude.'"

FRAME OF REFERENCE

Western Lists

Tim Dirks, in the "Western Films" section of his informative website filmsite.org, categorizes the subgenres of Westerns thusly: epic, singing cowboy, spaghetti, noir, contemporary, revisionist, comedy, post-apocalyptic, and science-fiction or space. The American Film Institute's (AFI) top ten Westerns, in order, are: *The Searchers* (1956), *High Noon* (1952), *Shane* (1953), *Unforgiven* (1992), *Red River* (1948), *The Wild Bunch* (1969), *Butch Cassidy and the Sundance Kid* (1969), *McCabe & Mrs. Miller* (1971), *Stagecoach* (1939), and (somewhat surprisingly) *Cat Ballou* (1965).

John Wayne, the original Rooster Cogburn, 1969.
© Moviestore Collection Ltd / Alamy

Out of the Past: A Cowboy Dude

So how does this discussion of the Western fit into *The Big Lebowski* beyond such set gags as a tumbleweed at the beach and a narrator in cowboy gear swigging sarsaparilla? Through the Dude, the Coens cleverly and comically invert Western archetypes.

The character of the Dude personifies a key trope of the Western genre, albeit in the body of a pot-smoking, White Russian–downing, antiestablishment slacker. On the surface he is quite the opposite of a traditional cowboy. His very moniker, as pointed out in the "The Dude's Seinfeldian Lexical World" by Mark Peters (see page 114), was once defined as "a non-westerner or city-dweller who tours or stays in the west of the U.S., esp. one who spends his holidays on a ranch; a tenderfoot"—in other words, a tourist in the ways of the rugged Wild West. As the Stranger says, "Now Dude, that's a name no one would self-apply where I come from." And certainly, his general

A way out west there was this fella, fella I want to tell you about, fella by the name of Jeff Lebowski. . . . Sometimes there's a man, wal, he's the man for his time'n place, he fits right in there—and that's the Dude, in Los Angeles.

befuddlement doesn't align with most people's conception of a cowboy (despite a history of the alcoholic cowboy, like Rooster Cogburn in *True Grit*), or even that of a settler, pioneer, rustler, or outlaw. But he does function as both an insider and an outsider, a man existing outside the established confines of society (in his own words, "a loser, someone the square community won't give a shit about"), yet needed by that community to solve the mystery of the plot. And the Dude also very much fits into Western iconography by being a man outside of his own time. He is a man of the past; a man who, by embodying obsolete values and skills, is on the cusp of being outdated; a man who fights the future—oftentimes a doomed battle.

The Stranger's assessment of the Dude as a man for his time and place is an interesting one. In 1991, on the heels of the "Me Generation" of the 1980s—an age of the rise of the Gordon Gekko *Wall Street* corporate culture, in a time of war when America was winning (and as such dissent was not much tolerated)—the Dude is a throwback to an older era, one of fighting for social change. He had occupied various administrative buildings, broken into the ROTC, was a member of the Seattle Seven, and coauthored the Port Huron statement. Throughout the film, he is continually berated for being out-of-step, and his lack of worth is called out by those he encounters. The Big Lebowski repeatedly characterizes the Dude as a "bum" and jeeringly points out that "the bums lost." The Chief of Police of Malibu, siding with the smooth gangster/pornographer who "draws a lot of water in this town," rebukes the Dude as a "goldbricker" and a "deadbeat," as do the doltish thugs who abuse him. Even the checkout girl at Ralphs looks askance at him, presumably because of his ratty clothes and

Different facial hair, same take-no-BS attitude.
© AF Archive / Alamy

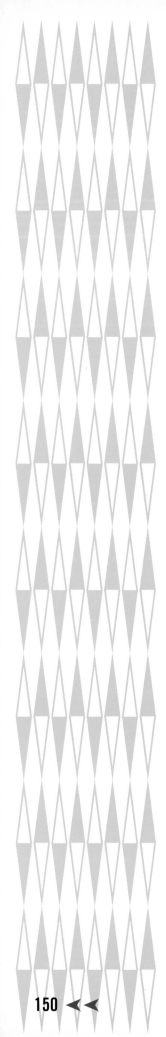

slouching demeanor, and perhaps because he deigns to write a sixty-nine-cent check.

So, the Dude, in his lifestyle and *raison d'etre*, is amassing a fight against the future, a future of greed and money and even technology (he still prefers to jerk off manually). This corresponds to such characters as Shane, who fights the robber barons; John Wayne in *The Searchers*, rebelling against the inevitable intermingling of the races with the catchphrase "That'll be the day"; and the *Wild Bunch* gang trying to exist in a new world order.

Right or wrong, the Dude aims to preserve the past in some measure, possibly a futile fight. His activities of choice—bowling (from the 1950s), drug use (from the 1960s, though certainly not relegated to them), and driving around with no discernable purpose—show his outdatedness, but they also evince his own set of values. The Dude has a code, like the cowboys of the classic Westerns. Most of the other characters in *The Big Lebowski* are motivated by greed of one kind of another: the Big Lebowski (in ripping off his Little Lebowski Urban Achievers); Bunny (like many a pretty teen runaway in the tradition of the Western); Jackie Treehorn; the various and sundry thugs; Walter, who tries to hone in on the ransom money; even Maude, who is greedy for sperm with no strings attached. The Dude, on the other hand, gets embroiled in the various financial entanglements of the other characters (albeit very ineptly), but ultimately realizes that he just wants his ratty little rug back. He embraces a simple, unencumbered lifestyle and doesn't ever seem to compromise his morals.

Noir Roots

"This damned burg's getting me. If I don't get away soon I'll be going blood-simple like the natives."—from *Red Harvest* by Dashiell Hammett

The first film in Sergio Leone's "The Man with No Name" trilogy, *A Fistful of Dollars*, was a remake of the great Japanese auteur Akira Kurosawa's 1961 *Yojimbo.* (This was the second Kurosawa film to be made into an American Western, after *The Seven Samurai* [1954] became *The Magnificent Seven* [1960].) But *Yojimbo* itself was an adaptation; the noirish detective writings of Dashiell Hammett, specifically *Red Harvest* (1929) and *The Glass Key* (1931), gave rise to the film. These Hammett works also inspired other filmmakers—notably, the Coens, who penned the title *Blood Simple* from a line in *Red Harvest* and fashioned the plot of *Miller's Crossing* from both. In fact, the Westerns genre has many intersections with that of noir, bringing us to . . .

The Big Lebowski
as Noir

Film noir translates from the French as literally "black film"; French critics were the first to recognize the inception of this film form, connecting it to a type of detective fiction called the *serie noire*. The genre is akin to the Western in that it is a form distinctly indigenous to America. Unlike Westerns, though, its films do not center on a specific period of history. They emphasize style and characters, with plot coming a distant last in importance. (This is certainly true of *The Big Lebowski*, which has a meandering, unimportant—in the end—plot, although it

> "Noir seemed to be the flavor of the narrative, with all these characters trapped by their pasts."
>
> —Ethan Coen in *The Big Lebowski: The Making of a Coen Brothers Film*

doesn't exhibit the typical stylization or types of characters to be found in the classic noir.)

The prototypical era of film noir began with *The Maltese Falcon* (1941) and continued

The Maltese Falcon starred Humphrey Bogart as private eye Sam Spade, Sidney Greenstreet as Big Lebowski–like "Fat Man" Kasper Gutman, character actor Peter Lorre as weasel-like Joe Cairo, and Mary Astor as *femme fatale* Brigid O'Shaughnessy.
© Moviestore Collection Ltd / Alamy

through Orson Welles' *Touch of Evil* (1958). It rose out of several factors. The German Expressionism movement came to America through exiled German film industry workers who emigrated to L.A. Stylistically, the expressionist films of the 1930s were infused with strong contrasts between dark and light, which created ominous shadows (one can see a minor example of such shadowing when the Dude rounds the corner, dancing to the strains of "Just Dropped In," at the beginning of his dream sequence). In addition to the Germans, the hard-boiled, gritty writings of Dashiell Hammett and Raymond Chandler gave rise to the best in noir movies. Noir also sprang from 1930s gangster pictures—at a time in which gangsterism in America flourished.

Finally, the mood from World War II and the start of the Cold War was one of distrust and disillusionment—some of the great themes of the noir picture. According to *A History of Narrative Film*, noir "carried postwar American pessimism to the point of nihilism" (though not typically in the form of German pancake-eaters). The negativity of McCarthyism, the fear of the atomic bomb, and the general cynical mood of the country fed the dark undercurrent of the genre. Tropes of the noir include a seamy urban landscape, filled with greed, lust, cruelty, brutality, violence, corruption, and sordid crime. Its films are peopled by *femme fatales*, neurotic characters, and, of course, the sound, strong detective.

Film Noirs and Westerns

The genres of film noir and Western have intersected frequently, perhaps in part due to their distinctly American sensibility. Howard Hawks, director of *The Big Sleep* (as well as other noirs such as *To Have and Have Not*), also directed the Westerns *Red River* (1948) and *Rio Bravo* (1959). *Ride the Pink Horse* (1947) is a traditional noir (including *femme fatale*) that takes place in the border town of San Pablo, when a mysterious stranger arrives. Robert Mitchum, a key noir figure from such classics as *Out of the Past*, appeared in two films that bridged the genres: *Pursued* (1947) and *Blood on the Moon* (1948). *Out of the Past* itself, though quintessentially noir, also includes tropes of the Western. A stranger comes to a small, dusty California town from the big city to escape his past, but when trouble appears he must use his old, what he thought were obsolete, unrestrained, and brutal "skills" to keep the peace.

To Have and Have Not, Slim (Lauren Bacall) famously offers instructions to Harry Morgan (Humphrey Bogart) on how to whistle.
© Sunset Boulevard / Corbis

The Muse: Raymond Chandler

Raymond Chandler was born in Chicago in 1888. After various travels, he moved to London and joined the civil service, which he eventually left to write for newspapers. In 1913 he landed in Los Angeles and worked as an executive for an oil company. During the time he lived there, through the 1950s, the city evolved from a town-like hamlet to an urban monolith hurtling toward vast proportions.

In 1932, at age forty-five, Chandler decided to become a writer after losing his job during the Depression. *The Big Sleep* (1939) was his first novel. He wrote numerous short stories (mostly for pulp magazines) and seven L.A.-based novels in which the protagonist was detective Philip Marlowe, most memorably portrayed by Humphrey Bogart in the movies. Exploring an underworld of chaos in Chandler's episodic plots, Marlowe exists as a strong, solitary figure who must untangle the most complicated intrigues, encountering no shortage of bizarre characters along the way.

Similarly, *The Big Lebowski* has a convoluted plot that is not integral to the movie in the end; instead, it is the diversions or detours that are at the crux of the film. Chandler often included hallucinations in his novels (like the Dude's dream sequences). The Chandler novel *Farewell, My Lovely* features a complex plot in which Marlowe is knocked unconscious throughout the story—which also happens to the poor Dude. In Chandler's L.A., there is always a central figure who possesses both wealth and power—like the Big Lebowski—and there are often sleazy nightclub owners who look and act a lot like Jackie Treehorn.

Chandler's novels are all told through first-person narration, but the Coens thought it wouldn't quite work to make the Dude the narrator—having his reefer-enhanced thoughts broadcast throughout the film would seem somewhat trite (and probably confusing). Throughout their filmography, the Coens exhibit a preference for voice-over narration, and in keeping with this tendency, they wrote

> **"When we were making *The Big Lebowski*, we were sort of thinking about Chandler—not so much the movies that have been made from Chandler's books, but Chandler's novels."**
>
> —Joel Coen

Raymond Chandler.
© Pictorial Press Ltd / Alamy

Bogart and Lauren Bacall in *The Big Sleep*.
© Moviestore Collection Ltd / Alamy

in the character of the Stranger to serve as an audience substitute. This enclosing of the story within a narration frame provides the same sort of distance from reality that noirs exhibit.

The Big Sleep-owski

Chandler's *The Big Sleep*, published in 1939 and released as a film in 1946 with stars Humphrey Bogart and Lauren Bacall, centers on a millionaire in Pasadena, General Sternwood (wheelchair-bound, like the Big Lebowski), who enlists Philip Marlowe to investigate a blackmailer named Geiger. The blackmailer claims to have illicit photos of Sternwood's depraved daughter Carmen. Carmen, like Bunny, tries to seduce Marlowe—in response to which, in the film, Marlowe jokes, "She tried to sit in my lap while I was standing up" (there were no cash machines back then). The plot becomes a confusing web of murder and blackmail, also involving an older daughter, a mature and sophisticated woman who is quite Maude-like. Typically, a Chandler plot involves the main character becoming romantically involved with this type of woman; *The Big Sleep* (like *The Big Lebowski*) is no exception.

Karate Kid Moves

The term "shamus," the self-designation of Da Fino (Jon Polito), was often used during the heyday of film noir to denote a private investigator. Da Fino's "Brother Shamus" scene was shot in just one night. Al Zaleski, who was the apprentice sound editor at the time, recalls that originally a Ralph Macchio–style karate kick was included, but this was ultimately left on the cutting room floor. Jon Polito, a Coen regular, shared his own memories of shooting the brief but memorable scene: "I do know that we did do different things in the battle in the beginning. I don't know how much longer [the scene] would have been, because we really didn't rehearse very much about what my defensive attack was going to be as I jumped out of the Volkswagen. But I do know that we did several takes, and what they settled on was me trying to be bigger than I was by putting my hands up as if I did karate—but you could tell from that round figure [that] I never touched karate a day in my life." Speaking of Polito's physique, the Coens, with their love for clashing juxtapositions, enjoy putting big men into small cars. Da Fino's little Volkswagen Beetle bears a striking resemblance to the one the hulking M. Emmet Walsh drives in their first film, *Blood Simple*. Polito continues, "I felt that I had to be taller because I was sort of round and sort of afraid of [the Dude], which was on script. So I kept on rising on the back of my feet, every time I would punctuate a line. . . . I kept on lifting up my heels, sort of making myself tall, or of equal height to him. . . . It certainly came out at the moment and it reads kind of strangely on camera."

Jon Polito has a long history working with the Coens. After first playing the gangster character Johnny Caspar in their third film, *Miller's Crossing*, he approached them about playing the blustery Jack Lipnick role in *Barton Fink*. According to Polito, they actually wanted him to play the small part of the wheedling assistant, Lou Breeze. He initially turned this down, thinking the part beneath him. He recalls, "It was a rainy night, and I remember I left the restaurant, and Frances McDormand ran after me and started calling me in the rain and I turned around under one of those stupid, small New York umbrellas that fold up, and she put her head under my umbrella with me and said, 'You've got to do this role. They wrote it for you. And it would be the best thing for your career.' So I basically said, 'All right, if Frances is going to hit me in the balls if I don't do it, I'd better do it.' And of course, that turned into being a wonderful variation from the Johnny Caspar character. I was blessed by being in any of the Coen brothers' films."

John Ridgely and Humphrey Bogart in *The Big Sleep*.
© Moviestore Collection Ltd / Alamy

The Big Sleep film had such a complicated plot that even its screenwriters, William Faulkner, Leigh Brackett, and Jules Furthman; director Howard Hawks; and Chandler himself professed not to quite understand all that was going on, including who killed one of the characters. Like *The Big Lebowski*, *The Big Sleep* is a distinctly L.A. story: "[Chandler] crafted *The Big Sleep*, like all his other novels set in Los Angeles, into a series of journeys across a mythical, motorized landscape of darkened bungalows, decaying office buildings, and sinister nightspots" (*Film Noir Encyclopedia*). The production crew very much had *The Big Sleep* in mind when outfitting the locations of *The Big Lebowski*. Rick Heinrichs, the production designer, was inspired by General Sternwood's palatial estate in creating the look and feel of the Big Lebowski's mansion.

Lebowski production designer Rick Heinrichs won an Oscar for Tim Burton's *Sleepy Hollow* (1999).
© Reuters / Corbis

The Precursor: The Long Goodbye

The Coen brothers delighted in putting a rumpled-looking, laid-back, pot-smoking character such as the Dude into this classic noir Marlowe role. The Dude is a glorious postmodern incarnation of Chandler's detective, but he wasn't the first. One of the Coens' favorite directors is Robert Altman, who did his own revisionist take on a Philip Marlowe Chandler novel: *The Long Goodbye* (1973), starring the incomparable Elliott Gould. Altman's conception of Marlowe was groundbreaking because he took the elegant persona cultivated by Humphrey Bogart and turned it on its head. Gould's characterization is of a laid-back, sarcastic private eye with the deadpan un-Marlowe-like mantra, "It's OK with me." Altman described his thought process on the shift in this famous character: "I decided that we were going to call him Rip Van Marlowe, as if he'd been asleep for twenty years, had woken up and was wandering through this landscape of the early 1970s, but trying to invoke the morals of a previous era.

> "You know how to whistle, don't you, Steve? You just put your lips together and blow."
> —Slim (Lauren Bacall) to Philip Marlowe in *To Have and Have Not*

> "Blow on them. . . . G'ahead. Blow."
> —Bunny Lebowski (Tara Reid) to the Dude in *The Big Lebowski*

I put him in that dark suit, white shirt and tie, while everyone else was smelling incense and smoking pot and going topless; everything was health food and exercise and cool. So we just satirized that whole time. And that's why that line of Elliott's—'It's OK with me'—became his key line throughout the film" (FocusFeatures.com). So the Elliott Gould character, as the Coens themselves have suggested, beyond being almost anti-Marlowe, is purposefully anachronistic. The Coens take this a few steps further with their own out-of-touch Marlowe—a figure who also exists in a twenty-year time warp, who although he doesn't say "It's OK with me," does abide.

Elliott Gould in *The Long Goodbye*, 1973.
© AF Archive / Alamy

Rolling on Screen

Bowling, although played throughout the world, has been the locus of very few films and television shows. It's rarely the main plot point of a good movie—not counting, of course, *The Big Lebowski*, and arguably the Farrelly brothers farce *Kingpin* (1996). Some of the most notable television shows that reference bowling include *Laverne & Shirley* (1976–1983, but set in the bowling heyday of the 1950s and 1960s), in which Laverne's (Penny Marshall) father runs the Pizza Bowl establishment, specializing in pizza and bowling. *The Simpsons* patriarch Homer, a cultural throwback as a husband and father, is also a bowler.

John Goodman has had a somewhat mystifying connection to many of the most memorable screen characters who bowl; perhaps his particular physique lends itself to bowling more than other sports. Ralph Cramden, the overbearing character played by Jackie Gleason in the legendary television show *The Honeymooners* (1953–1956), bowled on a team named "The Hurricanes" with his friend Ed Norton (Art Carney). Goodman played that Cramden character in a 1996 *Muppets Tonight* spoof called "The Lunarmooners." *The Flintstones*, the 1959–1966 children's show that was itself an imitation of *The Honeymooners*, featured a championship bowler in main character Fred. Goodman portrayed him in the 1994 live-action feature film *The Flintstones*. And Goodman's most famous character (rivaling

Ryan Gosling's character in *Lars and the Real Girl* would not last a second in Walter's presence—he bowls into the gutter … of another lane. © *AF Archive / Alamy*

Walter Sobchak), Dan Conner, on the influential television show *Roseanne* (1988–1997), was on a bowling team with Arnie Thomas (Tom Arnold)—though not a very good one.

The peak period of noir movies—the 1950s and 1960s—coincides with that of the proliferation of bowling as a sport. In addition, both bowling and noir were centrally located on the West Coast, and each has a somewhat seedy underbelly. Taking all of this into account, it stands to reason that bowling would be frequently referenced in noir pictures. While *Road House* is the only one of the following in which bowling is central to the plot, which sets the action in a bar/bowling alley, the following noirs incorporate the sport into their narratives: *Angel Face* (1952); *The Big Operator* (1959); *Cape Fear* (1962); *Crime in the Streets* (1956); *Criss Cross* (1949); *Double Indemnity* (1944); *Follow Me Quietly* (1949); *The Human Jungle* (1954); *Man in the Vault* (1956); *Nobody Lives Forever* (1946); *Pickup on South Street* (1953); *Pushover* (1954); *Red Light* (1949); *Road House* (1948); *Scarface* (1932); *Stakeout on Dope Street* (1958); *Tension* (1949); and *Try and Get Me*, aka *The Sound and the Fury* (1950) (from the essay "Bowling Noir" by Michael F. Keaney).

In *King Ralph*, John Goodman's lounge-singer-turned-royal has a bowling alley installed in Buckingham Palace. © *AF Archive / Alamy*

The Big Lebowski as . . . The Wizard of Oz?

"Every movie ever made is just an attempt to remake *The Wizard of Oz*."

—Joel Coen

Although the Coens tend to make pronouncements solely to amuse themselves, let's take Joel's comment at face value and examine *The Big Lebowski* through the lens of *The Wizard of Oz* (1939). Within the Oz formula, the Dude equates with the Dorothy character. Both D-named protagonists are thrust into a strange, often surreal world beyond their comprehension. For the Dude this is the complex mystery surrounding Bunny's disappearance, but also the bizarreness that is L.A., with its vibrant cast of characters, including *Miami Vice*–dressed pornographers and naked, harnessed women creating "art." This (techni-)colorful milieu is quite a contrast to the black-and-white (gray, really) photo of Bunny's family farm and the bleak surrounding landscape of Moorhead, Minnesota. Definitely Kansas-esque.

The Dude believes he has inadvertently endangered Bunny's life, much as Dorothy accidentally kills the witch. They both take their friends on their journeys. Of course, Dorothy and her companions help each other out, whereas the Dude, Walter, and Donny typically hinder one another—but at the very least they do offer a certain degree of solace through friendship.

The original Pomeranian, Donny, Dude, and Walter?
© AF Archive / Alamy

Unlike Cynthia's show dog, this is an actual Pomeranian.
Linn Currie / www.shutterstock.com

The Big Lebowski character parallels the Great Oz. Both men send the hero and their cohorts on a journey to solve a task that turns out to be false endeavor—a wild goose chase, if you will. Lebowski presents himself as an individual of great power and wealth, one who has lived a life of achievement that stems from a strong work ethic. Just as the great and powerful Oz is exposed as merely a regular man, so, too, is Jeffrey Lebowski uncovered as a fraud. His façade is all chicanery: he is not a man of his own means; he doesn't have a job, per se; and he can't even manage the small tasks given to him by his daughter, the real powerhouse of the family.

Walter's ex-wife Cynthia's show dog, although referred to as a Pomeranian, is in actuality the same breed of terrier as Toto. Toto pulls back the curtain to reveal Oz as a "humbug," and Walter's charge licks the face of the Big Lebowski when he's down and can't defend himself, similarly illuminating his ineffectuality and powerlessness.

Finally, a bit of apropos trivia: Steve Buscemi played the Cowardly Lion in his fourth-grade play.

The emerald toes.
© Moviestore Collection LTD / Alamy.
Courtesy of Universal Studios Licensing LLC

Walter and the Dude,
by Jordan Kerfeld
(look closely to see
what they're made of).
*Courtesy of
JordanKerfeld.com*

PART V
The Release and Its Aftermath

Initial Audience and Critical Reception

The Big Lebowski premiered at the prestigious Berlin Film Festival in February 1998, where it garnered Joel Coen a Golden Bear nomination for Best Director. It was released on March 6 in the United States, where it received a decidedly lukewarm reception. Spending a mere six weeks in theaters, the film barely recouped its budget with a total domestic gross of nearly $17.5 million—a figure that matched Titanic's haul over just Lebowski's opening weekend, even though James Cameron's behemoth had already spent twelve weeks in theaters. According to the IMDB website Box Office Mojo, among all of the 1998 domestic movie releases, The Big Lebowski came in at a distant ninety-sixth, after such stinkers as The Waterboy, Patch Adams, Dr. Doolittle, and You've Got Mail (a feature-length AOL commercial masked as a movie). Even just among other Coen films in the dark/black comedy category, Lebowski's gross ranks fourth after Burn After Reading, Raising Arizona, and The Ladykillers (widely considered the Coens' worst cinematic offering, even though its cast was headed by box-office golden boy Tom Hanks of You've Got Mail fame). Considering Lebowski came on the heels of the Oscar-winning Fargo, with a recognizable cast including Jeff Bridges (no box-office slouch himself), there is one inescapable conclusion to be drawn: audiences just didn't get it.

Film critics were also exceedingly mixed in their reactions to the Coens' post-Fargo endeavor, many comparing it unfavorably to the colder clime–set film. Though somewhat positive in his assessment, David Denby, then at New York Magazine, espoused that the filmmaking in Fargo showed "enormous discipline" compared to the more ragtag Lebowski. Roger Ebert found it "weirdly engaging," but in no way comparable to the excellent Fargo. His At the Movies cohort Gene Siskel found every aspect, from the acting, plot, to even the bowling, uninspired, and Kenneth Turan at the Los Angeles Times also lamented the film

The Coens and John Goodman at the International Film Festival in Berlin, February 1998.
Photograph by Hans Edinger / Associated Press

as being disappointingly lackluster. Several critics, ranging from the esteemed Jonathan Rosenbaum (*Chicago Reader*) to the more-often-than-not milktoasty *Variety*, lambasted it as cleverness for cleverness' sake—or, at least, for the Coens' sake. Some critics were confused and felt insulted; Peter Howell of the *Toronto Star* wrote that the Coens were "simply throwing weirdness at the screen."

But the critical disdain was not universal. In the "thumbs-up" category, Janet Maslin's *New York Times* review praised the cast, calling out Bridges' and Goodman's performances for successfully hitting the humor mark. Andrew Sarris, the venerable (and at times irascible) *New York Observer* critic, also enjoyed the comedy, and wrote in particular of the Coens' filmmaking virtuosity in the dream sequences:

"To go so far out on a limb stylistically, and not fall flat on your face, is a rare feat nowadays." But it was a somewhat hard-to-define quality of *The Big Lebowski*, one that's actually in keeping with the stylistically disparate *Fargo*, that made several critics sit up and take notice: that of the backbone of humanity running through the film, exemplified by the protagonist and the affection the Coens have for him. Throughout Joel and Ethan's careers, a chief complaint from many film writers and critics has been that the brothers people their films with characters they view with derision and contempt. This is a sentiment that still abides with some to this day; in 2007 the *TV Guide's Movie Guide* wrote of *Lebowski* (in that critic's opinion the Coens' worst film) that it was an "insult." Their insulting treatment of

Brandt, The Big Lebowski & Bunny, 2011 print triptych by Joshua Budich. *Courtesy Joshua Budich, www.joshuabudich.com*

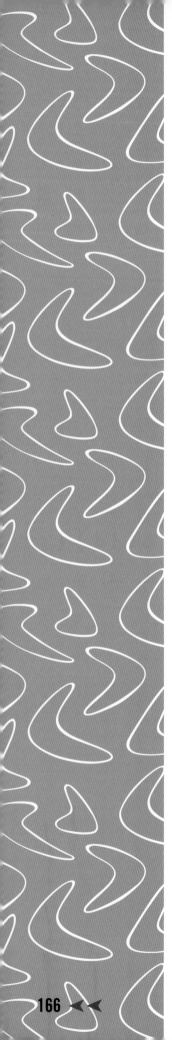

characters is an arguable point, and one that may possibly have been influenced by the "irreverent" manner in which the Coens deal with the press. At any rate, the brothers' whip-smart and oftentimes scathing sense of humor and skewed portrayals of reality contributed to the critical scoffing at their films' characters. However, with *Fargo*'s very winning and human Marge Gunderson (portrayed with heart and soul by Frances McDormand), the tide of this opinion on the Coens turned to a degree, if only in some circles. And the Coens' affection for the Dude—however addled and flawed he might be—is certainly evident, especially upon recurrent viewings.

A review in *Empire* articulates this idea, saying the Coens' response to their success was to "laugh in the face of populism and follow *Fargo*'s black on white trickery with a film as peculiar, original and unstintingly inventive as any on their twisted CV. Hollywood will be as perplexed by their genius as ever, this is a movie that will only make perfect sense if you happen to possess Coen genes . . . yet beyond the hysterical black comedy, scattered violence and groovy dialogue, there sounds the same song to human goodness which enriched *Fargo*. In the Dude's easy riding, people-loving approach to the mess of his life, you are witness to something no end of $200 mill sinking tubs could touch upon. In a perfect world all movies would be made by the Coen brothers."

Writer Rob Nelson eloquently concurred in *City Pages*, the alternative weekly based in the Coens' own Minneapolis, home to a populace of dispassionate, stalwart stock: "The big difference in *Lebowski* is the filmmakers' palpable affection for their caricatures. . . . Whether it's because the Coens hail from these parts, the expression of true feelings has never been their characters' strong suit—or their own. But as *Lebowski*'s climactic bear hug signals direct communication more warmly than anything in their oeuvre, I'd say the Coen Brothers have finally looked into their heart."

The Rise of the Cult of *The Big Lebowski*

After a quick exit from movie theaters, and ostensibly from the public consciousness, *The Big Lebowski* slowly, inexorably, began to creep back into the minds of moviegoers. Two years after its release, it started to make the second-run rounds at midnight showings. In July 2002, an article in *Metromix* identified the film's newfound, but still marginal, popularity. The author, Steve Palopoli, saw it at L.A.'s New Beverly Cinema, where audience members yelled out lines of memorized dialogue during a midnight screening. Late-night showings of *Lebowski* became an increasingly frequent occurrence around the country. Like other films such as *Fight Club* (1999), which had a short stint in the theater but was wildly successful on the second-run, midnight circuit, *The Big Lebowski* needed a word-of-mouth rollout and repeated viewings to truly come into its own.

"The most worshipped comedy of its generation."

—*Rolling Stone,* on *The Big Lebowski*

Tales from the Little Lebowski Shop

By Roy Preston

As the proprietor of the world's only shop dedicated entirely to all things having to do with *The Big Lebowski*, the level of affection, the outright devotion, the sheer lunacy, and the absolute joy that *The Big Lebowski* inspires in its many fans unceasingly amazes me. I see them every day, coming from near and far. It doesn't matter if it's hot or cold, cloudy or sunny; the Achievers—the nickname fans of the film have playfully given themselves—cross the threshold of my shop with a knowing wink and a smile. They come from France (where they call the Dude *Le Duc*, the Duke!), Germany, Italy (where, not having a word for "dude," they just made up the name Drugo), Belgium, and even a little country called Queens, all to share a quote or two from their favorite film. Some of these folks can do quite a bit more than share a quote or two; heck, they've memorized the entire film. Do you have any idea what it's like to be stuck between two men from different continents while they shout at one another, "*This is what happens when you fuck a stranger in the ass!*"? It's quite something to behold.

I can't think of another film that has spawned a festival, a religion, one very small store—ahem!—and numerous books, one of which is a Shakespearian adaptation of the screenplay. All of this is made even more remarkable if one remembers that the film, upon its release in 1998, was a complete box office bomb. *The Big Lebowski* came and went faster than a White Russian in the Dude's hand. I remember seeing the film on its opening night. When it was over I turned to my friend and said, "Well, that was almost a home run." I've seen *The Big Lebowski* many times since and am quite happy to say that the Coen brothers actually batted this one so far and so high that I couldn't see it leave the park.

With regard to the film's success, the overwhelming consensus among the people I've had the privilege of speaking with who were involved in the making of it seems to be one of bemused surprise. None of them ever expected *The Big Lebowski* to reach the level of popularity it has. John Cameron, one of the film's producers, told me they did the film as a lark. Even Jeff Bridges said to me with a straight face as he looked around the store, "Gee! There's a whole culture that's sprung up around this, huh?" It just goes to show that great films will always find their audience, even if it takes them awhile.

Another surprising thing about *The Big Lebowski* is its demographic. It doesn't have one. When people ask me who my target audience is for the store, I'm always left furiously scratching my head. I'm hard-pressed to give a straight answer and usually end up replying, "Everyone." Age is not relevant when it comes to the Dude. I suspect this has something to do with his being a Baby Boomer and a holdover from the sixties. He appeals to older folks who remember that period, as well as younger people who fancy themselves rebels and kindred spirits of the Dude. Frankly, I don't even advertise. People have proven themselves quite adept at finding the store without my help.

One day an elderly woman and her husband visited the shop. She told me, with an angelic smile spreading across her creased face, that *The Big Lebowski* was her and her husband's favorite movie, and that the two of them watched it together every Thanksgiving. She then told me that because it was her seventieth birthday, her husband was going to buy her a *Lebowski* T-shirt. It was

The Little Lebowski Shop in Greenwich Village, Manhattan, where new shit is always coming to light/retail.
Courtesy of store owner Roy Preston, www.littlelebowskishop.com

at this point that woman pointed to a stack of shirts and said to me, "Give me 'Nobody fucks with the Jesus.'"

On another occasion a gentleman in his twenties was visiting the store from Italy. First he looked about him in disbelief and then exclaimed proudly, "We lika the Dude in Italy because he no interested in success, and we no interested in success. But the Dude have alotta style, and we have alotta style." The happy fellow then raised his hand into the air and curled his delicate fingers, whereupon he touched them to his lips and blew a kiss to a nonexistent Dude.

And in another instance a middle-aged woman who had just purchased fifteen *Lebowski* shirts for her boyfriend blurted out at the cash register, "I'm so getting laid tonight!" (I've often wondered how many children have been conceived because of *The Big Lebowski*. This incident left me quite certain there is more achieving going on than we think.) One can only conclude from

all of this enthusiasm that people of all ages, and from all corners of the world, love *The Big Lebowski*.

All of this leads to a question: why *does* the Dude abide? How did a film with no marketing campaign behind it, a film that all but vanished during its theatrical release, become such a phenomenon?

On a cold winter day back in 2007, when the Coen brothers were doing press for *No Country for Old Men*, a disheveled woman entered the store. She looked as though she had just returned from an endeavor that had sucked every ounce of energy from her being. The exhausted woman took several breaths. It was some time before she could speak. When she had properly composed herself again she confided in me that she was a film journalist. "What a wonderful job," I remember telling her. She gave me a faint smile, as if to say "You're so naïve." She then told me she had just returned from a three-hour interview with the Coens. "Ah!" I exclaimed, eyes bulging out of my head. "That must have been exciting." Again she gave me that same smile that said, "Such a simple man. If he only knew what a lion's den I've just come from." She went on to tell me that the Coens were her least favorite directors to interview because they don't talk about their directorial methods, they don't talk about their past films, and they don't talk about their private lives. They will only discuss the film they are presently promoting. The journalist claimed that interviewing the Coens was like trying to extract teeth.

As I reflected upon this information I realized that while their silence is bad for journalists, it's a benefit to their many fans. How many times have we seen directors doing interview after interview for their films, telling us what every single frame of the film means? So often in films today all of the thinking is done for us. Audiences aren't allowed to decide for themselves what a movie is about. Any personal interpretation of the work is squashed. The Coen brothers consciously avoid telling us what their films are about and in doing so leave space for something richer to grow out of their work. I remember watching an interview with the Coens in which the reporter asked them why *The Big Lebowski* was set during the first Persian Gulf War. Their answer was shocking in its simplicity: "We wanted something for Walter to rant about." Would the film be nearly as much fun if they were telling us during every interview about how their deep-seated political beliefs feed into their work? Nah! In fact their answer left me with even more questions.

And what about the Dude himself? Isn't he an archetypal character? He's the lazy man who has never planned a day in his life, the drunkard polite society shuns, the fellow who does all the things we secretly want to do, the vulgar fool who is in actuality the very definition of kindness. Audiences have always loved to root for this sort of character. If you held up a drawing of Shakespeare's Falstaff (wasn't he after all just an Elizabethan abider?) next to the Dude, you would probably see

Print by Dave Perillo.
Courtesy of the artist, www.montygog.blogspot.com

a rather striking resemblance. Both are portly, bearded white men prone to a love of beverage. It sounds preposterous, but the film does feature a plot about mistaken identity and even a character called the Stranger who functions as a sort of Greek chorus. (Falstaff was so popular in his day that Queen Elizabeth I demanded the character be bought back for two more plays—much as fans today are always clamoring for the Coens to do a sequel to *Lebowski*.)

Of course a large portion of the film's success must be attributed to the brilliance of its writing. Why else would people quote the film endlessly? The Coen brothers have always displayed a deft ear for language, or more precisely a deft ear for how we mangle language. Their characters are constantly chomping on and spitting out English in pieces. Can you name a character in any of the Coens' films who doesn't speak in his own unique vernacular? The Coens understand, in a manner reminiscent of Mark Twain, that language is a powerful tool for revealing character and heightening a sense of time and place. Take, for instance, David Huddleston's fantastic line in *The Big Lebowski*: "By God, sir! I will not abide another toe." The line tells the audience that the old man is educated, a person of some social distinction, and a larger-than-life figure—in his own mind at least. Later, of course, the Dude repeats a variation of the old man's line when he tells the Stranger at the end of the film, "The Dude abides."

Now does anything I've discussed here amount to a hill of beans? Not likely. There isn't any one reason for *The Big Lebowski*'s success. Great works speak to people in a myriad of very personal ways that can't really be pinpointed. Maybe that elusive, inexplicable, and truly individual response the film elicits is why, after all this time, the Dude abides.

Catch ya later on down the trail.

Roy Preston is the owner of the Little Lebowski Shop in downtown Manhattan.

"By God, sir!" © *Moviestore Collection Ltd / Alamy. Courtesy of Universal Studios Licensing LLC*

What Have You

The same month that the *Metromix* article came out, a perfect storm of circumstances came together that would have an indisputably lasting effect on *The Big Lebowski*'s legacy in the cultural zeitgeist. The events took place at a Holiday Inn, no less.

At the Derby City Tattoo Expo convention in Louisville, Kentucky, two bored T-shirt venders, Will Russell and Scott Shuffitt, began one-upping each other by quoting lines from *The Big Lebowski* to pass the time. Before long, others joined in, until a small group of *Lebowski* aficionados formed. Russell and Shuffitt realized there were clearly other like-minded fans out there and figured if such as thing as a tattoo convention could exist, why not a *Lebowski* one? Surely it would be a more entertaining enterprise. So they organized their own kind of convention, slated for October 12, 2002, and named it the "1st Annual *Big Lebowski* What-Have-You Fest" (without actually expecting it to *become* an annual event—and with a vengeance). They thought small, renting the cheapest bowling alley possible (the Fellowship Lanes, run by Baptists), and gathering secondhand bowling trophies to hand out as prizes. Assuming the event would consist of an intimate group getting together in Louisville to bowl, drink White Russians, and watch the movie, the men were taken aback when 150 people showed up, some from far-flung areas of the country.

In the episode "The Big Cakeowski" of the television show *Ace of Cakes*, Head Chef Duff Goldman created a White Russian–flavored cake for a 2008 Lebowski Fest.
Courtesy Duff Goldman / Charm City Cakes

A Lebowski celebration in Jerusalem, 2011.
Photograph by Sebastian Scheiner / Associated Press

In 2003, Lebowski Fest made *SPIN* magazine's "19 Summer Events You Can't Miss," and the event blew up. Upwards of 1,200 "Achievers," as the film's fans call themselves (from the Little Lebowski Urban Achievers), from thirty-five states came to celebrate all things *Lebowski*. Since then, the Fest has expanded beyond the confines of Louisville, into such cities as Austin, Boston, Columbus, Denver, Las Vegas, Los Angeles, New York, Minneapolis, Orlando, Philadelphia, Portland, San Diego, San Francisco, and Seattle. Festivals have even gone international, with celebrations in Edinburgh and London. The typically two-day events now include live music performances in addition to the bowling party, as well as brain-numbingly challenging trivia contests and astonishingly creative costumes from obscure lines of the film.

A 2006 screening at the Somerset House in London drew two thousand attendees.
© Gideon Mendel / Corbis

The Many Faces of *Lebowski*

At Lebowski Fests, Achievers have gone beyond dressing as characters, props (e.g., rugs, Creedence tapes, homework in baggies, severed toes, marmots), or even scenes and use sheer resourcefulness and imagination to convert lines from their favorite flick into costumes. A few choice examples:

- A Chinese man carrying two severed legs, from the Big Lebowski's line: "I didn't blame anyone for the loss of my legs, some Chinaman in Korea *took* them from me"

- Men dressed in Iraqi war gear, with a stuffed animal camel, uh, attached to his nether regions, as in Walter's statement, "look at our current situation with that camelfucker in Iraq" (Saddam Hussein)

- Women in crowns, wearing bras and panties, from when the Stranger, referring to Los Angeles, says: "'Course, I can't say I seen London, and I never been to France, and I ain't never seen no queen in her damned undies as the fella says"

- A farm couple handing out leaflets for their missing daughter, Fawn Knutson (aka Bunny Lebowski)

- A roadie for Metallica wearing a T-shirt for the (nonexistent) "Speed of Sound Tour" that the Dude told Maude he worked

- A large-breasted woman wearing a blue, underwater-themed cape, representing the bosom of the Pacific Ocean ("And so, Theodore—Donald—Karabotsos, in accordance with what we think your dying wishes might well have been, we commit your mortal remains to the bosom of the Pacific Ocean, which you loved so well")

- White–clothing–clad women wearing ushankas (Russian caps): White Russians

- A man inside an empty laundry wringer (apparatus with rollers that squeeze water from washed laundry), from Walter's line during the botched ransom handoff, "The ringer cannot look empty!"

- A man in a lab coat, referencing the Auto Circus cop saying, "Leads, yeah. I'll just check with the boys down at the Crime Lab!"

- Three people dressed as pigs and wearing blankets, from the nihilists' breakfast order at the diner

- A masturbation guide or "Jerk-off Manual," as the Dude jokes to Jackie Treehorn, "I still jerk off manually"

"White Russians" in Redding, California.
© *Andreas Fuhrmann / ZUMA Press / Corbis*

The 2011 Lebowski Fest cast reunion in New York.
Photograph by Diane Bondareff / AP Images for Universal Studios Home Entertainment

There's been a wide variety of notable participants in Lebowski festivals. These include inspirations for some of the characters, like Jeff Dowd (who seems to be making a living off his Dude persona); muses of the Walter character Peter Exline and Big Lew Abernathy; and even Jaik Freeman, the basis for Little Larry Sellers. Freeman was reunited at a Fest with Exline, one of the men who confronted him about stealing a car back when he was a teenager.

Musical attendees to Lebowski Fests have ranged from fans such as They Might Be Giants and Louisville's own My Morning Jacket, to bands featuring actors from the film, like Blonde from Fargo, an alternative rock garage band with lead singer Peter Stormare (nihilist Uli Kunkel), and even Jeff Bridges himself, who performed the *Lebowski* title credits song, Bob Dylan's "The Man in Me," at a Los Angeles festival. "I had my Beatle moment when I played one of these Lebowski Fests, where everybody dresses up like different characters from the movie," Bridges said of the experience. "That was incredible. I played to a sea of Dudes and bowling pins" (*Marin Independent Journal*).

> "I played Gary the bartender at the bowling alley. I never appear on camera [author note: his face doesn't appear, but his back and side do], so in some respects I guess I'm a bit of a Trivial Pursuit question. I went to a Lebowski Fest and was quite amazed that they even knew who I was!"
>
> —actor Peter "Goose" Siragusa

Demonstrating the flat-out devotion of the Achievers, even the most minor characters have received adulation at festivals, including the Ralphs checkout girl (Robin Jones), Saddam Hussein (Jerry Haleva), Jesus' bowling partner Liam (James G. Hoosier), the owner of the smashed-up Corvette (Luis Colina), and the Auto Circus cop (Michael Gomez). Same goes for the more obscure crew, like Brian McCarty, the music playback operator for the film, who appeared at a Denver Festival and was peppered with questions about his (little known to non-movie-industry people) work on the film.

Rolling On, and On, and On . . .

The rollout of the various and sundry packaged editions of *The Big Lebowski* for home viewing speaks to its ever-increasing popularity—and corresponding lucrativeness. In 1998 it was issued on laserdisc and DVD, then again on DVD and VHS in 1999. Then, in 2000, it was screened on cable television (with the now infamous substitution for "Do you see what happens when you fuck a stranger in the ass!" with the wackily incomprehensible "Do you see what happens when you find a stranger in the Alps!"). In 2002 the marketplace gained another *Lebowski* DVD, and the following year a DVD "value pack" that included both *The Big Lebowski* and another 1998 "stoner" movie release, *Half-Baked*, came out. Even more DVDs were issued in 2005, including a special Coen Brothers Collection Edition and an Achiever's Edition, which assembled photo cards, character coasters, and a collectible bowling towel, in addition to the "making of"

The Dude Abides in VHS, by Erika Iris Simmons.
Courtesy of the artist

The Historical Mixology of White Russians, or "Hey, Careful Man, There's a Beverage Here!"

"It's essentially a liquefied ice cream cone that you can buy in a bar."—Jeff Dowd, in *The New York Times*

Historically, a "White Russian" is a Russian who fought against the Bolsheviks in the Russian Revolution. In the parlance of our contemporary times, it's a drink created through the combination of vodka, coffee liqueur, and cream served in an Old-Fashioned (lowball) glass. The coffee-flavored liqueur used in White Russians is characteristically the Mexican rum-based Kahlúa (est. 1936) or the slightly less expensive Jamaica-originating Tia Maria (first sold in 1950), but businesses that specialize in other beverages (such as Starbucks and Patrón) have attempted to branch out into the coffee liqueur market. For the cream, substitutes can include milk, Bailey's Irish Cream, vanilla soymilk, or half-and-half. The first appearance of the Dude in *Lebowski* is of him in a Ralphs aisle, opening a carton of half-and-half to ascertain its freshness before purchasing for future beverages. Later, he uses powdered creamer in lieu of cream—he's clearly not a stickler for following a prescribed recipe.

Other, similar drinks from which the White Russian seemingly derives existed back in 1930s America. According to *Esquire*, the "Russian" consisted of vodka and white crème de cacao with the then ever-

Palmer Kane LLC / www.shutterstock.com

popular and present gin, and the "Barbara" (later renamed "Russian Bear") combined two parts vodka, one part crème de cacao, and one part cream or half-and-half. The "Russian" in the drink's name derives from the natural connection of vodka to its nation of origin. At that time in U.S. history, vodka was still a little-known liquor, an egregious oversight that was rectified with an extensive marketing campaign in the 1950s to promote vodka-based cocktails. In 1961, the *Diner's Club Drink Book* added the word "black" to the noncream version of the Russian, implying that one with cream should necessarily be called "white." According to the *Oxford English Dictionary*, the first official reference to a "White Russian" in the cocktail sense of the word appeared in the *Oakland Tribune* on November 21, 1965, and was delineated as one ounce each of Southern vodka and cream.

Today's White Russian is a drink specially matched for both ends of the drinking spectrum—lightweights and lushes alike. The heavy, sweet cream masks the high alcohol content, ensuring the drink goes down the gullet easily—a little too easily, for those in the lightweight camp—and for the heavy drinkers (the Dude, as case in point), facilitating the imbibing for the imbibers.

In the fascinating *The Year's Work in Lebowski Studies*, Craig Owens' essay "On the White Russian" details two schools of thought in making a proper White Russian: floating the cream (the "floaters") or mixing it in (the "homogenizers"). Certainly, such details are not generally specified by a drinker at a bar, leaving it up to the mixologist to determine which type to make. Whether by preference or simply because of his laid-back persona, the Dude seems to fall into a lackadaisical version of the homogenizer category, perfunctorily stirring his "Caucasians" when given access to a stir stick.

Clearly not a measurement-precise drink, different sources have minor tweaks in their guidelines on creating this creamy concoction. Some recipes measure the ingredients in gills (a unit of volume introduced in the fourteenth century and equivalent to four fluid ounces), while others measure in centiliters or ounces. Recipes vary not only in whether or not the cream is floated or stirred (or hedging the bet by not really specifying), but also in the ratio of vodka to coffee liqueur (often specifically Kahlúa) to cream.

The International Bartenders Association (IBA, est. 1951) has selected the White Russian as an "official" cocktail, and as such it's one of many drinks used in the annual World Cocktail Championship (WCC) of bartending. It falls in the category of "After-Dinner Cocktail—Sweet."

"It's hard to think of a more boring drink, except, perhaps, when it's spraying from the Dude's mouth," said Martin Doudoroff, a historian for cocktaildb.com (and depending on the pronunciation, a very aptly named one for this discussion). *The Big Lebowski* devotees have been able to enliven the drink by inventing games to coincide with watching the movie—such as taking a drink when certain plot points occur or words are spoken. Popular drinking moments include when the Dude is punched; someone throws a bowling ball; Walter refers to Vietnam; such words as "Dude," "Shabbos," or "Lebowski" are uttered; or simply, when a White Russian is imbibed on screen.

Coasters for White Russians, or what have you.
Courtesy Kelly Puissegur, www.retrowhale.com

White Russian Variations

With Substitutions for Cream:
Anna Kournikova: skim milk
Blind Russian: Bailey's Irish Cream
Irish Russian: Coca-Cola, Guinness stout
Lara's Russian Quaalude: Bailey's Irish Cream, Frangelico
Banana Russian: Crème de banane (and with vanilla vodka)
Nutty Russian: Frangelico
Russian Iceberg: White crème de menthe, Rumple Minze
White Canadian: goat's milk
White Mexican: *horchata*

With Substitutions for Vodka:
Rebel Russian: Southern Comfort
White Cuban: rum
White Mexican: tequila

Lebowski Fest Variation—
White Trash Russian: Yoo-Hoo and vodka

Jeff Dowd's Variation—
Dirty Mother (the drink he moved to from White Russians in the 1970s): Kahlua and brandy over ice

STRIKES & GUTTERS

No Crying over Spilled Cream

For the scene in which the Dude is thrown into the Big Lebowski's limo while hanging onto a White Russian for dear life, the special effects crew built a trick magician's glass with a false liquid in it so he wouldn't spill all over the set. Since there is typically more than one take for a scene, they also wanted to ensure that Jeff Bridges didn't have to keep changing out of a sodden costume. According to Peter Chesney, the challenge for the special effects crew came in balancing the "real" look (i.e., that the liquid is actually in the glass and spilling because of the impact of the Dude being roughly tossed into the limo) with going too far in soaking the actor.

documentary from the original DVD, an introduction to the reissue by faux Coen persona Mortimer Young, and a piece on Jeff Bridges' on-set photography. In 2005 the movie was also included in a DVD collection of five Coen brothers films. *Lebowski* was released in 2007 in the short-lived HD DVD format, which lost out in the marketplace to Blu-ray. The following year several HD DVD packages came out: *Lebowski* with Monty Python's *The Meaning of Life*, with *Fear and Loathing in Las Vegas*, and with both *The 40-Year-Old Virgin* and *Shaun of the Dead*—all humorous but otherwise pretty disparate offerings. Of course, the tenth anniversary of the film necessitated a new special anniversary edition (both regular and a limited edition that was packaged in a fake bowling ball), with some new featurettes.

The 2011 release of the Blu-ray and a Limited Edition Blu-ray version had the most extras yet, rehashing some from the original DVD but also including such fun digital features as an on-screen counter to keep track of certain "Lebowski-isms" and a tool to create a custom playlist from the soundtrack. The hoopla surrounding the release was extravagant: the main actors from the film—Jeff Bridges, Julianne Moore, Steve Buscemi, John Goodman, and John Turturro, along with music producer T Bone Burnett—reunited for an onstage conversation and Q&A. At this point, the film had become so legendary that its legions of fans couldn't contain themselves at the event, shouting out lines of dialogue and drowning out the very stars they had come to hear.

STRIKES & GUTTERS

Mortimer Young of Forever Young Film Preservation

For reissues of both *Blood Simple* and *The Big Lebowski*, the Coens added a hilarious fake introduction to "explain" film preservation. It features Mortimer Young, an elderly man with Coke-bottle glasses, a Sherlock Holmes–style pipe, and a pink carnation in his buttonhole, sitting in a leather armchair in a stuffy, old library, waxing poetic about the company Forever Young Film Preservation. In the *Lebowski* intro, he discusses in serious tones a plant explosion (no more union labor for the company

henceforth), then gives a nonsensical explanation of the restoration process, including the "jiggle-bath" for the "toe scene" in *Le Grand Lebowski*. Young, played with panache by George Ives, a character actor who appeared in such classic television shows as *Green Acres, That Girl, Mod Squad*, and *Mannix*, as well as the Coens' *Intolerable Cruelty* and *The Man Who Wasn't There*, closes with the lines, "Restored, rejuvenated, and still smokin'."

Are You a Lebowski Achiever?: Awards and Acclaim

After the film's premiere, the accolades were slow in coming. Joel Coen (as the credited director of the film) was nominated for a Berlin Golden Bear at that city's international film festival, then later for a Screen International Award. But compared with other Coen films, the list of nominations was decidedly paltry. It wasn't until the film achieved full cult status that it started to make a few "best of" headlines. In our list-mad culture, just a few that tally *The Big Lebowski* include: "Funniest-ever Film," ranked seventh by *Guardian Observer* readers and eighth by *Entertainment Weekly*, the latter calling it a "masterpiece of anti-storytelling." *Lebowski* was listed as one of the "Top 50 Greatest Comedies of All Time" by the now-defunct yet influential *Premiere* magazine. It's thirty-fourth on *Entertainment Weekly*'s "Top 50 Cult Films," and fifteenth on their "Essential Left-Field Movie Hits since '83." As for *Lebowski*'s characters, *Empire* cites the Dude as the seventh "Greatest Movie Character," gushing, "There's nothing like him," and he ranks fourteenth in the "100 Greatest Characters of the Last 20

"It's great to be a part of something that's such an important part of pop culture."

—actor Torsten Voges, Franz (the tall nihilist)

STRIKES & GUTTERS

Dowd Gets *High* (*Times* Award)

The *High Times* Stony Awards have only been around since 2002, when Snoop Dogg won Stoner of the Year and *How High* received the honor of Best Stoner Movie. Despite being ahead of its time, *The Big Lebowski* has a strong presence in the *High Times Guide to Stoner Film History*, and in 2006, Jeff Dowd was awarded the Thomas King Forçade Award for stony achievement in film.

Years," with Walter Sobchak at forty-ninth (also in *Entertainment Weekly*, that great paragon of list-making). The *Los Angeles Times*, in their writers' survey of the "25 Best L.A. films of the last 25 Years," ranks it tenth (despite a somewhat tepid review upon release), for "encompassing a wide swath of L.A.'s crazy quilt of social milieus." It even appears on *Time* magazine's "All-Time 25 Best Sports Movies": "Joel and Ethan Coen, in their tribute to tenpins, recognized that the game is not so much an exercise opportunity as a social event—where beer is an essential accoutrement, like tobacco chaw to a baseball player; bringing a Pomeranian to the alley can risk sundering a friendship; and disputes on such issues as the one-toe-over-the-line rule are resolved with a show of firepower."

Effect on Cast and Crew: Recognition, Résumés, and Renown

And how did working on *The Big Lebowski* affect the cast and crew? From the top to the bottom, all the actors are recognized on the street—even those with no lines and a mere minute onscreen, like Carlos Leon, one of Maude's thugs who pops the Dude in the face. Julianne Moore, with an extensive filmography under her belt that includes the box-office smash *The Lost World: Jurassic Park*, says that it is one of the movies mentioned most frequently to her. On the creepier side, John Turturro receives explicit mail because of his Jesus Quintana character. Steve Buscemi talks about the unspoken language of *Lebowski*: "I'll pass three guys on the street, and they may just give me a nod. They don't even have to say a line from the movie. I know what movie they're thinking about" (*Rolling Stone*). Jack Kehler has similar experiences: "I get recognized a

> "I've been acting in film and television for more than a decade now, and have worked on a lot of wonderful projects, but no matter where I go, if someone looks at my résumé, they always say, 'Wow, what was it like to work on *The Big Lebowski*?'"
>
> —Wendy Braun, dancer

Dancer Wendy Braun with Jeff Bridges.
Courtesy of Wendy Braun

Marty the Landlord (Jack Kehler) and Brandt (Philip
Seymour Hoffman) reunited in 2002's *Love Liza*.
© AF Archive / Alamy

lot because of it, and I'll see that recognition
when somebody says to themselves, 'There's
the Dude's landlord,' or, 'There's Marty.' I can
appreciate people's appreciation. It's a certain
kind of person, and I don't even know how
to describe. . . ." He pauses before continuing,
"I'll use what a stage manager once said to
me: 'Allow me some geekdom moments here,'
and she proceeded to talk about *The Big
Lebowski*." Cast and crew also talk about how
it's the movie that jumps out on their résu-
més—no matter how long those might be.

Dancer Kiva Dawson discusses how
despite a decade having passed since her brief
stint on set, there is a common bond among
the female dancers that exists to this day:
"Whenever we run into each other, we have
that in common, *The Big Lebowski* thing."

The effects of the film have lasted among
other members of the production as well. A

group from C5 (the editing facility that has
worked on many Coen films) made bowling
outings a recurring activity that started during production and continued for several years
after the film's release. At these events, while
making the film, they hung around and quoted
lines from the film—precursors, in a way, to the
modern-day Achiever. When the movie actually
came out, the bowling alley workers recognized
what the group had been quoting and asked in
astonishment, "How did you know?"

Even the smallest of gestures betray the
film's impact. Brian McCarty, the film's playback operator, who relocated to Australia after
working on *Lebowski*, named his Bijon puppy
the Dude (not "Dude," but "the Dude") and
swears the pet has an uncanny awareness that
isn't doglike, but more Dude-like. As he says
today, "The picture affects everybody. So there
you go."

The Jesus, Donny, Walter, and the Dude, by Dax Norman. *Courtesy of the artist, www.daxnorman.com*

THE LEAGUE

Jeff Bridges Photo Album:
The Making of *The Big Lebowski*

"Another really unique thing about working with Jeff Bridges is that he creates a book out of the photos that he takes during the shoot and then sends a copy to all of the crew. No one else in twenty-five years of being in the business has ever done this that I know of."

—Kristina Soderquist, assistant accountant

"Usually on a movie you get a belt buckle or a T-shirt. *The Big Lebowski* was my last Hollywood picture before we left [for Australia], and as you probably know Jeff Bridges, who walked around the set every day taking pictures with this little panorama picture camera, made coffee-table books for everybody. . . . It's spectacular. That kind of epitomizes the kind of actors the Coen brothers are able to attract because of their skill at

making movies. It was Jeff Bridges' way of telling the crew, 'I know this was a tough picture for everybody, and I captured some of this difficulty with the pictures that I took, and I want to share them with you because you were an important part of this experience.'"

—Brian McCarty, music playback operator

"He takes pictures on the set, of just about everybody, all day long, and then after the shoot, in the mail came this really beautiful yearbook kind of thing, of photos— of everybody, of everybody on the crew, and every cast member, a whole page for each person, with a handwritten comment from him. He was just a total gentleman."

—actor Jack Kehler, Marty the Landlord

What Makes a Cult Classic?

Not all cult films follow the same formula. Some are movies so bad they're good. *Attack of the Killer Tomatoes!* (1978), with its legion of evil yet utterly nonthreatening squishy vegetables, is an archetypal example, but the contemporary *Showgirls*, which swept the 1995 Razzie awards, fits the bill just as well. These are films whose makers took themselves seriously, whereas 1975's *Rocky Horror Picture Show* (the film that should have its photo in the dictionary next to "cult movie") actually had fun at its own expense, embracing the campiness of the plot and acting. The film spawned a phenomenon of midnight theater showings, accompanied by audience costumes and antics orchestrated to specific moments in the narrative; these showings continue to this day. Despite some measure of critical disagreement about its worth at the time of its release, *The Big Lebowski* was never truly considered a "bad" film along the lines of these movies.

Showgirls, starring Elizabeth Berkley, is in the so-bad-it's-good category.
© AF Archive / Alamy

Because of its decades of midnight showings, *The Rocky Horror Picture Show* has had the longest theatrical run in movie history.
© Stuwdamdorp / Alamy

Cult films are often created outside of the mainstream Hollywood apparatus or are somehow distinctive or experimental in their techniques or plot structures. *Rocky Horror*, with its mélange of musical, transvestite, sci-fi, and sexualized elements, is a good example, as is David Lynch's *Eraserhead* (1977), with its bizarre narrative; grotesque, creature-like characters; and eerie sound design. While *The Big Lebowski* is certainly uncommon in many ways, it was distributed through the widely known Universal Pictures, and it had recognizable actors and a plot that, while unusual, wasn't terribly unconventional.

Another defining characteristic of cult films is a rabid fan base that is either small or specialized, or both, in its makeup. *Lebowski* has a broad and extensive fan base, and while it skews somewhat younger, male, and white, its devotees are from all walks of life, crossing economic lines with both white and blue collars, academics and the undereducated. A high percentage of people (well, white men) on the dating website OkCupid who list *The Big Lebowski* as a favorite film also cite NASCAR as a main interest—a little perplexing in light of the movie's hero, a liberal slacker. On the other hand, there are stories of those who have incorporated the movie into their job interview process and professionals who have made careers out of giving sales presentations and symposiums using the language of *Lebowski*. So while rabid, the broad swath of *Lebowski* followers are not a small, distinct group.

As it doesn't fit any of the aforementioned criteria, what argument can be made for *The Big Lebowski* as the ultimate in cult filmdom?

STRIKES & GUTTERS

Lebowski and Dating: "Special Ladies" and "Fucking Ladyfriends"

The perfect gift for a loved one. Earrings by Jessica Dallman. *Photo courtesy of the artist, www.mspink404.etsy.com*

"Telling someone on a first date that I was in *The Big Lebowski* goes over very well. Apparently a lot of men on match.com love that film."
—Jamie Green, dancer from the dream sequence

Dating and social networking sites are a fruitful setting to ponder the place of *The Big Lebowski* within our society. While the movie definitely shows up in (mostly) men's profiles on such dating sites as Match and Plenty of Fish, it is OkCupid, the fastest-growing free dating site in the United States, with its slightly younger, somewhat quirkier, possibly hipper user base, where *The Big Lebowski*'s hallowed status in the life of the American white guy is clearly exhibited.

A 2011 search for the word "Lebowski" found that over a thousand U.S. men mention it on their profiles (i.e., bios). More statistically significant analyses were done in 2010, when OkCupid amassed over a half-million profiles—which, all told, comprised 280 million words—divided the profiles into racial groups, then isolated the top fifty words and phrases that made each group's profiles distinct from the others. Of all the Hollywood fare ever to have graced our local theaters or living rooms, *The Big Lebowski* is the second-most mentioned movie by white men, after *Ghostbusters*. Even more mind-blowing is that "Lebowski" was the seventh-highest of *any* word or phrase listed for this group—after only "Tom Clancy," "Van Halen," "golfing," "Harley Davidson," the aforementioned "Ghostbusters," and "Phish." (Incidentally, "Coen brothers" is #33.) Other movies for this group, though much further on down the list, include *Blazing Saddles, Apocalypse Now,* and *Lock, Stock, and Two Smoking Barrels*.

Most subscribers seem to cite *The Big Lebowski* in the

"Movies I Like" category of OkCupid, but many reference it in a sentence of their profile like the semisweet, "I probably have a pretty unhealthy obsession with *The Big Lebowski*, seriously, I named my dog after the Great Lebowski himself," or the more indelicate "My ex 'wife' thought *The Big Lebowski* was the stupidest movie ever. Don't make the same mistake." (Ouch!) Very often, it's used in the context of a frank pronouncement on the frequency that the subscriber quotes this oh-so-quotable movie. Usually it's daily.

The website goes beyond matching singles based on the compatibility of their profiles, and endeavors to cultivate a subscriber base by making the process of online dating "fun" through quizzes and personality tests. *The Big Lebowski* is a theme for several such tests on OkCupid, the most popular panderingly calling the film "probably the most sublime work of art ever produced by any civilization," and identifying the test-taker as one of the characters (The Dude, Walter, Donny, Maude, or the Stranger) based on his or her ability to accurately answer crucial questions about toenail color and blunt objects wielded in the film. The quiz itself is fairly rigorous, and most takers are relegated to "Donny" rather than "Dude" stature.

Whether listing *Lebowski* in a man's profile actually increases his chance of getting a date is unclear. However, in regards to the wild world of Internet dating in our contemporary times, as the Stranger says, "I guess that's the way the whole durned human comedy keeps perpetuatin' itself. . . ."

Repeated Viewings: Am I Wrong? Am I Wrong?

Traditionally, the "cult" label suggests a movie that didn't succeed initially in the theaters. This was certainly the case with *The Big Lebowski*. It's been called the first cult movie of the Internet age, and the implications of this assessment are manifold. New technologies mean that unlike the time when a film such as *Rocky Horror* first rose to cult status, people can now watch movies over and over. They can watch scenes or listen to lines of dialogue repeatedly—on DVD or YouTube and other Internet outlets—with greater ease than they ever could with VHS tapes.

Most movies, though, don't hold up to repeated viewings. What makes this film—or any film, for that matter—improve with age? The crucial factor is that the movie is

"It became, stealthily, the decade's most venerated cult film. It's got that elusive and addictive quality that a great midnight movie has to have: it blissfully widens and expands in your mind upon repeat viewings."
—*The New York Times*

particularly rewatchable, an opinion widely shared by *Lebowski* fans, casual observers, and even the cast and crew of the movie. The "why," though, is not easily answered. Upon first viewing *Lebowski*, one has to follow a rather rambling, even convoluted plot, and it isn't until the denouement that it becomes clear that actually understanding the narrative isn't essential in the grand scheme of enjoying the movie. As Al Zaleski, apprentice sound editor on *Lebowski*, says of his first time watching it (without the music, no less): "*The Big Lebowski* on its own was just confusing. The first time I saw it I had no idea what the plot was or what was going on." (On the DVD extras, Joel dismisses the plot's importance.)

Watching it subsequent times, with attempts to comprehend the plot out of the way, the viewer can focus instead on such elements as the smartly written characters and the intelligent dialogue (Coen trademarks) that reference everything from other movies like *The Wizard of Oz*, *The Long Goodbye*, and *The Big Sleep* to Judaic texts, pot culture, Vietnam and 1960s peace movements, nihilism, Busby Berkeley, tropes of the Western genre, noir, and so on. The Coens are masters at infusing their movies with a plethora of enlivening details. There is great specificity in the script: the Dude and Walter drinking plastic cups of Bud; the nihilist swinging a cricket bat when smashing up the Dude's house; Knox Harrington, the video artist, reading a copy of *Architectural Digest* in Maude's apartment. Their storyboards are so precise that such details as the sneeze of the "marmot" were pre-planned. As actor Mark Pellegrino says, "It's one of those wacky films that gets better every single time you see it, and you recognize something in it that you didn't recognize before, like peeling back the layers of an infinitely layered onion." That repeated viewing enhances the experience of the film seems indisputable; even that stubborn subset of the population—film critics—who have been known to change their tune on *The Big Lebowski* over time seem to agree. Ten years after his original impugning *New York Magazine* review, David Denby wrote a piece in *The New Yorker* on the Coens' work in which he called the film a "harmonious masterpiece." Peter Howell, who had panned it, published an eloquent about-face in the *Toronto Star*, in which he wrote: "I [admitted] how wrong I had been . . . . The things I considered flaws upon first encounter, namely the episodic plot and the out-there eccentricities of the characters, are now what I consider to be the chief virtues of *The Big Lebowski*. . . . In fact, it may just be my favourite Coen Bros. film."

Lebowski has been a source of inspiration for many artists; the artistry extends to edibles.
Michelle Clausen / www.sugarswings.blogspot.com

"The Coens are like a great painting. You gotta see it more than once, and you gotta see it in a different light, and you gotta see it under different conditions, you know. Their films are not like seeing the sculpture of the Pietà or something where you say, 'Oh my god, it's beautiful and I'll never forget it.' They're not at all like that—it's necessary to witness their art in repeated viewings. And that will just give you more and more pleasure."

—actor Jon Polito (Da Fino in *The Big Lebowski*)

The movie is so dense with details and ideas that hundreds of academic papers have been written about it, and there was even a two-day symposium held in conjunction with the 2006 Lebowski Fest. The resulting collection of essays, with such erudite titles as "*Lebowski* and the Ends of Postmodern American Comedy" was published in the book *The Year's Work in Lebowski Studies*. The philosophy of the movie has even spawned a religion, Dudeism, with over 140,000 ordained Dudeist priests worldwide.

The Gospel According to the Dude:
How *The Big Lebowski* Inspired a Religion

By The Dudely Lama of Dudeism, Rev. Oliver Benjamin

BOOK I

1. Truth be told, Dudeism wasn't the first religion I created. That one was called "The Temple of Earth." I have to confess now that it was rather a failure. As it turns out, it's easy to start a religion, but not so easy to get people to believe in it. Perhaps I should have arranged a few phony miracles or at least taken out a few Facebook ads.

2. In retrospect, the problem should have been obvious: it was a religion for atheists. And as it turns out, atheists are a smug bunch who don't need a cool logo to help them identify their worldview. Nevertheless, down deep I still really wanted to be a religious prophet. I don't know what it was exactly. Perhaps because I was losing my hair I wanted an excuse to shave my head. Or, like many other religious leaders, I, too, wanted to get a lot of things for free.

3. Nevertheless, it wasn't long before I had a revelation that would install me as the leader of a significant religious movement: Dudeism—the Church of the Latter-Day Dude.

BOOK II

1. It all started in 2005 while watching a DVD of *The Big Lebowski* in a café in Thailand. Even though I'd seen the film before, I realized right then that it was without a doubt the greatest movie I'd ever seen in my entire life. And as a man who'd spent the last ten years as a travel bum, I'd seen more than my fair share.

2. Under the spell of the hilarious and insightful dialogue of the film, the collective enthusiasm of the audience, and five strong Thai beers, I experienced a striking revelation. It felt like a profound religious experience, just like the one Saint Paul had on the road to Damascus or the one Bob Dylan had after he banged his head in a motorcycle accident. Only instead of seeing Jesus Christ, I beheld Jeff Bridges in a ratty bathrobe playing a lazy antihero called "the Dude." The Dude, I felt, could truly be the savior of all mankind, man. Or some of it, anyway.

3. Like the foundation text of many an established religion, this extraordinary 1998 film by the Coen brothers was replete with pertinent examples of how to "abide" in the face of tough times. Its protagonist, the Dude, managed to "take it easy" in the face of outrageous misfortune, never letting the weight of the world drag him down. And so, inspired by the Dude attitude, I felt peace of mind wash over me like a warm ocean wave on a southern Thai shore.

4. The following day I visited an Internet café and discovered that I was not alone in my quasi-religious reverence for this largely underappreciated film. Though considered a total failure on its release in 1998, by 2005 a rapidly growing cult of fans had come out of the woodworks. Most surprising of all, there had been annual Lebowski festivals held in the United States since 2002! At these "Lebowski Fests" thousands of fans would show up dressed

Oliver Benjamin, aka the Dudely Lama.
Courtesy of Oliver Benjamin, www.dudeism.com

as characters from the film and imbibe the Dude's favorite drink (White Russians), practice his favorite pastime (bowling), and recite expletive-laced lines from the film to each other as feverishly as Christians quote the Bible.

5. The Church of the Latter-Day Dude (Dudeism) was founded shortly thereafter. With the Lebowski Fest fellows helping promote it, folks from all over the world flocked to the website to read the Dude word and get ordained for free as Dudeist priests. Many who didn't subscribe to any particular religion suddenly realized they'd been religious all their lives. I certainly didn't expect the flood of interest that continued. But I dug how it flowed.

BOOK III

1. What exactly was it that endeared this unlikely hero so much to myself and others? By most contemporary estimates he would be considered a total wreck of a human being—middle-aged and unemployed, never married, stoned and buzzed a lot of the time, and driving a piece of crap car. Moreover, he received no respect from anyone save a couple of hapless bowling buddies.

2. Despite his superficial failures, the Dude managed to resolutely "go with the flow," "keep his mind limber," and "take it easy" even in the most humiliating circumstances. And although he sometimes lost his cool, it would be only seconds before he once again donned his "deeply casual" attitude. It wasn't exactly a new philosophy—the more I looked into it, the more I realized how closely the "Dude Way" matched that of the ancient Chinese religion of Taoism. The Dude even resembled an old goateed Chinese sage, comfortable wearing a bathrobe and flip-flops when out in public.

3. But Dudeism didn't end with Taoism: Looking further into it, I discovered variations of the "Dude Way" running alongside the major currents of civilization down through the ages, across the sands of time.

4. Dudeism, in fact, was an ancient tradition that went by many names and fell under many guises. Around about the same time that Lao Tzu's Taoism sprung up in China, ancient Greece birthed the philosophies of Heraclitus ("ups and downs, strikes and gutters"), Epicurus ("just take it easy, man"), and the Stoics ("can't be worried about that shit"). Soon afterward, in the Levant, Jesus Christ preached an extremely Dudely way of life before the Church brushed aside his "lilies of the field" message of mellowing out and celebrating the meek.

5. Later on, the European Middle Ages celebrated wandering troubadours who were like Western

incarnations of Taoist priests, singing songs and tramping 'round the countryside in tattered tunics as they sang paeans to all things natural. When the Middle Ages ended, Dudeism was brought out in the open with the philosophical movements of Humanism, emphasizing individual liberty, and ultimately the Enlightenment, all of which freed mankind from superstition and exalted the power of perception and the senses.

6. More recently, the Romantic poets, the American Transcendentalists, the Beatniks, the Hippies, and even aspects of the modern Rave culture have all carried the torch (and sometimes burned the roach) of the holy Dudeist creed. And though its central message has often been coopted and perverted for commercial ends, Dudeism is always rediscovered and reinvigorated by succeeding generations of easygoing but revolutionary *relaxionaries,* both male and female. (Note: Dudeism doesn't recognize the feminine epithet "dudette.")

7. Yet despite its extensive pedigree, Dudeism has long remained marginalized—it's a fringe philosophy with no strong economic base to support it and a freethinking outlook that's hard to couch in concrete terms.

8. For many of us, the religions of old no longer "tie the room together." The result is that, like Sisyphus rolling that big boulder up and down the hill repeatedly and to no apparent end, most people end up stuck playing a game they don't even enjoy. So unlike poor Sisyphus, perhaps more of us should follow the teachings of *The Big Lebowski,* saying instead, "Fuck it, dude. Let's go bowling," and letting the boulder roll down the mountain instead of up.

9. The yin/yang bowling ball, by the way, is Dudeism's super-cool logo. Despite the failure of the Temple of Earth, a good religion still depends partly upon a suitably far-out symbol.

Rosary by Stella Maris.
Photo by the artist, www.polyesterstella.etsy.com

BOOK IV

1. For years, Dudeism existed only on the Internet and in the minds of its disciples. Then, in May 2009, I was invited to deliver the opening benediction to the Los Angeles Lebowski Fest. Some three thousand fans repeated after me as I recited lines from the Dude's Prayer, a modified version of the Lord's Prayer of Catholic tradition that incorporates lines from the film.

2. The second night of the festival, an advertising agency asked if they could film me discussing Dudeism for a Volkswagen ad campaign to support independent cinemas in the UK. It became a viral hit on YouTube and helped secure a book deal for *The Abide Guide,* a philosophical investigation into *The Big Lebowski* and what it all means to me and many of my fellow Dudeists.

3. Today, the Church of the Latter-Day Dude has over 140,000 ordained Dudeist priests with about 10,000 more signing up every month. And while many of those are just ordaining for a laugh or because it's easy to do, clearly this film and its characters have touched a chord in the hearts of many who would otherwise not even consider themselves religious in any sense of the word.

4. As implied earlier, Dudeism is trying to reignite a tradition that has stretched back from the dawn of civilization—namely, a humanistic rejection of civilization itself, or at least, of its worst excesses. It goes without saying that civilization is an inherently unnatural mode of living for human beings—we're genetically designed to "take it easy" and pick fruit on a tropical African savannah, not live in cities and toil away in cubicles.

5. To this end, Dudeism is currently investigating ways to expand its influence, bringing the natural yin/yang roll of the Dude's bowling ball into the lives of those who would seek it. Plans currently include a social network ("The Rug"), an institution of higher learning ("Abide University"), more books (*The Tao of the Dude, Lebowski 101*) and other what-have-you. Of course, given our Dudeist proclivities, it's all taking quite a bit longer than anticipated.

The Dudefish.
Courtesy Oliver Benjamin, www.dudeism.com

6. Wrapping 'er all up, if Dudeism has one central message about life, it is this: No problem, man. That is, life is only a drag if we make it so. It's our roll, Dude, and up to us not only to score, but to have a good time while doing so and deal with the consequences when gutterballs are thrown. We can choose to enter a "world of pain" or we can "take it easy." As the Dude puts it, it's all "just, like, our opinion, man." The Buddha (also considered a great Dudeist prophet) said precisely this a long time ago.

Amen to that, man. And abide.

For more information, please visit: www.dudeism.com as well as Dudeism's official publication, *The Dudespaper* (www.dudespaper.com).

Oliver Benjamin is the founder of the Church of the Latter-Day Dude and author of The Abide Guide.

The Quotability Quotient

Umberto Eco wrote about the cult movie, "It must provide a completely furnished world so that its fans can quote characters and episodes as if they were aspects of the fan's private sectarian world . . . so that adepts of the sect recognize each other through a shared expertise" ("*Casablanca*: Cult Movies and Intertextual Collage"). *The Big Lebowski* is so chock-full of hilarious dialogue—witty turns of phrase, puns, definitional disagreements, wordplay, absurdism, and both hyperbole and extreme understatement—that there is no end to the quoting possibilities. Certain moments of the film are so funny that the audience drowns out

Jesus wall art by Amanda and James Miller.
Courtesy of Flex Family Arts, www.flexfamilyarts.com

"Say, Dude, where is your car? Where's your car, Dude?"
—Walter, in *The Big Lebowski*, 1998

"Jesse: Dude, where's my car?
Chester: Where's your car, dude?
Jesse: Dude, where's my car?
Chester: Where's your car, dude?"
—Ashton Kutcher and Seann William Scott, in *Dude, Where's My Car?*, 2000

Lebowski, a bar in Berlin where ice cubes are shaped like toes.
Courtesy Aki Karkkainen

the next few lines of dialogue, and so upon the next viewing new witticisms are uncovered, and so on with each subsequent viewing. While the characters may all be bumbling, each has a distinct comic vernacular: Walter with his theorizing on Judaism and compulsion to associate everything with the Vietnam War ("Well, there isn't a *literal* connection, Dude"); Maude with her range of sex parlance ("Sex. The physical act of love. Coitus"); Jesus Quintana with his in-your-face ribald epithets ("It's bush-league

---

"*The Big Lebowski* is fuckin' hilarious, and habitually so, surrendering more of its plethora of verbal and visual jokes (including misidentifications, misunderstandings, mis-trickery, and mis-posturing) each time. "

—*Sidevue*

---

psych-out stuff! Laughable, man! I would've fucked you in the ass Saturday, I'll fuck you in the ass next Wednesday instead! Whoo! You got a date Wednesday, baby!"); and the Dude, with his deadpan sarcasm (regarding the conclusion of *Logjammin'*, "He fixes the cable?").

The abundance of details in the film corresponds to the density of its language, which tells its own story of the characters and creates the world they live in. The lines are what prompted the first-ever Lebowski Fest, and they continue to serve as the backbone of the event. The language has also spawned hundreds of parodies and mash-ups. On YouTube, there exist montages of every "Fuck" and one of every "Dude" in the movie; animated tributes; mash-ups with *Star Wars*, *Office Space*, *The Simpsons*, and even *Sesame Street*; and a great parody of *Tron Legacy* (a film also starring Jeff Bridges). Reenactments range from kids uploading videos of themselves in their basements to art videos created by college students for upper-level film courses.

And somehow the *Lebowski* comedy translates around the world. Quotes from the film appear on the walls of an Icelandic hotel, White Russian–themed parties have been held at the Amerika Häuser (now closed) in West Germany, and there is a Lebowski-themed bar in Berlin. Kristina Soderquist, the film's assistant account, recalls, "I actually saw it again on the big screen while working in Romania—with much laughter."

Donny Was a Good Bowler, by Misha.
Acrylic on velvet canvas board.
Courtesy of the artist, www.misha-art.com

What happens to Bunny in the sequel? Only Tara Reid may know.
© AF Archive / Alamy. Courtesy of Universal Studios Licensing LLC

PART VI
The Coens after *Lebowski*

fter the Coens won the Best Original Screenplay Oscar for *Fargo*, which happened midproduction of *The Big Lebowski*, their subsequent movies had bigger budgets and some bigger-name stars. The era of their true "indie" phase was over, although they continue to work with their core stable of actors and crew and maintain final cut privilege.

> ## "I'm glad she's working on it. . . . We'll watch it when it comes out."
>
> —Ethan responding to Tara Reid's (Bunny Lebowski) public assertion of a *Lebowski* sequel, on austin360.com

O Brother, Where Art Thou? (2000)

The title is a teasing reference to a line in Preston Sturges' *Sullivan's Travels* (1941), in which a director abandons a socially conscious movie in favor of pure entertainment. *O Brother, Where Art Thou?*, though overtly comedic, is a sly meditation on race, class, and friendship. The film was noted for its distinctive look (color corrected by Roger Deakins to give it a sepia tint reminiscent of faded photographs) and for a hilarious, Clark Gable–esque George Clooney, who, as a prison escapee looking to reunite with his wife, is the Ulysses of this Odyssey. The film includes a breathtaking Ku Klux Klan sequence with *Wizard of Oz* overtones, which was shot in the middle of the night with a black military regiment dressed as the KKK. It's "a tribute to, and an example of, the persistent vitality of the American imagination" (A. O. Scott, *The New York Times*). The evocative soundtrack, with bluegrass, country, gospel, blues, and folk music suitable to the 1930s time period of the film, became a bestseller and spawned a tour and a documentary film, *Down from the Mountain*. (It was produced by T Bone Burnett, who worked with the Coens on *The Big Lebowski* and later *The Ladykillers*.)

Tim Blake Nelson in *O Brother, Where Art Thou?*, the fifth collaboration between the Coen brothers and cinematographer Roger Deakins.
© AF Archive / Alamy

Billy Bob Thornton in *The Man Who Wasn't There.*
© AF Archive / Alamy

The Man Who Wasn't There (2001)

Extortion is the name of the game in this twenty-first-century homage to vintage film noir. At the center is Billy Bob Thornton's dead-on, deadpan portrait of malaise and yearning in small-town 1940s California. Shot on color negative film that was then printed in incandescent, stunning black and white (another ingenious effort by Roger Deakins), the film garnered the Coens their third Best Director award from the Cannes Film Festival. Nonetheless, in usual Coen fashion, the movie received mixed reviews, in part for its moments of absurdity reminiscent of pulp-fiction writer Jim Thompson, including what appears to be an alien abduction. The lawyer's (Tony Shalhoub) speech about the "the Uncertainty Principle," and how the simple act of looking at something changes it, is a Coen theme that reappears in *A Serious Man*.

Intolerable Cruelty (2003)

This overlooked gem was based on a script developed by others and rewritten by the Coens, who usually fare best with their own original writing. It's a modern-day Howard Hawkes–ian, screwball battle-of-the-sexes romp between a divorce lawyer and a divorcée. George Clooney and Catherine Zeta-Jones conjure the charisma of 1930s Hollywood stars, and their war of words "fizzes with arch wit and sexual-financial-Darwinist treble entendres" (*The Guardian*).

The Ladykillers (2004)

This remake of a 1955 British heist film is a farce set on the boundary between old and new Mississippi, with a typical Coen cast of misfits and bungling miscreants, here including Tom Hanks as the loquacious professor G. H. Dorr. "In his first truly comedic role in years, Hanks summons up an unforgettable caricature of Southern gentility turned foul" (*The Onion*). *The Ladykillers* is generally looked upon least favorably of any film in the Coen brothers' repertoire.

No Country for Old Men (2007)

Based on the Cormac McCarthy novel of the same name, *No Country for Old Men* is a bracing thriller/Western set near the Rio Grande. The film is distinguished by Javier Bardem's legendary performance as hit man Anton Chigurh. "This movie never lets up. . . . [It is] essentially a game of hide-and-seek, set in brownish, stained motel rooms and other shabby American redoubts, but shot with a formal precision and an economy that make one think of masters like Hitchcock and Bresson" (David Denby, *The New Yorker*). *No Country* swept the Oscars, garnering statuettes for Best Director, Screenplay, Supporting Actor for Bardem, and Motion Picture. It also introduced Josh Brolin into the Coens' stable of regulars; he went on to act in their remake of *True Grit*.

Anton Chigurh (Javier Bardem), a character created by Cormac McCarthy, is a relentlessly psychopathic hit man; he fits perfectly in the Coen universe.
© AF Archive / Alamy

Burn After Reading (2008)

Always ones to change it up, after their triumph in the genre of serious Western, the Coens made a return to raucous black comedy with *Burn After Reading*, based on that inspiration from childhood, *Advise and Consent*. Covering familiar ground with its story of a scheme gone awry, the film is replete with espionage, infidelity, and Internet dating. *Slate*'s review invoked parallels to *The Big Lebowski*'s plot with its failed blackmail and greed, but distinguished the two films in their attitudes: "The contrast in tone, though, is stark. There's no real friendship in the world of *Burn After Reading*, there's even less heroism, and paranoia abounds. No one mentions 9/11 or the war in Iraq, but these characters, like their audience, are living in a darker world. The cult of *Lebowski*, I've begun to suspect, has more than a little nostalgia in it—for a decade when one could poke brilliant fun at the national disposition and the stakes didn't feel so high."

A Serious Man (2009)

The Coens' most personal film is set in a Midwestern Jewish community with an academic father as the protagonist. According to Ethan, "This is where we grew up, the familiar environment to our story, although the characters are all made up." Marko Costanzo, foley artist on *The Big Lebowski*, recalls Ethan telling him that the brothers took episodes directly out of living in Minnesota, being Jewish, and being a minority as inspirations for much of the film.

Set in the 1970s, it is an absurdist contemporary story of Job, the Biblical character whose faith is severely tested by God. Larry Gopnik (Michael Stuhlbarg), a math professor who tries to be a good and serious man, looks for answers to his troubles, but, like Job, he is thwarted at every turn. The quote at the beginning of the film, by medieval Jewish scholar Rashi—"Receive with simplicity everything that happens to you"—is akin to the Dude's outlook on life.

A Serious Man is set in St. Louis Park, the Minneapolis suburb where the Coen brothers grew up.
© Photos 12 / Alamy

True Grit (2010)

In the Coens' remake of the 1969 film, Jeff Bridges played the role of tough-yet-flawed U.S. Marshal Rooster Cogburn, originated by John Wayne. Joel and Ethan's version stayed truer to the Charles Portis novel by emphasizing the role of protagonist Mattie Ross, a young, strong woman out for justice. Similar to *The Big Lebowski*, *True Grit* has themes of friendship and undertones of the redemptive power of goodness and humane behavior. Like other classic Westerns, the wicked characters don't hold together as a group; instead, they turn on each other and destroy everything in their path, and "flee when none pursueth" as says the line from Solomon, Proverbs 28:1, which opens the film. Nominated for ten Academy Awards, *True Grit* was praised by *The New York Times* as being a "parable about good and evil. Only here, the lines between the two are so blurred as to be indistinguishable, making this a true picture of how the West was won, or—depending on your view—lost."

Jeff Bridges in *True Grit*.
© AF Archive / Alamy

"You said it, man. Nobody #&%!$ with The Jesus,"
said The Jesus.

The Jesus, by Josh Cooley.
Courtesy of the artist. www.cooleycooley.blogspot.com

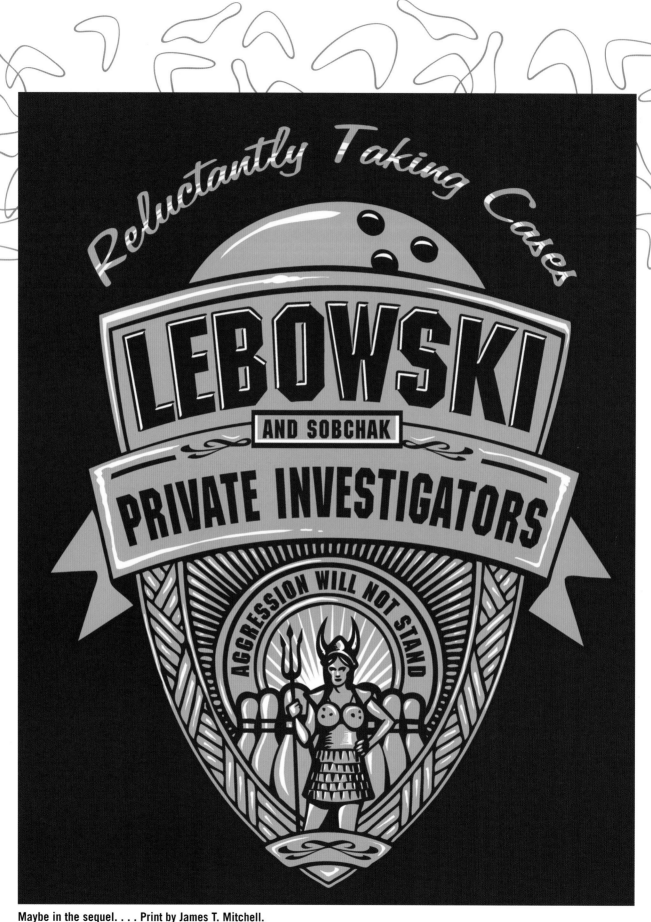

Maybe in the sequel. . . . Print by James T. Mitchell.
Courtesy of the artist

Epilogue

The end of *The Big Lebowski* brings us back to the beginning—full circle, if you will. Walter eulogizes Donny, grasping his remains in a Folgers coffee can from Ralphs—the same grocery store in which we first encounter the Dude. What's clear from Walter's eulogy is that he didn't know Donny all that well—beyond his being a surfer and a bowler. The important point: he was "one of us." There is an *esprit de corps* among the friends of *The Big Lebowski*, which is, at its core, a film about friendship. Despite the ups and downs, the strikes and gutters of living, it's our friends who sustain us. And Walter's suggestion, "Let's go bowling," both diffuses their conflict and sadness, and epitomizes the free-spirited, easygoing, and carefree way in which this man, the Dude, lives his life.

In the final scene, the Stranger reappears in the bowling alley, closing the narrative frame. He expresses the comfort he takes in knowing that the Dude abides, "Taking 'er easy for all us sinners." Acknowledging he's rambling (much like this rambling, shaggy dog of a film), the Stranger promises to catch us "later on down the trail." With the film closing on a lone bowler, the hypnotic sounds of balls hitting pins overlaid on the plaintive melody of the Rolling Stones' "Dead Flowers," we are not left with any particular lessons from the machinations of the plot or the meaningless money chase the other characters took part in. But the Dude abides, and his simple philosophy of being at ease with himself and the universe lives on. *The Big Lebowski* abides as well, in the hearts and imaginations and funny bones of countless fans around the world.

Bibliography

"The 100 Greatest Movie Characters." *Empire*. http://www.empireonline.com/100-greatest-movie-characters/default.asp?c=7

Allen, William Rodney (Ed.). *The Coen Brothers Interviews*. Jackson: University Press of Mississippi, 2006.

Anderman, Joan. "How 'The Big Lebowski' became a cultural touchstone and the impetus for festivals across the country." *The Boston Globe*, September 15, 2009. http://www.boston.com/lifestyle/articles/2009/09/15/the_big_lebowski_spawns_its_own_subculture/

Armbruster, Jessica. "Dude, Big Lebowski Fun Facts." *City Pages*, October 30, 2009. http://blogs.citypages.com/gimmenoise/2008/10/dude_big_lebows.php

Asia Carrera Buttkicking Homepage! http://www.asiacarrera.com/index3.html

Basinger, Jeanine. *American Cinema: One Hundred Years of Filmmaking*. New York: Rizzoli International Publications, Inc., 1994.

Bergan, Ronald. *The Coen Brothers*. New York: Thunder's Mouth Press, 2000.

Bernstein, Richard. "Ideas and Trends; The Rising Hegemony of the Politically Correct." *The New York Times*, October 28, 1990. http://www.nytimes.com/1990/10/28/weekinreview/ideas-trends-the-rising-hegemony-of-the-politically-correct.html?pagewanted=all&src=pm

Boucher, Geoff. "L.A.'s story is complicated, but they got it: The 25 best L.A. films of the last 25 years." *Los Angeles Times*, August 31, 2008. http://www.latimes.com/entertainment/news/movies/la-ca-25films31-2008aug31,0,70218.htmlstory

Bowling Lingo / PBA.com. http://www.pba.co/Resources/BowlingLingo/

Bowling Noir. http://wesclark.com/ubn/bowling_noir.html

Box Office Mojo. http://www.boxofficemojo.com/?ref=ft

Carolee Schneemann.com. http://www.caroleeschneemann.com/uptoandincluding.html

Carr, David. "They Keep Killing Steve Buscemi, but He's Not Complaining." *The New York Times*, March 23, 2006. http://www.nytimes.com/2006/03/23/movies/23busc.html

Chandler, Raymond. *The Big Sleep and Other Novels*. London: Penguin Books, 2000.

Cocktail DB: The Internet Cocktail Database. http://cocktaildb.com/

Coen, Ethan, and Joel Coen. *The Big Lebowski*. London: Faber and Faber Limited, 1998.

"The Comedy 25: The Funniest Movies of the Past 25 Years." *Entertainment Weekly*, August 27, 2008. http://www.ew.com/ew/gallery/0,,20221235_17,00.html

Comentale, Edward P., and Aaron Jaffe (Eds.). *The Year's Work in Lebowski Studies*. Bloomington and Indianapolis: Indiana University Press, 2009.

Cook, David A. *A History of Narrative Film*. London and New York: W.W. Norton & Company, Inc., 1990.

Cooke, Tricia (Ed.), and William Preston Robertson. *The Big Lebowski: The Making of a Coen Brothers Film*. London and New York: W.W. Norton & Company, Inc., 1998.

"The Cult 25: The Essential Left-Field Movie Hits Since '83." *Entertainment Weekly*, September 3, 2008. http://www.ew.com/ew/gallery/0,,20221982_10,00.html.

Dargis, Manohla. "Wearing Braids, Seeking Revenge." *The New York Times*, December 21, 2010. http://www.nytimes.com/2010/12/22/movies/22true.html?pagewanted=all

Donohue, Walter. "Rip van Marlowe: Robert Altman's *The Long Goodbye*." FocusFeatures.com, October 28, 2009. http://focusfeatures.com/article/rip_van_marlowe__robert_altman_s__em_the_long_goodbye__em_

Ebert, Roger. "*The Big Lebowski*." *Chicago Sun Times*, March 6, 1998. http://rogerebert.suntimes.com/apps/pbcs.dll/article?AID=/19980306/REVIEWS/803060301/1023&AID1=/19980306/REVIEWS/803060301/1023&AID2=/20100310/REVIEWS08/100319989/1023

Ebert, Roger. "*Fargo*." *Chicago Sun Times*, March 8, 1996. http://rogerebert.suntimes.com/apps/pbcs.dll/article?AID=/19960308/REVIEWS/603080302

Ebert, Roger. "*The Hudsucker Proxy*." *Chicago Sun Times*, March 25, 1994. http://rogerebert.suntimes.com/apps/pbcs.dll/article?AID=/19940325/REVIEWS/403250301/1023

Family Media Guide. "Freeze Frame: *The Big Lebowski*." http://web.archive.org/web/20070506173334/http://www.familymediaguide.com/media/onDVD/media-433568.html

Filmsite.org. American Movie Classics Company LLC. http://www.filmsite.org/westernfilms.html

Fischer, Lucy. "City of Women: Busby Berkeley, Architecture, and Urban Space." *Cinema Journal*, 49, no. 4. (Summer 2010): 111–130.

Garner, Dwight. "Dissertations on His Dudeness." *The New York Times*, December 29, 2009. http://www.nytimes.com/2009/12/30/books/30lebowski.html?_r=1

Gibson, Brian. "Sidevue: Citizen Dude: How the Coens' slice of slacker-noir shuffled on beyond 'cult-classic'" (Expanded Version). *Vue Weekly*, Aug. 03, 2011. http://www.vueweekly.com/film/story/sidevue_citizen_dude_expanded_version/

Gilbey, Ryan. "Jeff Bridges: 'He's a real chameleon': From stoner to alien to all-American hero, Jeff Bridges immerses himself in every role. Here, his friends, co-stars and directors uncover the man behind the movies." *Guardian*, May 26, 2011. http://www.guardian.co.uk/film/2011/may/26/jeff-bridges-career

Googie Architecture Online. http://www.spaceagecity.com/googie/

Green, Bill, Ben Peskoe, Will Russell, and Scott Shuffitt. *I'm a Lebowski, You're a Lebowski: Life, The Big Lebowski, and What Have You*. New York: Bloomsbury USA, 2007.

Greene, Andy. "Decade of The Dude: *Rolling Stone*'s 2008 Feature on 'The Big Lebowski'—How the Coen brothers' 1998 stoner caper became the most worshipped comedy of its generation." *Rolling Stone*, August 15, 2011. http://www.rollingstone.com/movies/news/decade-of-the-dude-rolling-stones-2008-feature-on-the-big-lebowski-20110815

Haglund, David. "Ranking the Coen Brothers' Movies." *Slate Magazine*, August, 10, 2011. http://www.slate.com/articles/arts/the_completist/2011/08/ranking_the_coen_brothers_movies.single.html

Haglund, David. "Walter Sobchak, Neocon." *Slate Magazine*, September 11, 2008. http://www.slate.com/id/2199811/

Hess, Alan. *Googie: Fifties Coffee Shop Architecture*. San Francisco: Chronicle Books, 1985.

Hodgkinson, Will. "Dude, let's go bowling." *The Guardian*, May 11, 2005. http://film.guardian.co.uk/features/featurepages/0,,1481323,00.html

Hoggard, Liz. "Get with the Dude's vibe." *The Guardian*, July 22, 2007. http://film.guardian.co.uk/features/featurepages/0,,2131837,00.html

Howell, Peter. "Howell: I love *The Big Lebowski*: even though the Wikipedia says I don't." *Toronto Star*, July 7, 2011. http://www.thestar.com/article/1020896--howell-i-love-the-big-lebowski-even-though-the-wikipedia-says-i-don-t

IMDBPro.com: *The Big Lebowski*. http://pro.imdb.com/title/tt0118715/maindetails

Jeff Dowd. http://www.jeffdowd.com/thedude/thedude.html

Jewish Virtual Library: Theodor (Binyamin Ze'ev) Herzl. http://www.jewishvirtuallibrary.org/jsource/biography/Herzl.html

Jones, Amelia. "'Presence' in Absentia: Experiencing Performance as Documentation." *Art Journal*, 56, no. 4. (Winter 1997): 11–18.

Jones, Jenny. "Joel and Ethan Coen: Raising Cain." *Walker* magazine, September/October 2009. http://www.walkerart.org/calendar/2009/joel-and-ethan-coen-raising-cain

Klinger, Barbara. "Becoming cult: *The Big Lebowski*, replay culture and male fans." *Screen*, Spring 2010. http://libweb.uoregon.edu/index/cms-filesystem-action/guides/english/klinger_lebowski.pdf

Konigsberg, Ira. *The Complete Film Dictionary*. New York: Meridian, 1989.

Lahr, John. "The Thin Man." *The New Yorker*, November 14, 2005. http://www.newyorker.com/archive/2005/11/14/051114fa_fact_lahr

Lebowski Fest.com. http://www.lebowskifest.com/

Levine, Josh. *The Coen Brothers: The Story of Two American Filmmakers*. Toronto: ECW Press, 2000.

Liberatore, Paul. "Lib at Large: The Dude and the Abiders." *Marin Independent Journal*, August 19, 2011. http://www.marinij.com/lifestyles/ci_18712403?source=pkg

Marijuana Dictionary. www.marijuanadictionary.com

Maslin, Janet. "*Blood Simple*, A Black-Comic Romp." *The New York Times*, October 12, 1984. http://movies.nytimes.com/movie/review?res=9502E6DB1639F931A25753C1A962948260

Maslin, Janet. "A Bowling Ball's-Eye View of Reality." *The New York Times*, March 6, 1998. http://www.nytimes.com/1998/03/06/movies/film-review-a-bowling-ball-s-eye-view-of-reality.html

McDonald, William. "Brothers in a Movie World of Their Own." *The New York Times*, March 3, 1996. http://www.nytimes.com/1996/03/03/movies/brothers-in-a-movie-world-of-their-own.html?pagewanted=all&src=pm

Morgan, Robert C. "Carolee Schneemann: The Politics of Eroticism." *Art Journal*, 56, no. 4. (Winter 1997): 97–100

Nathan, Ian. "Review of *The Big Lebowski*." *Empire*, May 1998. http://www.empireonline.com/reviews/reviewcomplete.asp?DVDID=117203

Nelson, Rob. "Dada, Dalí and the Dude: Feeling Minnesota . . . Not!: Jeff Bridges and John Goodman in Joel and Ethan Coen's *The Big Lebowski*." *City Pages*, March 4, 2007. http://www.citypages.com/1998-03-04/movies/dada-dali-and-the-dude/

Nietzsche, Friedrich. Bernard Williams (Ed.). *The Gay Science*. Cambridge: Cambridge University Press, 2006.

Nietzsche, Friedrich. *On the Genealogy of Morality. A New Translation by Douglas Smith*. Oxford: Oxford University Press, 1998.

OKCupid: Free Online Dating. http://www.okcupid.com/

O'Neal, Sean. "Random Roles: John Turturro. *The Onion*, June 28, 2011. http://www.avclub.com/articles/john-turturro,58178/2/

Palopoli, Steve. "The Last Cult Picture Show." *Metro Santa Cruz*, July 25–31, 2002. http://www.metroactive.com/papers/metro/07.25.02/lebowski1-0230.html

The Pew Forum on Religion and Public Life. http://www.pewforum.org/

"Playboy Interview: Steve Buscemi." *Playboy*, August 10, 2011.

Porfirio, Robert, Alain Silver, James Ursini, and Elizabeth Ward (Eds.). *Film Noir: The Encyclopedia*. New York and London: Overlook Duckworth, Peter Mayer Publications, Inc., 2010.

Rohrer, Finlo. "Is *The Big Lebowski* a cultural milestone?" *BBC News Magazine*, October 10, 2008. http://news.bbc.co.uk/2/hi/uk_news/magazine/7662943.stm

Rosenbaum, Jonathan. "L.A. Residential." *Chicago Reader*, March 6, 1998. http://www.chicagoreader.com/movies/archives/1998/0398/03068.html. http://www.chicagoreader.com/chicago/la-residential/Content?oid=895709

Ross, Jenna. "Drugstore has role in lives, film of Coen Brothers." *Star Tribune*, November 9, 2007. http://www.startribune.com/local/west/11550951.html

Rovzar, Chris. "OKCupid Study Reinforces Vague Racial Pop-Culture Stereotypes." *New York Magazine*, September 8, 2010. http://nymag.com/daily/intel/2010/09/okcupid_study_reinforces_vague.html

Rubin, Martin. *Showstoppers: Busby Berkeley and the Tradition of Spectacle*. New York: Columbia University Press, 1993.

Russell, Will. "Hey Dude: The Lebowski Festival." *The Independent*, August 15, 2007. http://www.independent.co.uk/arts-entertainment/films/features/hey-dude-the-lebowski-festival-461663.html

Sante, Luc. "Reaching for It." *The New York Times Magazine*, November 11, 2007. http://www.nytimes.com/2007/11/11/magazine/11wwln-lede-t.html

Sarris, Andrew. "A Cubist Coen Comedy." *New York Observer*, March 8, 1998. http://www.observer.com/node/40253

Scott, A.O. "First Passive and Invisible, Then Ruinous and Glowing." *The New York Times*, October 31, 2001. http://www.nytimes.com/2001/10/31/movies/film-review-first-passive-and-invisible-then-ruinous-and-glowing.html

Stone, Doug. "The Coens Speak (Reluctantly)." *IndieWIRE*, March 9, 1998. http://www.indiewire.com/article/the_coens_speak_reluctantly/

Tenpin Bowling.org: All About Bowling. http://www.tenpinbowling.org/view.php?page=the_game.history

Tobias, Scott. "The New Cult Canon: *The Big Lebowski*." *AV Club*, May 14, 2009. http://www.avclub.com/articles/the-big-lebowski,27984/?utm_source=channel_the-new-cult-canon

Tyree, J. M., and Ben Walters. *The Big Lebowski*. London: British Film Institute, 2010.

UNODC / United Nations Office on Drugs and Crime. World Drug Report 2011. http://www.unodc.org/unodc/en/data-and-analysis/WDR-2011.html

Urban Dictionary. www.urbandictionary.com

Vary, Adam B. "The 100 Greatest Characters of the Last 20 Years." *Entertainment Weekly*, June 4–11, 2010. http://popwatch.ew.com/2010/06/01/100-greatest-characters-of-last-20-years-full-list/

Von Busack, Richard. "Vanishing Act: The Coen brothers disappoint with *The Man Who Wasn't There*." *Metroactive*, November 8–14, 2001. http://www.metroactive.com/papers/sonoma/11.08.01/manwho-0145.html

The Webtender: An On-Line Bartender. http://www.webtender.com/

"Whatever man." *Boston Globe*, October 27, 2005. http://www.boston.com/ae/movies/articles/2005/10/27/whatever_man/

Wills, Nadine. "'110 per cent woman': The Crotch Shot in the Hollywood Musical." *Screen*, Summer 2001.

Wondrich, David. "The Wondrich Take: Expert Commentary from Esquire's Resident Cocktail Historian: White Russian." *Esquire*, http://www.esquire.com/drinks/white-russian-drink-recipe

Acknowledgments

This book came about from the efforts of many, many people—all "Achievers" in their own right. I'd like to thank my editor Grace Labatt, who offered me a dream project and was immensely supportive during the process. She did a masterful job with both the words and images of the book. Josh Leventhal got me into this business and contributed useful insights. Dick Jones and Jeanne Jones Michael brought me into the world, and kept me going through the difficult times. My brilliant daughter Madeline was a bright star throughout.

Thanks to Drew Houpt, credited in *A Serious Man* for being "the last of the just," for his words of encouragement and for relaying that Joel and Ethan Coen gave me "neither their blessing nor their curse" on the project. Several members of the cast and crew and others "in the know" offered personal anecdotes. They were all amazingly gracious and open: Wendy Braun, Marko Costanzo, Jamie Green, Jack Kehler, Bill Landrum, Carlos Leon, Brian McCarty, David Orr, Mark Pellegrino, Jon Polito, Bruce Pross, William Preston Robertson, Peter Siragusa, Kristina Soderquist, Chris Spellman, Torsten Voges, Al Zaleski, and most especially Peter Chesney and Kiva Dawson, who took much time out of their busy lives to give me guidance.

Essayists who contributed were Oliver Benjamin, Joe Forkan, Gail Levin, Todd Martens, Roy Preston, and Mark Peters.

Designer (and *Lebowski* fan) Brad Norr really ran with the project, creating a unique look that pulls together so many of the film's visual elements with panache. Thanks also to the Walker Art Center for giving me permission to use elements of the essay on the Coen brothers and their work that I wrote for the *Walker* magazine.

I have a vast network of exceedingly smart and supportive friends who served as my gang of roving researchers: Joe Beres, Dave Good, Rembert Hueser, Verena Mund, Colin Petit, Melissa Schedler, and Alice Swenson. Emily Taylor was a great guide through the intricate subculture of online dating. Pearl "Rampage" Rea provided haikus, helpful analyses on the Dude's drink of choice, and also made many a mean (and I mean *mean*) White Russian. Sharon Broscha was instrumental in keeping me fed and nurtured.

Both Robert Cowgill, my film mentor, and Ben Geffen, one of the ones who talked me into this, walked me through their love of Westerns. Greg Blue did a thorough analysis of the shooting script against the finished film. Jeremy Meckler was a jack-of-all-trades and did an astute job assisting with aspects of the book too numerous to list, as well as bolstering me with anecdotes, clips, and by channeling Werner Herzog with the inspiring words: "Let's get this showboat over the Andes!"

And, finally, to Alice and Joe: you're the best.

Index

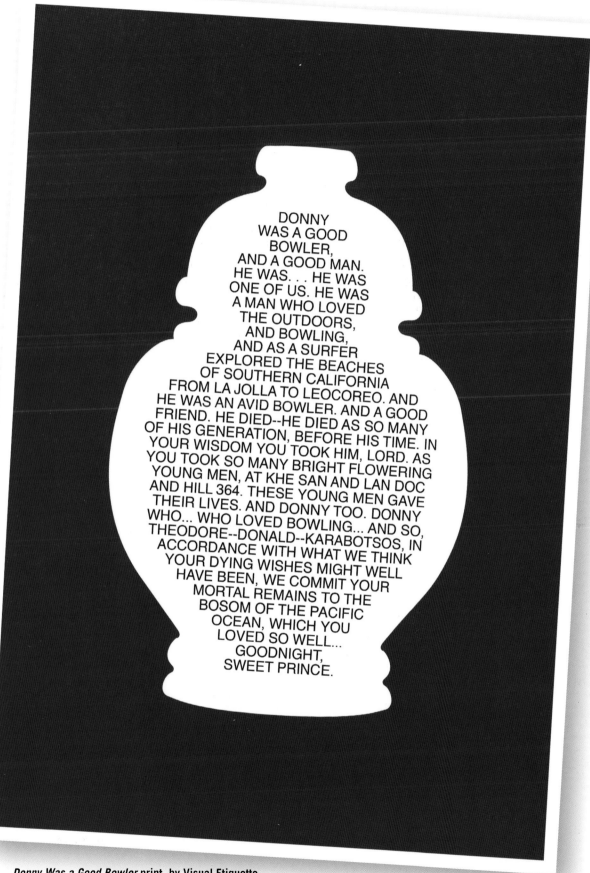

DONNY
WAS A GOOD
BOWLER,
AND A GOOD MAN.
HE WAS. . . HE WAS
ONE OF US. HE WAS
A MAN WHO LOVED
THE OUTDOORS,
AND BOWLING,
AND AS A SURFER
EXPLORED THE BEACHES
OF SOUTHERN CALIFORNIA
FROM LA JOLLA TO LEOCOREO. AND
HE WAS AN AVID BOWLER. AND A GOOD
FRIEND. HE DIED--HE DIED AS SO MANY
OF HIS GENERATION, BEFORE HIS TIME. IN
YOUR WISDOM YOU TOOK HIM, LORD. AS
YOU TOOK SO MANY BRIGHT FLOWERING
YOUNG MEN, AT KHE SAN AND LAN DOC
AND HILL 364. THESE YOUNG MEN GAVE
THEIR LIVES. AND DONNY TOO. DONNY
WHO... WHO LOVED BOWLING... AND SO,
THEODORE--DONALD--KARABOTSOS, IN
ACCORDANCE WITH WHAT WE THINK
YOUR DYING WISHES MIGHT WELL
HAVE BEEN, WE COMMIT YOUR
MORTAL REMAINS TO THE
BOSOM OF THE PACIFIC
OCEAN, WHICH YOU
LOVED SO WELL...
GOODNIGHT,
SWEET PRINCE.

Donny Was a Good Bowler print, by Visual Etiquette.
Courtesy Visual Etiquette

About the Author

Jenny M. Jones is the author of *The Annotated Godfather: The Complete Screenplay.* She has worked in film exhibition at the Northwest Film Center in Portland, Oregon; the late, great Oak Street Cinema in Minneapolis; and the Walker Art Center. At the Walker, she helped organize a complete 35mm retrospective of the work of Joel and Ethan Coen and an onstage conversation with the brothers. Like Ethan, her work history also includes a brief stint at the legendary Embers Restaurant. She currently resides in St. Paul, Minnesota, with her daughter, Madeline.